Men *to* Men

Companion Books by African-Americans

The Black Family: Past, Present, and Future (edited by Lee N. June, Ph.D.)

Men to Men: Perspectives of Sixteen African-American Christian Men (edited by Lee N. June, Ph.D., and Matthew Parker)

Women to Women: Perspectives of Fifteen African-American Christian Women (edited by Norvella Carter, Ph.D., and Matthew Parker)

Men *to* Men

PERSPECTIVES OF SIXTEEN
AFRICAN-AMERICAN CHRISTIAN MEN

LEE N. JUNE, Ph.D.
Editor

MATTHEW PARKER
Consulting Editor

ZondervanPublishingHouse
Grand Rapids, Michigan

A Division of HarperCollinsPublishers

Men to Men
Copyright © 1996 by the Institute for Black Family Development

Requests for information should be addressed to:

 ZondervanPublishingHouse
Grand Rapids, Michigan 49530

Library of Congress Cataloging-in-Publication Data

Men to men : perspectives of sixteen African-American Christian men / Dr. Lee N. June, editor,
    Matthew Parker, consulting editor.
        p. cm.
        ISBN 0-310-20157-8 (pbk.)
        1. Afro-American men—Conduct of life. 2. Afro-American men—Religious life. I. June,
    Lee N. II. Parker, Matthew, 1945– .
    E185.86.M46 1996
    248.8'42'08996073—dc20   95-44004
                                                                                         CIP

Authors use various translations of the Bible in this book. The versions cited are identified in the
reference lists at the end of the chapters and in the text as needed. KJV stands for the *King James
Version*. NASB stands for the *New American Standard Bible*. NIV® stands for the *Holy Bible:
New International Version*.

Copy editing by Jan M. Ortiz
Interior design by Sherri L. Hoffman

Printed in the United States of America

---

00 01 02 /❖ DH/ 10 9

Dedicated to Dr. Lloyd Blue,
who has invested his life in so many people

Contents

Preface by Matthew Parker   9

Introduction by Lee N. June, Ph.D.   11

PART 1: Developing Life Enhancement Skills

  1. The Importance of Moral Character   15
    Lee N. June

  2. Risk and Failure as Preludes to Achievement   29
    Henry Lee (Hank) Allen

  3. Keys to Sound Financial Planning   51
    Allen T. Sheffield

  4. Sanctifying Our Sexual Energy   65
    Haman Cross Jr.

  5. Male Bonding: Men Relating to Men   79
    Rodney S. Patterson

PART 2: Strengthening Relationships Within Families

  6. How to Romance Your Wife   99
    Lloyd C. Blue

  7. Building Powerful Families   115
    Michael R. Lyles and Larry Purvis

  8. The Meaning of Fatherhood   129
    Claude L. Dallas Jr.

  9. Balancing Career and Family   149
    Kenneth B. Staley

10. The Commitment to Marriage   161
    J. Derek McNeil

11. Male Leadership in the Home and Family   179
    Willie Richardson

PART 3: Dealing with the Criminal Justice System

12. Avoiding Arrest and Prison   197
    Kenneth McDaniel

13. Surviving the Criminal Justice System   209
    Clifford E. Washington

PART 4: Facing Contemporary Challenges

14. Concepts of Manhood   225
    Warren E. Williams

15. Rebuilding the Walls: An Action Plan   237
    John M. Wallace Jr.

16. African-American, Afrocentric (Africentric), Christian,
    and Male?   257
    Lee N. June

Preface

The best leaders I know accomplish goals without making people feel that they have been led. In 1970 Lloyd Blue, a pastor, became my spiritual dad. Dr. Blue taught me about authority, how to have a good attitude toward pastors, and how to evangelize and disciple African-American males. He also taught me what it means to be faithful and obedient to God. I learned through our relationship what it means to be under the authority of God: How can I really be responsive to God, whom I cannot see, if it is difficult to respond to someone I can see?

This book is by African-American men who have mentored and networked with people across the United States. They have shared their knowledge, wisdom, discernment, and understanding to enhance personal lives and ministries around this country.

As you read this book, it is my desire that you share these experiences with others.

Matthew Parker, President
Institute for Black Family Development, Detroit

Introduction

The overall purpose of this book is to provide a forum for African-American Christian males to speak to the critical issues and challenges facing the African-American male community in particular and the Christian community more generally.

The book offers profound and penetrating insight into the thoughts, opinions, and proposed solutions as to how the African-American male can avoid common pitfalls and live a productive life as a Christian and a citizen.

We believe this book will be useful to African-American males and females, pastors, Bible institutes, seminaries, Christian workers, church study groups, Christians in general, and anyone else seeking to understand the issues facing the African-American male and wanting to find and implement solutions.

Even though the book is written by and to men, African-American females (and others) will find it highly useful as well because they can get a firsthand view of both the issues facing males and our thoughts on dealing with them.

The book is divided into four sections. Part 1, "Developing Life Enhancement Skills," contains five chapters covering topics which, if understood and implemented, can help us to live more effective lives. Having a moral character, taking calculated risks and not being devastated by failures, using sound financial planning, exercising sexuality properly, and having quality male friendships are necessary in the world in which we live.

Part 2 is titled "Strengthening Relationships Within Families" and has six chapters. With the increasing divorce and separation rates and with the all too often poor quality of life within families, we need to have the skills to strengthen family life and to carry out family responsibilities effectively. This section includes discussions on the importance of and tips on romancing your wife; how to build powerful families; the challenges, responsibilities, and rewards of fatherhood; how to balance career and family; how to maintain a commitment to marriage; and the proper exercise of male leadership in the home.

Part 3 is intended to equip African-American males to deal with an issue that disproportionately affects us—the criminal justice system. One chapter describes what to do if you are arrested. The other chapter, written by a former prison inmate who is now living a full and productive life, is intended to give hope to those who are currently in jail or prison or have had involvement with the criminal justice system.

Part 4, "Facing Contemporary Challenges," contains three chapters. The first of these talks about the challenge of spiritual manhood, choosing between the worldly view and the biblical view. The other chapters deal with "rebuilding the walls," a plan of action for strengthening the family and the community and the African-American male identity.

This project is sponsored by the Institute for Black Family Development. The Institute provides tools for the success of the Black community and family. Special thanks go to Matthew Parker, the institute's president and the consulting editor for this volume, and to the members of the board of directors for embracing this project. Thanks also are extended to Ms. Velma Ferguson, who assisted in some of the word processing.

As editor, it has been a joy to assemble this volume and to work with these diverse writers, who come from a variety of backgrounds. As we face the closing of the twentieth century and anticipate the dawn of the twenty-first, I believe that the 12,246,371 Black males in America (*U.S. Census Report*, 1990) can be "saved" as we march (the Million Man march), work, write, unite, and accept God as He is and become even more of a positive force in the next generation. It is in that conviction that this volume is presented. It is my hope that this book will be used by God to further develop and enhance His kingdom and His people on earth.

Lee N. June, Ph.D.
Editor
Lansing, Michigan

PART 1

DEVELOPING LIFE ENHANCEMENT SKILLS

Lee N. June

The Importance of Moral Character

LEE N. JUNE is a professor at Michigan State University and currently serves as Assistant Provost for Student Academic Support Services, Racial, Ethnic, and Multicultural Issues, and is Interim Vice President for Student Affairs and Services. He was director of a university counseling center for eight and a half years. Born and reared in Manning, South Carolina, Lee holds a bachelor of science degree from Tuskegee University, a master of education degree in counseling, a master of arts degree in clinical psychology, and a doctor of philosophy degree in clinical psychology from the University of Illinois (Champaign-Urbana). He did postgraduate study in psychology at Haverford College (1966–67) and was a special student during a sabbatical leave at the Duke University Divinity School (1981). He is editor of *The Black Family: Past, Present, and Future* (Zondervan, 1991). A member of the New Mount Calvary Baptist Church (Lansing, Michigan), Lee is married to Shirley Spencer June, and they have two sons, Stephen and Brian.

Chapter 1

Lee N. June

The Importance of Moral Character

A good name is rather to be chosen than great riches. (Proverbs 22:1)

In those days ... every man did that which was right in his own eyes. (Judges 21:25)

And the LORD said unto Satan, Hast thou considered my servant Job, that there is none like him in the earth, a perfect and upright man, one that feareth God, and escheweth evil? (Job 1:8)

INTRODUCTION

Morality has to do with what is right and what is wrong. The word *moral*, according to *Webster's Ninth New Collegiate Dictionary* (1985), is defined as "relating to principles of right and wrong in behavior." A synonym for *moral* is the word *ethical*. The word *morality*, according to Webster, is defined as "a doctrine or system of moral conduct." The word *character* is defined by Webster as "the aggregate of distinctive qualities or characteristics of a breed, strain or type; the complex of mental and ethical traits marking and often individualizing a person, group, or nation." A closely related word to character is *reputation*. Thus, as the definitions imply, one can think of the moral character of an individual, group, organization, or nation.

Few of us would disregard the importance of moral character. If we were to examine the moral character of our nation, however, we would probably have to agree that it has received some severe blows over time. These blows have come from the legacy of slavery, segregation, and discrimination as well as from scandals such as Watergate.

Moral character is something that can be taught and learned. As men, we can all look back to our upbringing and see the values that we were taught. We can also examine ourselves and determine the values that have been incorporated into our lives. Even though values can be taught (Lofton 1991), they do not automatically become a part of our lives. We all have occasionally seen examples of children who, in spite of having had "good" parents, become "bad." We have also occasionally witnessed the reverse—wherein bad parents ended up having good children. However, parents and role models contribute significantly to the development of moral character.

MORAL CHARACTER AS A CONCEPT

We frequently hear persons speaking of reputation, character, or integrity, though they are too often downplayed as central virtues. Even though we often hear these terms, there seems to be another central value that supersedes them. That value is success—making it—and doing whatever it takes to be successful.

During the 1970s, situation ethics became popular because of the work of Joseph Fletcher (1974). Fletcher described situation ethics in the following manner:

> The situationist enters into every decision-making situation fully armed with the ethical maxims of his community and its heritage, and he treats them with respect as illuminators of his problems. Just the same he is prepared in any situation to compromise them or set them aside in the situation if love seems better served by doing so.
>
> Situation ethics goes part of the way with natural law, by accepting reason as the instrument of moral judgment, while rejecting the notion that the good is "given" in the nature of things, objectively. It goes part of the way with Scriptural law by accepting revelation as the source of the norm while rejecting all "revealed" norms or laws but the one command—to love God in the neighbor. The situationist follows a moral law or violates it according to love's need. For example, "Almsgiving is a good thing if . . ." The situationist never says, "Almsgiving is a good thing. Period!" His decisions are hypothetical,

not categorical. Only the commandment to love is categorically good. "Owe no one anything, except to love one another" (Romans 13:8). (p. 26)

Although situation ethics is still visible, the ethic that seems to be modeled today is captured by the following five phrases:

1. "Do whatever needs to be done, don't get caught."
2. "Do to others before they do to you."
3. "Right and wrong are relative—survival is absolute."
4. "Money is more important than principles."
5. "Principles are good, but only money pays the bills."

If one attempts to state a moral or ethical position, he or she is often accused of moralizing. The word *moralizing* means to explain or interpret morally or to give a moral quality or direction to. In counseling and teaching situations, moralizing is often an issue that is raised. While I agree that moralizing in the sense of denying individuals their right to certain behaviors is wrong, there are times when one must take a moral position.

Traditional religions place tremendous value on morals or codes of ethics. While the specific morals and practices vary among religions, all religions have a systematic code of ethics. Religion in turn tremendously influences societies and their laws. The Bible and Christianity place a high value on personal and moral character as the following biblical passages show:

A good name is rather to be chosen than great riches, and loving favour rather than silver and gold. (Proverbs 22:1)

A good name is better than precious ointment. (Ecclesiastes 7:1a)

(Today, we might paraphrase this to say, "A good name is better than being a chief executive officer if it takes doing wrong to become one.")

Pure religion and undefiled before God and the Father is this, to visit the fatherless and widows in their affliction and to keep oneself unspotted from the world. (James 1:27 paraphrased)

A bishop then must be blameless . . . *of* good behavior. *Moreover, he must have a* good report *of them that are outside* . . . *Deacons, being found* blameless. (1 Timothy 3:2, 7, 10 paraphrased)

I, therefore, the prisoner of the Lord, beseech you that ye walk worthy *of the vocation to which you are called, with all lowliness and meekness, with long-suffering, forbearing one another in love; Endeavoring to keep the unity of the Spirit in the bond of peace.* (Ephesians 4:1–3 paraphrased)

DEVELOPING AND MAINTAINING MORAL CHARACTER: A GENERAL VIEW

Most persons would agree and evidence would support the hypothesis that the development of moral character is dependent on three things: Morality must be taught; morality must be modeled; morality must be reinforced. Each of these, other people do for us; each is extremely helpful in setting the framework for the development of moral character. To complete the process, however, one must determine that the development of moral character is valuable and then incorporate morality in one's life. Hence morality, besides being taught, modeled, and reinforced, must become a personal value.

Several theories regarding moral development have been formulated. These theories tend to suggest that morality is learned in stages and through a developmental process. Lawrence Kohlberg's theory (1973), for example, postulates three levels—preconventional, conventional, and postconventional. At the preconventional level, the person is responsible to cultural rules and labels. From these rules, the person acquires a concept of right or wrong. At the conventional level, the major focus is on meeting and maintaining the expectations of the individual's family, group, or nation. This is done regardless of other consequences. At the postconventional level, an individual begins to define moral values and principles beyond those that are simply derived from the group.

W. G. Perry (1970) outlined a four-stage theory of morality—dualism, multiplicity, relativism, and commitment in relativism. At the dualism stage, a person views the world in a strict right/wrong perspective with no room for alternative or conditional reasoning. At the multiplicity stage, one sees that there may be several ways of looking at life. The relativism stage allows for relative, multiple, and comparative answers and contexts. The final stage—commitment in relativism—involves developing and living with a series of commitments and senses of identity that function simultaneously.

Both the Kohlberg and the Perry theories assume that one moves through the stages in sequence and that the final stage is descriptive of the more mature person.

N. Branden (1969) made the following comments regarding the development of character and the importance of values in developing one's self-worth.

> A man's *character* is the sum of the principles and values that guide his actions in the face of moral choices.
>
> Very early in his development, as a child becomes aware of his power to choose his actions, as he acquires the sense of being a *person* he experiences the need to feel that he is *right* as a person, right in his characteristic manner of acting—that he is good.
>
> As I have stressed, no other living species faces such questions as: What kind of entity should I seek to become? By what moral principles should I guide my life? But there is no way for man to escape these questions. *Man cannot exempt himself from the realm of values and value-judgments*. Whether the values by which he judges himself are conscious or subconscious, rational or irrational, consistent or contradictory, life-serving or life-negating—every human being judges himself by *some* standard; and to the extent that he fails to satisfy that standard, his sense of personal worth, his self-respect, suffers accordingly. (pp. 113–14)

When one fails to develop a conscience, a super-ego, or a set of moral or ethical principles based on the good of the group and society while also considering the self, one becomes what the psychologist and psychiatrist describe in clinical terms as the antisocial personality. In times past, such individuals were referred to as sociopaths or psychopaths. Among other characteristics, the antisocial personality exhibits the following (see *Diagnostic and Statistical Manual of Mental Disorders 4th ed.*, 1994, pp. 649–50):

1. Failure to conform to social norms with respect to lawful behaviors as indicated by repeatedly performing acts that are grounds for arrest
2. Deceitfulness, as indicated by repeated lying, use of aliases, or conning others for personal profit or pleasure
3. Lack of remorse, as indicated by being indifferent to or rationalizing their having hurt, mistreated, or stolen from another

DEVELOPING AND MAINTAINING MORAL CHARACTER: A CHRISTIAN PERSPECTIVE.

Earlier, I mentioned several Bible verses that indicate the importance that the Scriptures place on moral character. However, a Christian must be careful to put moral character in its proper perspective. That is, as important as it is, moral character must not become God.

From the perspective of developing and maintaining an orderly society having upright and good citizens, a moral person is in and of itself valued. The Bible supports the concept of laws in a society. However, from the standpoint of biblical Christianity, being moral in and of itself is of no lasting consequence. Moral character for the Christian must be a *result* of a relationship with Christ and not a condition for acceptance by Christ. Ephesians 2:10 captures well this idea: "For we are his workmanship, created in Christ Jesus unto good works, which God hath before ordained that we should walk in them." Thus, good works and moral character for the Christian must *flow from* a relationship with Christ Jesus and become an integrated part of one's life. Christian men and women are expected to live moral and consistent lives and will be judged by works not in terms of salvation, but in regard to rewards.

MORAL CHARACTER AS A LIFESTYLE

How then is the Christian able to exhibit moral character as a lifestyle? There are several prerequisites that are critical to this process.

First, there must above all be the certainty of salvation. The Scriptures are clear that one can know that one is saved. The following Scriptures speak to this fact:

> *That if thou shalt confess with thy mouth the Lord Jesus, and shalt believe in thine heart that God hath raised him from the dead, thou shalt be saved.*
> *For with the heart man believeth unto righteousness; and with the mouth confession is made unto salvation.*
> *For the scripture saith, whosoever believeth on him shall not be ashamed.*
> *For there is no difference between the Jew and the Greek, for the same Lord over all is rich unto all that call upon him.*
> *For whosoever shall call upon the name of the Lord shall be saved.* (Romans 10:9–13)

Whosoever believeth that Jesus is the Christ is born of God: and everyone that loveth him that begat loveth him also that is begotten of him.

He that believeth on the Son of God hath the witness in himself: he that believeth not God hath made him a liar, because he believeth not the record that God gave of his Son.

And this is the record, that God hath given to us eternal life, and this life is in his Son.

He that hath the Son hath life; and he that hath not the Son of God hath not life.

These things have I written unto you that believe on the name of the Son of God; that you may know *that ye have eternal life, and that ye may believe on the name of the Son of God.* (1 John 5:1, 10–13)

Neither is there salvation in any other: for there is none other name *under heaven given among men, whereby we must be saved.* (Acts 4:12)

Therefore, the certainty of salvation is critically indispensable to the development of biblical moral character. We have to know whose we are. If we know our Anchor, we will be able to develop an appropriate and consistent worldview, stating with the confidence of Paul in 2 Corinthians 5:17, "Therefore if any man be in Christ, he is a new creature."

Second, we must understand and carry out God's general and specific (personal) wills. God's general will refers to those things that are expected of all Christians. All Christians are expected to (1) pray (one ought to always pray); (2) study ("study to show thyself approved . . ." [2 Timothy 2:15]); (3) witness; (4) love (they will know we are Christians by our love); and (5) give (of our talent, time, and money). When we are doing those things we are fulfilling the general will of God.

To be *fully* effective, however, we must be open to and do God's specific will and the unique tasks that he has called us to do. The specific will of God is often a troublesome area for many people. I believe that as people are assured of salvation and likewise assured of their role in God's plan, their walk will be better and more confident. Earlier, I quoted Ephesians 4:1 wherein Paul admonishes us to walk worthy of the vocation to which we are called.

We can determine God's specific will by going to God in prayer and requesting that he reveal his specific will to us. James 1:5–6 tells us that "if any of you lack wisdom, let him ask of God, that giveth to all men liberally, and upbraideth not; and it shall be given him. But let him ask in faith, nothing wavering."

We can also determine God's specific will by studying the list of roles and gifts that are given by the Holy Spirit, to see which we are exemplifying (see Ephesians 4:11; 1 Corinthians 12). That list includes apostles, prophets, evangelists, pastors, teachers, word of wisdom, word of knowledge, faith, gifts of healing, working of miracles, prophecy, discerning of spirits, diversities of tongues, interpretation of tongues, helps, and government.

One conclusion from a close study of gifts and the giving of gifts by the Holy Spirit is that everyone has a gift and everyone has a ministry whether or not one knows what they are.

Third, one must clearly understand God's view of the Christian *as a witness*.

> *But ye shall receive power, after that the Holy Ghost is come upon you: and ye shall be witnesses unto me both in Jerusalem, and in all Judea, and in Samaria, and unto the uttermost part of the earth.* (Acts 1:8)

> *Ye* are *the salt of the earth: but if the salt have lost its savour, wherewith shall it be salted? It is henceforth good for nothing, but to be cast out, and to be trodden under foot of men. Ye* are *the light of the world. A city that is set on a hill cannot be hid. Let your light so shine before men, that they may* see your good works, *and glorify your Father which is in heaven.* (Matthew 5:13–14, 16)

If one pays close attention to these verses, one will note that they indicate that a Christian, by virtue of one's being or essence, is a witness. Being a witness is not optional. Our character and our witness is on open display. So, the issue is not whether we are witnesses but rather what types of witnesses are we.

Fourth, one must have the right concept of ministry. Vine, in the *Expository Dictionary of Old and New Testament Words* (1981), defines *ministry* or *minister* as a "servant, attendant, or deacon." Hence, the biblical concept of ministry is service. Our society has, in too many cases, unfortunately equated ministry with ministers and ministers with preachers. Such narrow concepts of ministry have resulted in Christians' belittling the need to "walk worthy" and therefore they have left walking worthy up to "preachers," deacons, and other leaders rather than seeing themselves *as* "ministers" and *in* the ministry in the generic and biblical sense of the term (see also Feucht 1974; Myers 1994).

Fifth, we must debunk the myth of "full-time" and "part-time" ministry. The general idea of full-time or part-time ministry gives the wrong impression to many Christians who are in so-called secular settings, serving only to help compartmentalize life in a way that runs counter to the biblical view presented earlier of our witness as being a lifestyle.

When we compartmentalize ourselves it is easier to rationalize our inconsistent moral character. Over time we can be led to believe that we can be one type of person in our church or Christian community and another type of person in our professional life.

Compartmentalizing is inconsistent with traditional African religion, early Black American Christianity, and biblical Christianity. Mbiti (1970) made the following comments about our African heritage:

> Africans are notoriously religious, and each people has its own religious system with a set of beliefs and practices. Religion permeates into all the departments of life so fully that it is not easy or possible always to isolate it.
>
> ... African peoples do not know how to exist without religion. One of the sources of severe strain for Africans exposed to modern change is the increasing process (through education, urbanization and industrialization) by which individuals become detached from their traditional environment ...
>
> It is not enough to learn and embrace a faith which is active once a week, either on Sunday or Friday, while the rest of the week is virtually empty. It is not enough to embrace a faith which is confined to a church building or mosque, which is locked up six days and opened only once or twice a week.
>
> Unless Christianity fully occupies the whole person as much as, if not more than, traditional religions do, most converts to these faiths will continue to revert to their old beliefs and practices for perhaps six days a week ...
>
> Since traditional religions occupy the whole person and the whole of his life, conversion to new religions like Christianity must embrace

his language, thought patterns, fears, social relationships, attitudes, and philosophical disposition, if that conversion is to make a lasting impact upon the individual and his community. (pp. 3–4)

These observations are a challenge to us as Christian and Black men. The extent to which we implement them is the extent to which we exemplify a consistent moral character.

Sixth, one must be willing to suffer for righteousness' sake. It is stated:

Blessed are they who are persecuted for righteousness' sake: for theirs is the kingdom of heaven. Blessed are ye, when men shall revile you, and persecute you, and shall say all manner of evil against you falsely, for my sake. Rejoice, and be exceedingly glad: for great is your reward in heaven: for so persecuted they the prophets which were before you. (Matthew 5:10–12)

One must be prepared to suffer for righteousness, if the situation presents itself.

Seventh, there must be a personal ministry. A personal ministry follows from God's specific will for our lives. Each of us must develop in such a way that we know how we are contributing to the body of Christ.

Eighth, one must understand and draw upon the power of the Holy Spirit.

Howbeit when he, the Spirit of truth, is come, he will guide you into all truth: for he shall not speak of himself; but whatever he shall hear, that shall he speak: and he will show you things to come. He shall glorify me: for he shall receive of mine, and shall show it unto you. All things that the Father hath are mine: therefore said I, that he shall take of mine, and shall show it unto you. (John 16:13–15)

Ninth, one must know how to be *in* the world but not *of* the world. Jesus in his high priestly intercessory prayer recorded in John said:

And now come I to thee; and these things I speak in the world, that they might have my joy fulfilled themselves. I have given them thy word; and the world hath hated them, because they are not of the world, even as I am not of the world. I pray not that thou shouldest take them out of the world, but that thou shouldest keep them from the evil. (John 17:13–15)

The key to being in the world but not of the world is by abiding totally in Christ.

> *I in them, and thou in me, that they may be made perfect in one; and that the world may know that thou hast sent me, and hast loved them, as thou has loved me.* (John 17:23)

> *Thy word have I hid in mine heart, that I might not sin against thee.* (Psalm 119:11)

CONCLUSION

Moral character for an individual is critically important. Our effectiveness as "light" and "salt" is enhanced by our integrity. One sees the importance of moral character in the song *Lift Him Up.*

The apostle Paul beseeches us in Romans 12:1–2 to present our bodies a living sacrifice to God that is holy and acceptable. He described this as a reasonable service. King David, in many of his psalms, also proclaimed this virtue. In Psalm 1, he portrayed the blessedness of walking in the "way of the righteous."

For this and future generations, we need more Black men *and* women who will *walk worthy.*

REFERENCES

Branden, N. 1969. *The psychology of self-esteem.* New York: Bantam.

1994. *Diagnostic and statistical manual of mental disorders.* 4th ed. Washington, DC: American Psychiatric Association.

Feucht, O. E. 1974. *Everyone a minister.* St. Louis: Concordia.

Fletcher, J. 1974. *Situation ethics: The new morality.* Philadelphia: Westminster.

June, L. N. February 1987. The importance of moral character. Paper presented at the Christian Professional's Conference, sponsored by

Christian Research and Development. Philadelphia, Pennsylvania. (The original source for this chapter.)

The King James version of the Bible.

Kohlberg, L. 1973. Continuities in childhood to adult moral development revisited. In *Life span developmental psychology: Personality and socialization,* edited by P. B. Baltes and K. W. Schaie. New York: Academic Press.

Lofton, F. 1991. Teaching Christian values within the Black family. In *The Black family: Past, present, and future,* edited by L. N. June. Grand Rapids: Zondervan.

Mbiti, J. S. 1970. *African religions and philosophy.* Garden City, NY: Doubleday.

Myers, W. H. 1994. *God's yes was louder than my no: Rethinking the African American call to ministry.* Trenton, NJ: Africa World Press.

Perry, W. G. 1970. *Forms of intellectual and ethical development during the college years: A scheme.* New York: Holt, Rinehart, and Winston.

Vine, W. E. 1981. *Vine's expository dictionary of Old and New Testament words,* edited by F. F. Bruce. Old Tappan, NJ: Revell.

1985. *Webster's new ninth collegiate dictionary.* Springfield, MA: Merriam-Webster.

Henry Lee (Hank) Allen

Risk and Failure
as Preludes
to Achievement

HENRY LEE (HANK) ALLEN is assistant professor in the Warner Graduate School of Education and Human Development at the University of Rochester in New York State. He has a biblical studies degree from Wheaton College and a doctor of philosophy degree from the University of Chicago. Born in Joiner, Arkansas, and raised in Phoenix, Illinois, he is married to Juliet Cooper Allen. They have eight children: Jonathan, Jessica, Janice, Justin, Julia, Janel, Joseph, and Judith. Hank is actively involved at Bethel Full Gospel Church in Rochester, New York. He has served on the faculty at Bethel College (Minnesota) and Calvin College (Michigan).

Chapter 2
Henry Lee (Hank) Allen

Risk and Failure as Preludes to Achievement

During the 1980s, two prominent social psychologists publicly questioned whether Black Americans had, in the aftermath of the Civil Rights Movement, been their own worst enemy by failing to grasp the hidden dimensions of success. These scholars reasoned that the ability of Black Americans to solve many of their social problems was being jeopardized by Black Americans themselves! The culprit was the failure of many Blacks to meet rigorous intellectual and professional challenges. Instead, Howard and Hammond (1985) found that Black youth were opting for mediocrity rather than disciplining themselves en masse to take advantage of the strategic opportunities that occurred in their lives. These authors are not alone in exposing this tendency toward underachievement. D. Glascow (1980) had done so years earlier.

A prominent educator, John Ogbu (Gibson & Ogbu 1991), has echoed this same sentiment, based on over twenty years of extensive research of various Black communities. Ogbu suggests that many Blacks underachieve in schools precisely because they practice an oppositional culture that stigmatizes obedience to authority, middle-class aspirations, and scholastic achievement as "acting White." Moreover, Professor Elijah Anderson (1994) has reported on how some Blacks have been intimidated by those who adhere to the most degrading aspects of "street culture." In the meantime, the sinister allurements of abject poverty are deliberately celebrated in the name of Black ethnicity or consciousness! The Black community cannot advance itself for long against even greater opposition by ignoring this spiritual cancer of lethargy plus ignominy. Wisdom dictates that we expose and reduce counterproductive tendencies among Black males. There can be no virtue in the solidarity of fools.

The above ethnographic depictions are not meant to impugn all segments of what we call the Black community. All of us are aware that the majority of African-Americans in this country labor against and have overcome tremendous odds in order to achieve what we have. None of my comments herein are meant to dispel the positive role models. Obvious detractions aside, however, there is ample empirical evidence to substantiate that many of us are squandering the precious opportunities we have, even though we in this current generation have fewer obstacles to face than most of our ancestors did. Insecurity, a damaged self-image, and the refusal to develop competencies have been the seedbeds of fatalism and neglect for far too many of us for far too long.

Yet the observations cited earlier and other similar renditions cause me to speculate: Why do some Blacks place a premium on pathological underachievement? Admittedly, barriers to opportunity do exist as does the specter of racial discrimination; yet, why do some of us neglect to develop those talents, capabilities, and challenges that are directly under our control? Why do not more of us learn success from our failures and risk being vulnerable enough to learn new skills? The exponential loss of talent in our community is compounded like exorbitant interest charges in the collective accomplishments of each new generation. Sad to say, many Black males in my generation—even my own schoolmates—failed to grasp how and why underachievement could be detrimental to their future and our collective progress.

All of this has led me to wonder anew whether this generation of young Black males has grasped two vital sociological truths: (1) often a person must take a risk in order to achieve (see Ecclesiastes 11:1); and (2) failure or humility is most often a necessary prerequisite to eventual success or honor (see Proverbs 15:33 and 18:12). The tenets of *authentic Christianity* offer a positive, constructive agenda that can lead to a transformation of any human tragedy, including those that are the direct consequence of our own failures and weaknesses. Those who fail to respond correctly to even the most miserable circumstances and fail to learn the lessons of risk and failure will be imprisoned needlessly in the misery of mediocrity.

My aim in this chapter is to discuss how risk and failure can be preludes to achievement. In fact, in the ways of God, it is often our weaknesses, failures, problems, and setbacks that will be used—by His intent and design—to humble us in preparation for success. Like a parent eagle who knocks a young eagle off its nest or perch in order to teach it to soar, God teaches us to risk the comforts of our current niche in order to develop our character and talents for success in the future. Moreover, we will observe the truth of what Edward Lord Phelps said long ago: "The man who makes no mistakes does not usually make anything" (quoted in Partington, 1992, p. 28).

We will see that many of the most successful people or organizations either failed many times, took several risks, or both—before they achieved. My plan therefore in this chapter is to clarify what I mean by risk and failure, deduce their most salient aspects or characteristics, elaborate their principles, and discuss their possible effects on the lives of Black men, young and old. Throughout, I will intersperse several personal and biblical examples to indicate how God uses both of these conditions to teach us to depend on Him, His wisdom, and His power. Only then is achievement possible!

DEFINING RISK

What is risk? How can it be differentiated from recklessness or wanton disregard? Does risk invariably lead to dereliction of duty or irresponsibility? How is failure different from laziness? What role do motives play in my failures? Can simplemindedness be transformed into wisdom? Can poor planning be overcome by supernatural guidance in Christ?

Risk involves having the faith to attempt something new or different even though it might be hard or lead to failure. Taking a risk means allowing yourself to be vulnerable; it means admitting that you do not have an exaggerated sense of your own worth and competence. Risk is not recklessness; recklessness involves little or no forethought. Recklessness derives from not taking the time to evaluate the outcome of one's choices or acts. In contrast, those who take risks are aware that they face enormous obstacles to achievement; yet, the rewards seem well worth the effort (Matthew 5:41).

The Bible is replete with examples of people who took risks in order to achieve great things. What they have in common is a tremendous faith in God prior to taking the risk that was in accord with God's plan for their lives. Peter took a risk by walking on the water. Likewise, Daniel took a gigantic risk agreeing in advance to interpret an angry ruler's dream. The beautiful Queen Esther took a risk in order to save her people Israel from certain genocide! King David, as a young man, took an enormous risk by challenging and defeating Goliath. Elijah risked all in a contest with the enemies of God at Mount Carmel. Our Lord Christ risked His life in order to serve and save us all (John 3:17). All were rewarded for their faith in God. It seems that you cannot have real faith or love without an element of risk!

The secular world we live in also illustrates how risk is often a prelude to success (Proverbs 12:24). Alex Haley, the renowned author of *Roots* (1976), risked bankruptcy in order to obtain the information necessary to complete his saga about Kunta Kinte. Haley was almost evicted from his residence and was tempted to abandon the project, immediately before a philanthropist gave him the funds he needed to complete his research. The entire nation has benefited from his extraordinary efforts and sacrifice as the story of enslavement was dramatized via television for millions to watch. Berry Gordy took a risk in creating and marketing Motown Records and saw it become one of the most successful businesses of its kind. Along the way, Gordy encountered Joseph Jackson, the father of a large family of boys who were talented musically. This family endured risk and hardship in order to become one of the most successful groups of entertainers ever—the Jackson Five!

In school, too, we must take risks in order to better ourselves through achievement. Frequently, unanticipated opportunities accompany the new skills or understandings we develop in reading, writing, and mathematics. At each level of achievement, there is a corresponding structure of incentives and rewards. We meet new people and establish crucial social contacts that may sustain us in the struggles associated with our work. Moreover, we are able to comprehend our own narrow world in a much deeper fashion. We discover deeper dimensions to the world around us, uncover great complexities in even the mundane affairs of our existence.

The calculus of life at work demands risk. Promotions are risky ventures, too. Those who achieve set goals in order to attempt or risk more of themselves. In fact, sociologists have discovered a tendency that we call "the Matthew Effect." It depicts the processes by which achievers in any field stand out, thereby accruing a disproportionate share of resources, opportunities, contacts, and communications—all due to their greater productivity. In most fields of endeavor, the productive few provide a disproportionate set of contributions for the many. Unfortunately, assuming a legitimate risk does not automatically guarantee a reward. We must develop patience while waiting on our Lord to open the doors of opportunity or promotion (see Psalm 75). God encourages and expects our integrity along with our productivity (John 15:1–8).

Risk is inevitable in the worlds of business, education, entertainment, sports, and science as the biographical histories of successful people or companies will document. Explorers like Columbus took tremendous risks in order to come to the land we now call America. Throughout the centuries, great discoveries have been made by men and women who took considerable risks (Boorstin 1983; McDonald 1993). During the 1960s, the United States took perhaps the ultimate human risk in preparing to land men on the moon. Despite the naysayers and incredible odds against it, *it happened!* Muhammad Ali took a substantial risk in regaining his boxing title—*three times*. More recently, the owner of Black Entertainment Television (BET), a cable channel, took a risk to start the first national television channel dedicated to our cultural interests. Of course, the surgeon Ben Carson has taken enormous risks to become an expert in medicine. Doubtless, General Colin Powell had to assume risk in order to learn the expertise he needed to command the United States armed forces.

Great achievements appear to correlate significantly with carefully assumed risks. In my university office, I have a plaque that reminds me of this:

EXCELLENCE can be attained if you ...
CARE more than others think is wise ...
RISK more than others think is safe ...
DREAM more than others think is practical ...
EXPECT more than others think is possible.

Choosing to risk time or effort to do what seems difficult or impossible is never easy. Christ's disciples did not have an easy time with the risks associated with spreading the gospel. Yet, because of their success, you and I have been confronted with the opportunity to know Christ as our Lord and Savior. Without risk taking, many of the amenities of the modern world would not have been possible: computers, television, radio, aircraft, electric lights, nuclear energy, and automobiles. Even the great republic that we live in was birthed at great risk to those who founded it.

Risk-taking is not compatible with laziness or insecurity. Laziness squanders opportunities, a lesson as old as the Scriptures. Insecurity causes one to seek isolation for fear of being exposed. To avoid failure, many people are reluctant even to try anything new or different. Risk-taking may sometimes lead to the embarrassment of failure. We may damage our lofty reputation. Others may ridicule us for daring to try some task beyond our initial threshold of capability. Risk may indeed lead to adversity, misunderstanding, and isolation, especially as one pioneers certain ventures.

Many times you feel like the proverbial tortoise in one of Aesop's fables. As you will recall, a race was sponsored between the tortoise and the rabbit. The rabbit ran ahead immediately, only to lose the race because he took an undue break to mock the tortoise's slowness. The tortoise was rejected by many as a legitimate contender. Why should an animal with its characteristic weakness (slowness) even bother to engage in a contest with a more advantaged adversary? The tortoise in the fable took a tremendous risk, but the story also indicates that its gain was great! It faced overwhelming odds. It received jests. Running the course was not at all easy. Still, going beyond these negative stimuli, the tortoise was able to rejoice in its victory and achievements.

Taking a risk could sometimes invigorate us; it could—under the proper circumstances—give creativity or freshness to our thinking. Nonetheless, we should normally not take any risk that involves harm to another or loss of life or property. Our earthly authorities, especially those most responsible for caring for, mentoring, and nurturing us, need to be notified about our intentions and plans. We must be accountable to others, despite whatever risks we take. Rebellion distorts our judgment and jeopardizes our achievement.

DEFINING FAILURE

Failure is determined mainly by how we respond to the mistakes we make or setbacks we encounter along the road of life. The National Aeronautics and Space Administration (NASA) failed many times before it developed the technology appropriate for launching spacecraft to the lunar surface. It is said that J. C. Penney was broke and bankrupt until he finally beheld success when he was in his nineties. Thomas Edison tested the lightbulb over a thousand times before he was successful. Yet millions on this planet have enjoyed the fruits of his labor. Alexander Graham Bell, the inventor of the telephone as we know it, failed miserably before obtaining his goal. Thus, failure is determined ultimately if and when we give up on something we are attempting. By our responses, therefore, we are—to a large extent—the masters of our destiny before Christ.

We can fail because we doubt our self-worth. We feel that we lack something. Sometimes we fail because we listen to what others say negatively about us. For Blacks, this means that we cannot allow those who make disparaging or distasteful remarks about our ethnic heritage or traits to dictate to us what our identity should be. We can fail because we feel angry about how God made us: about how we look, the family He placed us in, or our innate weaknesses. We can become bitter over our errors. We can foolishly blame others for our problems.

Moses had similar sentiments about his self-image. When God called him to go to Pharaoh, Moses felt stupid and inadequate. Yet, God built up Moses' self-esteem by declaring His control and support for Moses, no matter what might transpire. Moreover, God has shown that He can curtail racists by the fate He allowed for Haman via Queen Esther, and Nebuchadnezzar via Daniel. Peter testifies that Christ is against racism (Acts 10:34–35).

The biblical character Joseph, son of Jacob, did not react to his undeserved troubles in an abusive manner. Jesus Christ teaches us that failure accrues to the person who rejects his words of truth (Matthew 7:24–29). Failure occurs only when we give up on responding to our situations in a godly manner or refuse to obey the inner prompting of the Holy Spirit who, as Romans 8 says, lives inside each Christian to help him or her with their weaknesses. We are in control of our responses to life's situations!

Failure, however, does not mean that it is wrong to redirect our efforts or interests. Many students enter college with the intent to become a physician, only to be disabused of that notion by their grades in biology or physiology. Some continue on despite the setbacks and actually become doctors; others decide that their talents are more appropriate for another vocation. Both types made valid decisions in light of the fact that failure can cause you to intensify or modify your plans. One must not wallow in self-pity, whatever the outcome. One must act proactively to failure, choosing instead to maximize its lessons by responding to the good aspects in every situation.

In my own life, my failure to make my high-school basketball team was painful and disheartening at the time; yet, I learned to redirect my affections toward improving my academic studies. Although I did not know it at the time, my enhanced proficiency at studying would lead—within just five years—to my receipt of a scholarship to attend graduate school at one of the nation's most rigorous universities. God uses our most severe failures to accomplish His positive plan for our lives, as long as we acknowledge our ultimate dependence on Him for wisdom, protection, guidance, and power.

Over the years, I have learned that one must risk "going the extra mile" in order to be diligent and creative. Therefore, being a minority group member is no excuse for failing to take advantage of the opportunities we have, no matter how great or small. God builds the character of mighty servants in the most debilitating circumstances. (Remember that David was a mere shepherd before he became ruler of Israel.) He displays His awesome sovereignty by placing a "minority" over the affairs of the majority: Witness Daniel, Joseph, and Esther in the Old Testament. I do not think He has changed His agenda to conform to modern times. The Bible indicates repeatedly that a godly minority can rule an ungodly majority at God's direction.

DEFINING ACHIEVEMENT

Achievement occurs when we use our skills, talents, and aptitudes to accomplish something that is worthwhile to God and others. Each achievement, no matter how modest or insignificant to others, represents a steppingstone that God will use to guide us toward eventual success. We must learn to be faithful in the most trivial, mundane tasks assigned to us by those in authority over us. The greater our achievements in this regard, the greater is our success. Great athletes, musicians, artisans, intellectuals, and others are distinguished by their tenacious attention to details that most people would ignore. In short, they must practice or work at developing their competencies from the simplest level to extraordinary levels of mastery.

Our achievement is enhanced by developing skills and sensibilities; education—whether from school, experience, apprenticeship, or the laboratory of life—is instrumental to this task. Achievement is not based on outward appearances, selfishness, popularity, or pride. It is derived from service, predicated on our willingness to discover and to meet the needs of others. Success and achievement are reflections of our spiritual maturity (Matthew 5:13–16; Colossians 3:17, 23). Virtue exudes from the discipline of working diligently at our assignments during times of obscurity. God knows that struggling to overcome obstacles and challenges refines our character. It teaches us also to cooperate with others in our areas of weakness and need, thereby inculcating authentic humility. Notoriety brings its hidden costs, pressures, vices, and vanities soon enough.

Achievement results from faith and vision. We ought to have visions of what we can do, of what Christ seeks to accomplish in and through us. We should not hide, neglect, or bury our talents like an unfaithful servant (Matthew 25:14–30). We ought to expect great things for ourselves as Black men in Christ. The greater the obstacles or problems in our families, the greater our vision should be in resolving them as the indwelling Christ directs us. We need a spirit like Caleb, who even after forty years of waiting on God in the desert, had the faith, courage, and vitality to compete for the Promised Land that he envisioned. Through faith and vision, Christ's disciples evangelized a Roman empire that sought originally to obliterate all believers.

Without question, Black men have achieved great things in entertainment, music, and sports. Black men have also accomplished terrific things in lesser-known areas of endeavor such as science, technology, and business. We have done so from scratch, given the aberrant legacy of slavery and segregation mounted against us. Every hall of fame in these arenas includes Black men of tremendous dedication and accomplishment. Given what Black men have been up against in this society, our accomplishments have been no less than phenomenal! Booker T. Washington and Frederick Douglass were stalwarts who began their lives in slavery. The technological activities of George Washington Carver and Benjamin Banneker were impressive, if not impeccable.

Look at what Charles Drew, W. E. B. Du Bois, Ralph Bunche, and Dr. Martin Luther King Jr. have achieved against the odds. Witness what Black soldiers, astronauts, and scientists such as Walter Massey have done. The accomplishments of prominent Black conservatives like Shelby Steele, Thomas Sowell, and Walter Williams are noteworthy. Elsewhere in the academy, I cite C. Eric Lincoln, John Hope Franklin, Allison Davis, St.

Clair Drake, Edgar Epps, James Blackwell, William Julius Wilson, Harry Edwards, Charles Willie, and Clifton Wharton Jr. as recent exemplars. I challenge the reader to become aware of the legacies established by these Black men.

We are also aware of "ordinary" Black men who have achieved great things in their work, families, and jobs without the deserved accolades or fanfare. Our fathers have worked hard at menial jobs in order to provide for our welfare. Black pastors have taught us about salvation and obedience to God. Our police have risked their lives protecting our neighborhoods. Our storekeepers have defied the odds and brought groceries as well as other necessities to our communities. Our teachers have instructed us, giving us the skills to cope or earn a decent living in a hostile modern society. Indeed, regular, common Black men have across the generations governed and rescued us from oblivion in the aftermath of slavery!

Thus, African-Americans need not be ashamed of our progenitors' accomplishments in this nation, whether skewed or not. We ought not to be dismayed by those who are dismissive of our historical contributions, nor of those who disabuse our interests. An unbiased view of our achievements would reveal an indisputable reality: *No ethnic group has in modern times achieved more than we have with fewer resources or less opportunity in a nation with such a pernicious legacy of racism.* Yet there is far more to be done and a new reality of multiculturalism has made it imperative that we accomplish even more. We need to cultivate the best lessons of the past in order to inspire us to higher pinnacles of achievement.

Canvass the successful persons, women and men, that you know in your church or neighborhood. Ask them to tell you about their experiences with risk and failure. Interview them to create a hall of fame for Black achievers in your school, church, or neighborhood center as well as your home. Keep a diary of your own experiences. Read the biographies or autobiographies of great achievers. Invariably, you will learn that risk and failure are the inevitable ingredients of achievement.

KEYS TO ACHIEVEMENT

Let me add here that achievement is not a unidimensional construct. It involves nurturing, learning, and sponsorship between and within various generations. Economists have used the term *human capital* to refer to investments in our assets of talent, expertise, experience, and education (along with its formal and informal aspects). James S. Coleman (1990), a prominent sociologist, has talked about the need to maintain "social capital," to identify the advantages we learn from our heritage, to listen to the lessons taught to us by those parents and others to whom we are accountable. Lessons imbued from failure contribute positively to our human and social capital if accepted in the correct manner.

Psychologists teach us that motivation is also instrumental to our achievement (Fleming 1984). Motivation is a type of human capital that is priceless in any worthy endeavor. We must be motivated to do our best no matter how arduous the task. There is simply no credible alternative to being as productive as we can be. We cannot be the best at everything, but we can develop our weaknesses into basic competencies. We can also learn what Dr. Martin Luther King Jr. taught decades ago: "Everybody can be great because everybody can serve." When I was a child, both my father and uncle taught me: Whatever you do, give it your best effort.

Social-science research, too, has much to say about the achievement levels of Black men. Traditionally, this literature has measured achievement by focusing on the factors influencing educational and occupational attainment. Income is also a measure used to evaluate achievement. Altogether, these measures indicate statistically that—despite many impressive gains over recent decades—many Black men are not achieving their potential! While we may quibble with the assumptions undergirding these measurements or the inferences scholars draw from them, the incontrovertible truth is that there are far too many Black men leading unproductive lives. Still others have lives fraught with chronic underachievement. Admittedly, these conditions may happen through no fault of their own but by virtue of racist barriers in society. Yet, despite these impediments, God holds us accountable for the stewardship of our lives. This fact necessitates that we must never give up achieving—no matter what it takes or how it hurts. For survival's sake, we simply cannot afford to be less than our best.

Suffice it to say, I am not now inclined to rehearse in meticulous detail the empirical findings of voluminous studies that document the achievement of Black males on all these various dimensions of endeavors (Blackwell 1981, 1990; Farley 1984; Farley & Allen 1987; W. J. Wilson 1987; National Research Council 1989; Hacker 1992; R. Wilson 1994). However, I do have some stern, quite vitriolic things to say about the parasitic dimensions of certain behavior. (I preface the following comments with love and with an understanding of how difficult our sojourn in this racist, oppressive society has been. My comments might offend a few readers so I apologize in advance for the graphic nature of my generalizations below. These depictions will not win me any popularity contests, and my liberal political reputation will probably be nullified.) Following are some unpleasant things that Black men must correct!

WHAT BLACK MEN MUST CORRECT

The litany of the woes resulting from our underachievement is insulting to civilization. Our unemployment levels are at depression levels. We do not have sufficient numbers of assets, businesses, or experts. Our net worth is abysmal in comparison with others. We depend far too much on public schools and institutions in a nation where private affairs are paramount. We waste too much time on athletics and music. Far too many of us are fathering children out of wedlock we do not parent or provide for. There is too much crime menacing our neighborhoods. We tolerate too many slurs against our women. We are the laughingstock of other ethnic groups who chide us for having a disproportionate percentage of our youth in prisons and our families on welfare. They are perceptive.

On top of this we deride those who have sacrificed themselves to achieve a mere modicum of success. We are vitriolic at defending our rights but deafly silent about assuming our responsibilities. Many of our youth are wild and indecent, trying to take the easy way out of a hard situation or trying to manipulate a buck. Character often takes a back seat to rhetoric. Our most heinous youth intimidate us via gangs, acting as if they have tacit authority over their elders. Brothers, we have to end this mess; it is a cancer that is destroying us all (Proverbs 14:34). I know these are not popular statements, but they depict actuality for too many Black men.

The degradation in some of our communities is an absolute disgrace. Like a bloodthirsty, voracious predator, some of us are foolish enough to rob and murder our ethnic kin. No amount of mythology or delusions can excuse such indecency. Such raunchy behavior is morally inexcusable for any among us, yet many of us continue to sanction it in the name of ethnic solidarity. These are harsh realities that too many of us rationalize away. In short, persistent patterns of underachievement among Black men are contributing exponentially to a loss of virtue in the Black community.

Many Whites and others seek to avoid us or isolate themselves from us—not because of racism—but because of unmitigated evil. The problem of evil in our communities, the loss of virtue among many of us, is often regarded as a sacrosanct issue within our confines. Meanwhile, others laugh, fear, or cry over our pathology. We must face the truth in love; truth is neither liberal nor conservative in its content. We have more to fear today from the cultural cannibalism and internecine violence of our worst ethnic kin than from our external enemies.

Whether we lost ground as a society in the conservative 1980s or not does not really matter since this point is moot! The issue is that other minorities do not stand still while we languish in complacency or self-flagellation. Neither wallowing in pity nor grumbling against others will change our lot. Jealousy and envy will be a cancer that will corrode our best achievements. We must refute the insolence of imbeciles who prey on our community's moral innocence and wealth. Lazy men must stop drinking, and they must abandon their loitering on corners. Such deviance should never be the litmus test for Black orthodoxy. No amount of allegiance to Afrocentrism should obscure the apostasy of those who demean the good we have.

This is not to say that a doomsday scenario is inevitable; however, the advent of increased local and global competition does not argue well for those Black men who lag behind. Political realities, dictated by new patterns of immigration, have allowed other minorities to usurp the nation's exclusive focus on Black issues. Moreover, global competitors may not be very sympathetic to the plight of Blacks as we seek economic and political hegemony. African-American men must plan ahead for a world characterized by increasing ethnic diversity to such an extent that our concerns may become peripheral to the nation and world.

SUCCESS FROM RISK AND FAILURE

How then do we allow risk and failure to breed success, given our current problems? What steps are involved? God gives beauty for ashes; He restores the years that the locusts have eaten. We must experiment with new strategies to promote achievement, all of them involving risk to our egos and capabilities. Like ancient Israel, innovation within the confines of God's purview is our only recourse against our woes and foes. We need spiritual, technological, scientific, psychological, economic, political, and sociological expertise. Our strategies must be targeted—within and across generations—at the individual, group, organizational, and systemic levels. We must anticipate a range of scenarios requiring exquisite planning and action. Black men must commit themselves morally to integrity and excellence whatever job we might have.

To begin with, Black men must risk ego to obtain the humility that pertains to godliness. We must first repent of our reliance on our own devices before consulting God's commands, confessing our sins to him. *Repentance means to change our mind and direction about what we are doing wrong.* Many kings in Israel had to take this step before God intervened to bless them. Daniel confessed his sin and repented, too (chap. 10). Repentance begins the healing process in our lives. It cleanses our failures, allowing us to start anew like the apostle Paul did after his conversion. We are rescued from the emotional poisons of bitterness and self-pity to the extent that we repent.

Repentance allows us free access and a direct claim on God's helping power and vast repository of resources, which greatly exceed our own. Unless we repent thoroughly, I fear that ominous days are ahead for all Black people as the unfolding of the negative trends documented by empirical research ensues unabated. Repentance clears our mind of the debris of failure, permitting us to see what risks are worth taking en route to reinvigorating our vision. Moses had to repent in the wilderness before he learned to rely on God's power, wisdom, and strength to deliver His people. We have much to repent for collectively as Black men. Only through such repentance can we visualize how our self-worth and competencies can alleviate our plight.

Second, we need to develop or rediscover a culture that accents and celebrates moral virtue. Something is wrong when we can have a church on every corner of a city and yet have crime rates, family dissolution statistics, and test scores that reflect chronic patterns of underachievement. There is no glory in this type of buffoonery. The apostasy at work in many of our churches and among our clergy must be exposed and eradicated so that the gospel might produce more abundant fruit in our families and communities. There is simply no substitute for the gospel for the ailments of an oppressed people. When understood and obeyed fervently, the gospel is the most dynamic fulcrum to success in any area of endeavor ever devised. We must use the tenets of the gospel to rebuild our families (Allen 1991).

Third, we must invest in social, intellectual, and other types of human capital, even though this is risky! Humanly speaking—when you have little, it takes faith and courage to risk it in ventures with a high probability of failure. Yet, as the most important achievers within science and business will attest, you cannot have great benefit without substantial risk. Black men must risk getting a superior education by rigorously applying our best energies to what educational or professional opportunities we now have at our disposal. We should seek out and help achievers succeed wherever they are located in our domain. Human capital is what we learn via expertise and experience; social capital refers to the storehouse of contacts that we develop in relationships with others who can augment what talents or expertise we lack. We must risk becoming productive, even though failing many times on the way toward that destination. No one can be excused for attempting less than their best.

Fourth, we must cultivate and respect leadership that is effective and of good character. We must increase accountability. Black men are notorious for allowing petty differences to divide and conquer them. We are often distracted from our most crucial goals by implosion; we turn on ourselves! The least competent among us are unwilling to defer to the most competent. We are skeptical of those with elite credentials or pretensions. No wonder we are in such a mess with regard to our panorama of leaders. We must learn to *trust* those who sacrificially and skillfully lead us in planning new ventures. Moreover, we must diversify the array of leaders that we include beyond just clergy.

Fifth, we must develop strategic plans to use whatever resources we have as efficiently and effectively as possible. Our conferences and forums must accomplish this agenda rather than emote in rhetoric. Pontification is a vain substitute for coordinating our individual, financial, organizational, and other resources toward a strategy that will reduce our failures and problems. We must finance and build our own houses, schools, stores, and hospitals in enough numbers to stimulate us to be self-sufficient, which will increase our employment base. We must create jobs to fill the vacuum created by having available in our communities mainly the most difficult or least desirable jobs in the marketplace.

Sixth, we must decrease our quixotic, systematic dependence on public-sector institutions like the public schools. Public institutions have

superordinate, multicultural goals to negotiate among multiple con-
stituencies, a factor that nullifies their particular effects for us. We must
not disengage from politics; rather we need to instigate plans to promote
and elect the best and the brightest political leaders among us. But this
talented elite must be prepared primarily in schools that cater to our own
interests and developmental needs. Private schools for Black men must
not be places where mythologies are perpetuated without challenge;
rather, they must have domestic and public policies. Creating fantasies
from the past will not help us cope with the realities of tomorrow. On the
domestic side, these private schools must deal strategically with the interests of Blacks; on the public side, they must address the legitimate concerns of outsiders. Private and public institutions must be asymmetrical,
coordinated in purpose and impact within our jurisdictions. Time and
space do not permit me the luxury of saying more about these complicated
remedies.

Like it or not, the best accomplishments of Black men can be tainted
irreparably by the deviant antics of a disproportionate few. Our achievements are often obscured or devalued by the preponderance of irresponsibility that fatalistically afflicts far too many of us during the prime of life.
Collectively, we must realize that as far as ethnicity is concerned, the status of the whole of us is affected by the sum of our parts. Black men must
close out this century by risking good no matter what social forces impede
our progress. This intestinal fortitude is what made our ancestors great in
the midst of colonialism, slavery, racism, segregation, and the mytholog-
ical onslaught of White supremacy. Failure, the rejection of hope, need not
be our legacy to kith and kin.

PERSONAL REFLECTIONS AND CONCLUSION

Let me end this chapter somewhat autobiographically by describing
how real events in my life have been affected by my responses to risk and
failure. I have failed many, many times in my life. Moreover, I have taken
risks that I did not want to take and watched these arduous situations
turn out to my benefit. All of these experiences have humbled me, developed my character, and increased my level of skills—*I have responded
with obedience to Christ's authority over my life situations and learned
godly attitudes.*

During my childhood, I envisioned myself becoming a scientist or
professor. However, the odds against my attaining that goal seemed astro-

nomical. Why? I was a Black male from a working-class family of eight; moreover, three of my siblings were mentally retarded. My father had a sixth-grade education, my mother had a ninth-grade education. I believed that my vision was inspired by my salvation in Christ, but it seemed so fantastic and therefore impossible.

Instead of trusting God to accomplish the vision, I became disillusioned and rebellious during adolescence, thereby short-circuiting the very discipline and character I would ultimately need to be successful. I began to slack off in my studies, doing far less than my best. I was confused, grumpy, belligerent, and stupid—until I started to obey God's Word. God led my family to move away from my favorite neighborhood to an obscure place that I initially hated. The Lord engineered a series of traumatic events that brought pain and suffering in my life in order to purify my motives and conduct. Then slowly, over the decades, the vision has been miraculously fulfilled! From the most unlikely circumstances, Christ had given me success (Psalm 126:5).

My personal journey to success has not been easy; in fact, I almost ruined my life many, many times by indulging in episodes of pride, temporal values, moral impurity, and profanity. As a youth, I was a disillusioned failure in almost everything other than school, where I was performing lackadaisically below my potential. Moreover, I seemed incessantly to attract bullies at every grade level during elementary and high school. During troubled times in my family—due to alcoholism, violence, poverty, ignorance, abuse, and confusion—I frequently contemplated suicide. I was depressed, listening jingoistically to the depressing rhythms of sensual and rebellious music. In short, during much of my adolescence, my life was a mess because (I learned after I became a Christian) I misunderstood God's will and plan via His Word and the prompting of the Holy Spirit. At several junctures in my life I wanted to give up. Life was hard; I had to struggle.

I have seen our community at its worst and its best! Based on my own risks and failures, I know that Christ gives beauty for ashes. In retrospect, my gain has been more than my pain by far. Christ, via His Word and Holy Spirit, restores those who repent sincerely before Him. He knows the risks you take. He heals all those who come to Him in failure. Let Him do the same for you! Black men, as we do this collectively, we will watch God transform our families, kith and kin, into a virtuous and prosperous nation.

REFERENCES

Allen, H. 1992. The sociology of prejudice. *Faculty Dialogue* 18: 91–111.

————. 1991. The Black family: Its unique legacy, current challenges, and future opportunities. In *The Black family: Past, present, and future,* edited by L. N. June. Grand Rapids: Zondervan.

Allen, W. R., E. G. Epps, and N. Z. Haniff, eds. 1991. *Colleges in Black and White: African-American students in predominantly White and in historically Black public universities*. Albany: State University of New York.

Altbach, P. G., and K. Lomotey, eds. 1991. *The racial crisis in American higher education*. Albany: State University of New York.

Anderson, E. 1994. The code of the streets. *Atlantic Monthly* 273 (May): 80–94.

Blackwell, J. 1990. Current issues affecting Blacks and Hispanics in the educational pipeline. In *U.S. race relations in the 1980s and 1990s: Challenges and alternatives,* edited by G. Thomas. New York: Hemisphere.

————. 1985. *The Black community: Diversity and unity*. 2d ed. New York: Harper and Row.

————. 1981. *Mainstreaming outsiders: The production of Black professionals*. Bayside, NY: General Hall.

Boorstin, D. 1983. *The discoverers*. New York: Random House.

Coleman, J. S. 1990. *Foundations of social theory*. Cambridge: Belknap.

Devine, J., and J. D. Wright. 1993. *The greatest of evils: Urban poverty and the American underclass*. New York: Aldine.

Farley, R., 1984. *Blacks and Whites: Narrowing the gap?* Cambridge: Harvard University Press.

Farley, R., and W. Allen. 1987. *The color line and the quality of life in America*. New York: Russell Sage.

Fleming, J. 1984. *Blacks in college*. San Francisco: Jossey-Bass.

Gibson, M. A., and J. Ogbu. 1991. *Minority status and schooling*. New York: Garland.

Glascow, D. 1980. *The Black underclass*. San Francisco: Jossey-Bass.

Hacker, A. 1992. *Two nations: Black and White, separate, hostile, unequal*. New York: Scribner's.

Haley, A. 1976. *Roots*. New York: Dell.

Howard, J., and R. Hammond. 1985. Rumors of inferiority. *New Republic* 193 (September): 17–21.

Jencks, C. 1992. *Rethinking social policy: Race, poverty, and the underclass*. Cambridge: Harvard University Press.

Kretovics, J., and E. J. Nussel, eds. 1994. *Transforming urban education*. Boston: Allyn and Bacon.

Lynch, J., C. Modgil, and S. Modgil, eds. 1994. *Cultural diversity and the schools: Prejudice, polemic, or progress?* London: Falmer.

Massey, D., and N. Denton. 1993. *American apartheid: Segregation and the making of the underclass*. Cambridge: Harvard University Press.

McDonald, L. 1993. *The early origins of the social sciences*. Montreal: McGill-Queens University Press.

Mead, L. 1992. *The new politics of poverty*. New York: Basic.

National Research Council. 1989. *A common destiny: Blacks and American society*. Washington, DC: National Academy Press.

Orfield, G., and C. Ashkinaze. 1991. *The closing door: Conservative policy and Black opportunity*. Chicago: University of Chicago Press.

Partington, A., ed. 1992. *The Oxford dictionary of quotations*. 4th ed. Oxford: Oxford University Press.

Peshkin, A. 1991. *The color of strangers, the color of friends*. Chicago: University of Chicago Press.

Payne, C. 1984. *Getting what we ask for: The ambiguity of success and failure in urban education*. Westport, CT: Greenwood.

Slaughter, D., and E. G. Epps. The home environment and academic achievement of Black American children and youth: An overview. In *Transforming urban education,* edited by J. Kretovics, and E. J. Nussel. Boston: Allyn and Bacon.

Thomas, G., ed. 1990. *U.S. race relations in the 1980s and 1990s: Challenges and alternatives*. New York: Hemisphere.

Wilson, R. 1994. The participation of African-Americans in American higher education. In *Minorities in higher education,* edited by M. J. Justiz, R. Wilson, and L. Bjork. Phoenix: Oryx Press.

Wilson, W. J. 1987. *The truly disadvantaged*. Chicago: University of Chicago Press.

Allen T. Sheffield

Keys to Sound
Financial Planning

ALLEN T. SHEFFIELD is a certified public accountant and former manager in the international accounting and consulting firm Coopers & Lybrand, L.L.P., in Detroit, Michigan. He is currently corporate internal audit manager for Kmart Corporation. He was born in New Orleans, Louisiana, and grew up in Detroit. Allen is a graduate of Eastern Michigan University with a bachelor of business administration in accounting. He is married to Paula Sheffield, and they have one daughter, Leah Nicole.

Chapter 3
Allen T. Sheffield

Keys to Sound Financial Planning

INTRODUCTION

What do you think of when you hear the words *African-American male*?

I think of men who have confidence, pride, talent, wisdom, and strength. Most of America and even most African-Americans would not agree that these attributes describe the African-American male. But, believe it or not, God made each one of us with those attributes. What we have to do is believe that it is so and live up to it.

African-American males are known for being employees rather than employers, spending money rather than investing it, squandering money rather than saving it. Sadly, even our African-American women are generally viewed as being more responsible and knowledgeable when it comes to handling finances. After all, they have had to not only nurture but provide financially for our families in the absence of husbands in too many cases throughout our history. It is time for African-American men to step up to the plate, so to speak, and provide financial leadership.

One of my dreams for the African-American male is that we would develop a reputation for having wisdom when it comes to managing our resources. Think of what an impact that will have on the relationships that we have with our wives, with our children, and with God. Think of what a witness that will be for God in this day and time if we become an "army of King Solomons," known for our wisdom and riches, demonstrating to the world not only His love but also the spiritual and material riches that He bestows on those who love and follow Him. If you are not a good steward of little, there is no way that God will make you a steward over much.

"If we fail to plan, we plan to fail." How many times have we heard this saying? Or how about, "If we aim for nothing, we will hit it every time." It would do us good to memorize these sayings so that we will stay focused on our financial goals. Financial planning is a must if we are to be good stewards of our finances. "But," you say, "I hate planning, I work better when I shoot from the hip." Just take a moment and think about that statement. Look at the seriousness of the subject you are applying it to—your welfare—and if you are married, the welfare of your wife, your children, and God's calling for your life.

Think about that. Each of us is going to be held accountable for what we have done with the time, treasure (finances), and talent that God has given us. When we meet our Maker, this is one of the things He is going to ask us about (see Romans 14:11–12). If, after thinking about what I've just said, you still want to shoot from the hip in this area, then go on to the next chapter in this book; there is no need for you to read any further here.

The goal of this chapter is simply to put you in touch with the keys to financial planning and their practical application. Financial planning covers several areas: investment, insurance (risk management), tax, estate, and retirement planning. The keys to sound financial planning apply to each of these areas. These keys are faith, goal setting, budgeting, research, and discipline. Within this chapter, we will also review typical pitfalls and provide helpful hints associated with financial planning.

FAITH AND FINANCIAL PLANNING

I know you are probably thinking, *What in the world does faith have to do with sound financial planning?* It has everything in the world to do with it. Faith in God and our Lord and Savior Jesus Christ not only yields spiritual blessings but it can also produce confidence, contentment, focus, wisdom, and peace in handling our finances. Our trust and dependence on God for guidance and favor is no joke. Our faith can take the feeling of desperation out of the decision-making process and keep us focused on being good stewards of our resources rather than focused on being some financial tycoon.

Faith is probably the most difficult and the most important key to apply on a consistent basis. Our faith in God should impact every decision we make in regard to saving and spending the money that God has made available to us. What we do with our finances should be consistent with His will. It should help to accomplish His goals. Most people tend to think that God's will for their finances will not give them any pleasure or security. I hope that is not you, because that mind-set could not be further from the truth. God has called us to live an abundant life. The problem is we do not believe Him.

The typical reaction once we achieve any type of financial success is to abandon God and rejoin the world and its ideals and practices. This is the worst possible reaction, because God cannot allow those who abandon Him to prosper for very long. Once we make it to the "king's castle," we must be like Daniel, Shadrach, Meshach, and Abednego and remain faithful and dependent on God. In doing so, we free His hands to bless us without measure. Our faith should not be set aside when handling our finances. It should be included in every facet of our financial planning.

SETTING GOALS

After God is in His rightful place, it is time to establish goals. What are your needs, dreams, desires, and fantasies? Do you have your eyes on some major item—a house, car, vacation? The goals you set should be specific and have a timetable for accomplishment associated with them. Your goals should include tithing consistently on your gross income, improving your record keeping, saving more and regularly, reducing debt, having adequate insurance coverage, and reducing taxes.

Write out your goals. They should be in three categories: short-term (within the next two years), intermediate (two-to-five years from now), and long-term (five-to-ten years from now). The level of detail that you use in documenting your goals is of course up to you, but there should be at least enough information that a year from now you will be able to evaluate which short-term goals you have met and how much progress you have made on intermediate and long-term goals without having to rely on memory for an accurate indication of what you were trying to achieve.

Establishing your long-term goals will give insight as to what some of your intermediate and short-term goals should be. Each goal should be specific and measurable. For example: "Reduce my credit-card debt by $2,500 by December 31, 1996" is better than "Reduce credit-card debt." The reduction goal is a short-term goal. The related intermediate goal could be: Pay off all credit-card debt by June 30, 1998. The related long-term goal could be: Live debt free except for the mortgage on my home.

To start, I would recommend that enough goal setting be done so that five-to-seven short-term goals and their related intermediate and long-term goals are *specifically* laid out. After the goals have been set, you should *prioritize* them. What is most important? Which one should I meet if I cannot realistically, at this juncture, meet them all? (See table 3.1 for a sample format of a goal-setting document.)

If you have a family, they should be included in this goal-setting session. The sacrifices and successes of your family's financial planning will

Table 3.1
Financial Goals

Achievement
Specific Short-term Goals   *Amount*   *Date*
_____   _____   _____
_____   _____   _____
_____   _____   _____
_____   _____   _____

Achievement
Specific Intermediate Goals   *Amount*   *Date*
_____   _____   _____
_____   _____   _____
_____   _____   _____
_____   _____   _____

Achievement
Specific Long-term Goals   *Amount*   *Date*
_____   _____   _____
_____   _____   _____
_____   _____   _____
_____   _____   _____

be shared by the entire family. It is important that each family member understand and submit, even if they do not agree, to the goals set by the family as a whole and those set by you as the head of the household. Although you may be leading the charge as a husband and father, each family member's submission to the plan will be crucial to your success.

The most important thing to realize in the context of the family is that we, as African-American males, have been called by God to lead our families in this area by example, with faith, love, patience, peace, and wisdom. Finances should not be a source of discord within the family. God is in control. He will see you and your family through. All He wants you to do is take responsibility for yourself and be an encourager and leader to your family. Do not, however, put financial goals before the spiritual and emotional needs of your family. Your family needs to see themselves, not some job or financial goal, as being what is most important to you, after God. Therefore, there will be times when forgoing the plan of reaching a financial goal will be the best thing to do. Since you know this will happen, you should plan for it by providing a cushion in your budget for these situations.

With each of your financial goals you should pray and ask, "Is this goal consistent with what I believe is God's will for my life?" If a goal is not, change it so that it is. Seeking a goal that is not consistent with God's will is foolish. It is a major waste of time and energy. Keep in mind that you are serving God, not yourself. Although He allows the benefits of your work and His blessings to flow through your hands, remember it is always for His glory and your good. When we seek things that are outside His will, we are then seeking only for our own good. We must seek both God's glory and our good. What we have to realize and believe is that if something is good, it will be in His will.

Each of your goals will cost you something. Achieving your goals will take hard work and sacrifice. You must determine what that cost or sacrifice is and decide up-front whether you are willing to pay the cost and/or make the sacrifice. (See Hank Allen's discourse on risk and failure in the previous chapter.)

BUDGETING, AN EXCELLENT FINANCIAL-PLANNING TOOL

Now that you have established where you want to be, you need to find out where you are, investigate what options are available, and decide how you can get there. You should ask: How much do I spend per month on necessary items? How about on personal items? What about debt repayment? What is my net worth? These questions can be answered by setting up a personal balance sheet and income statement. A balance sheet is a financial statement that shows what your assets, liabilities, and net worth are at a given point in time. Your assets are the things you own (such as your car, house, cash in the bank, investments, and clothing). You should list your assets at their fair market value (that is, what you could get for them if you sold them today). Your liabilities are what you owe (credit card, mortgage, and other debt). Your net worth is the difference between your assets and your liabilities. If your liabilities exceed your assets, you have negative net worth. This means that if you sold all your assets, you still could not pay all of what you owe. If your assets exceed your liabilities, you have positive net worth. In either case your goals should serve to get you to a positive net-worth position if you are not already there. From that position continue to increase your net worth, that is, the amount by which your assets exceed your liabilities. (See table 3.2 for a sample balance sheet.)

An income statement lists all sources of income and all expenses, the difference of which is net income if income exceeds expenses. You have a net loss if expenses exceed income for the month, year, or whatever period of time being evaluated. If you do not already know what you take in and spend on a monthly basis, you should track your spending habits for the next month or two. Write down by category each expenditure. Once you have a handle on where your money has actually been going, you will need to identify which expenses were (1) fixed expenses (a set amount that does not vary, e.g., debt and children's tuition); (2) variable expenses (amounts that change each month, e.g., utilities and phone bills); and (3) discretionary expenses (those that are totally up to you and that require no payment, e.g., entertainment, vacation, and recreation).

All of your specific spending categories may not fit neatly under the three headings above, but the idea is to determine which expenses you have no control over (at this point), which expenses you have some control over, and which expenses you have total control over. With this understanding, you are now ready to begin examining where spending cuts can be made and what changes in your lifestyle and the lifestyle of your family will be necessary to achieve the savings.

An excellent planning tool for the documentation of what spending cuts, savings, and other changes to your income statement you are

Table 3.2
Personal Balance Sheet

Name: _____

Balance Sheet as of (date): _____

Assets	*Amount*
Cash at home	_____
Cash and investments in bank accounts	_____
_____	_____
_____	_____
_____	_____
_____	_____
_____	_____
Fair market value of:	
Household appliances	_____
Furniture	_____
Car	_____
Home	_____
Other assets:	
_____	_____
_____	_____
Total assets	_____

Liabilities	*Amount*
Credit-card debt:	
_____	_____
_____	_____
_____	_____
Loans:	
Car loan	_____
Home mortgage	_____
_____	_____
_____	_____
_____	_____
Total liabilities	_____
Net worth (total assets minus total liabilities)	_____

considering is a monthly income statement and budget. This budget should list all anticipated expenses and amounts to be put away for savings, vacations, and other goals each month. Instead of paying bills as they come in, you should consider paying bills twice per month. Your monthly budget would indicate, based on the bill's due date, when you will make the payment. (See table 3.3 for a sample budget.)

Table 3.3
Budgeted Income Statement

Name: _____

Period:___ *April 199x* _____

Income	*Actual Amount*	*Budgeted Amount*
Total net pay for *April 199x*	_____	_____
Other income:		
_____	_____	_____
_____	_____	_____
Total income	_____	_____
Expenses		
Tithe	_____	_____
Credit-card debt:		
_____	_____	_____
_____	_____	_____
_____	_____	_____
Car-loan payment	_____	_____
Mortgage payment	_____	_____
Utilities	_____	_____
Entertainment	_____	_____
Deposit into savings	_____	_____
Vacation	_____	_____
Spending money	_____	_____
Other:		
_____	_____	_____
_____	_____	_____
_____	_____	_____
Total expenses	_____	_____
Net income (loss)	_____	_____

Establishing a monthly budget can help ensure that all bills for the month are paid, give you comfort as to the grip you have on your finances, and help identify when available cash will be tight or nonexistent. Remember to be realistic when establishing your budget. You are not trying to impress anyone or improve your financial situation overnight. Your plan should be to cut out the excess and unnecessary spending and make sacrifices that may be uncomfortable but endurable.

African-Americans have a long-standing reputation of living beyond our means. We have a reputation of exhibiting wealth through ownership or rental of expensive material possessions, while all the while sinking further and further into debt and financial ruin. The most important thing to do is live within your means. Do not spend more than you earn. The exercise of preparing a personal income statement will point out whether you are living beyond your means. You probably already know, but putting it down on paper will help you see how much and where you can make cuts.

In order to maintain your current balance sheet and net worth, you must live within your means. In order to improve your net worth and reach your financial goals, you will have to live *beneath* your means. The savings achieved by living beneath your means will fuel your financial success. Instead of aspiring for an outward demonstration of wealth, which will drive you deeper into a financial hole, aspire to do that which will improve your net worth and reach your long-term goals. This has to be your focus.

You must look at every item in your budget and investigate how the expenditure can be reduced. Discretionary expenditures will be the easiest to reduce or eliminate. The next will be variable expenses. Cutting back on the length of phone calls, using less electricity, and turning down your thermostat are just a few ways you can cut back on variable expenses. Fixed expenses will be the hardest to reduce.

Whatever you do, stop using your credit cards. The last thing you need is more debt and interest payments. Weigh carefully the costs and bondage involved in getting deeper into debt. You should pay off the debt that has the highest interest rate first. Carefully investigate the options of consolidating debt to reduce monthly payments and interest rates you are being charged. You should also investigate the possibility of utilizing a home-equity loan (the interest on it being tax deductible in most cases) to pay off credit-card debt (the interest or finance charges not being tax deductible). Make sure you can afford the home-equity loan. If you cannot, you will be putting your home in jeopardy.

Avoid renting appliances and other household items. This is money that is gone forever. Seek to own, not rent. If you cannot afford to pay cash, do without for now and save until you can. Whenever you shop, shop for bargains.

Make an extra payment on your home mortgage principle each month, even if it is only $25. On a $100,000, thirty-year mortgage at an interest rate of 10 percent, your combined monthly interest and principle payment would be $877. If you paid an extra $25 a month on the principle, you would save $33,600 in interest and pay off the mortgage four years early. The same idea applies to other debt. As long as there is no penalty for early repayment, do not just pay the minimum required. Always pay at least a little extra on the principle balance.

If you have been receiving tax refunds over the past few years, you have been giving the Internal Revenue Service (IRS) an interest-free loan. As an example, someone who received a $1,200 refund actually loaned the IRS this money throughout the previous year. He could have taken the $100 per month and paid debt. If this is you, consider increasing the number of allowable exemptions claimed on Form W–4 filed with your employer. This will reduce the amount of taxes withheld from your paycheck each pay period. Be careful not to have the amount of withholdings reduced so much that you have to pay when you file your tax returns. You may not have the cash to do so.

For more cost-cutting ideas see the books listed in the reference section of this chapter.

DOING YOUR HOMEWORK

Now that you know where you want to be and where you actually are, before finalizing the areas you plan to cut in your budgeted-income statement, make sure that you research the decisions you are considering. Do your homework. Read. Pray. Consult with those knowledgeable about finances. There is a wide variety of resources available—many of which are in layperson's terms—to help you better understand the consequences of the actions you are planning.

Be extremely careful when considering going to a financial advisor. Many advisors receive sales commissions and management fees for getting their clients to buy into certain investments. Take your time. Do not let anyone rush you into anything.

DISCIPLINE

You will need every one of the fruit of the Spirit listed in Galatians 5:22–23 to effectively carry out your financial plan. The last fruit listed is discipline, or self-control. Without it you will never realize your goals. Whatever you do, my African-American brothers, do not give up. Once you have established your plan, stick to it. At least every three months, evaluate how you are doing and make appropriate changes. If you get off the track, do not stay off. It will take plenty of discipline to achieve your goals. Take one day at a time, one step at a time.

Remember, God is in control. Your faithfulness is unto Him, not your budget or your goals. Keep your relationship with Him solid. He will honor this. His wisdom and favor bestowed on you are what will make the difference. If you do not believe in yourself, believe in Him. He wants to do some great things through you. "For God has not given us a spirit of timidity, but of power and love and discipline" (2 Timothy 1:7).

SUMMARY

Financial planning is not rocket-science-type material. Even if it were, we as average African-American men would find a way to get through it. The principles of financial planning are quite basic but if applied consistently; the results can be quite profound.

Set goals, put them on paper. Make a genuine assessment of your financial position. Develop a plan as to where you can reduce expenses. Document this plan using a monthly budget, and monitor your adherence to that plan. Do your homework. Seek to understand those things that are impacting your cost of living. Maintain self-control. Live beneath your means. Seek to *be* wealthy, not *look* wealthy. Save regularly. Like the apostle Paul, have faith, learn to be content in whatever situation you are in. Seek to live debt free. Debt and its close friend interest are bondage, a form of slavery.

God has riches stored up in heaven just waiting for us to improve in the area of stewardship. Let us be like Solomon and seek wisdom. God is waiting to bless us with more than we could imagine. I hope you believe Him. I do.

REFERENCES

Bodnar, J. 1993. *Money, smart kids (and parents, too)*. Washington, DC: Kiplinger Washington Editors.

Broussard, C. D. 1991. *The Black woman's guide to financial independence*. Oakland, CA: Hyde Park Publishing.

Gelb, E. 1994. *Eric Gelb's checkbook management: A guide to saving money*. Woodmere, NY: Career Advancement Center.

1978. *New American standard Bible*. Chicago: Moody Press.

Tyson, E. 1994. *Personal finance for dummie$*. Foster City, CA: IDG Books Worldwide.

Haman Cross Jr.

Sanctifying
Our Sexual
Energy

HAMAN CROSS JR. grew up in Detroit, Michigan. He is a graduate of William Tyndale College and the founding pastor of Rosedale Park Baptist Church. He is married to Roberta Cross and they are the parents of Haman III, Corey, and Sharyl. Haman has traveled and lectured extensively in the United States and abroad. His publications include *Sanctified Sex* (with D. Scott and E. Seals, 1991) and *Wild Thing: Let's Talk About Sex* (with D. Scott and E. Seals, 1992).

Chapter 4
Haman Cross Jr.

Sanctifying Our Sexual Energy

One of the crimes that Satan has committed against creation is his removing the presence of God from the bedroom. Whenever God's presence is absent in any part of life, it will never be what it could be. This includes our sexuality.

Too many Christian men see sex as a curse rather than a blessing. In fact, many single men are surprised to find out that many married men are just as frustrated as they are. That is because very few people, married or single, know how to bring God's presence into their sexuality. We have to invite God into our sexual life before marriage. Having a marriage license will not guarantee your enjoyment of this gift. Countless married men tell me that their biggest frustration is not being able to have sex when they want it or how they want it. Their wives often say that they too are frustrated with their sex lives. In such cases, neither knows how to satisfy the other's sexual needs or desires.

Many Christian men are terrible lovers. They know how to penetrate, roll over, and fall asleep. This is because they do not know how to possess their vessel as outlined in 1 Thessalonians 4. The word *possess* means manage. Men often are terrible managers of their sexuality. We go from one extreme, "God, just help me control my raging hormones," to the other, "God, just castrate me, I wish I had no sexual organs at all." Satan distorts sex, one of the greatest gifts God has given to us (Penner & Penner 1981), however, by causing us either to worship sex or to be angry toward it.

SANCTIFIED AND SECULAR SEX

As Christians, we should be preaching and teaching what God has to say about sex. Christ should make a difference in our sexuality. Through Him, secular sex (Cross, Scott & Seals 1992) can become sanctified sex (Cross, Scott & Seals 1991).

When one is engaging in sanctified sex, there is no guilt. There is no fear of contracting AIDS or of getting someone pregnant. There is no reason to be involved in any form of illicit sexual behavior. Sanctified sex is practicing the presence of God in your bedroom as a married couple. When you sense His OK, you are free. You and your wife will want to holler, "Thank you, Jesus!" In the privacy of your home, you can imagine all of heaven saying, "Go for it, go for it!"

Satan, however, wants to keep our communities addicted to secular or so-called recreational sex. This addiction causes us to forfeit all that God has prepared for those who save sex until marriage. What many of us learned about sex was from the streets, the media, or the men's locker room. With pornography, masturbation, and one-night stands filling too many heads, we think we are good lovers, but in reality we are messed up.

God has been using my wife and me to counsel thousands of people. However, before this I was involved in secular sex and also practiced recreational sex. But nothing compares with the sanctified sex that my wife and I now enjoy. We have learned that sexuality is not a curse. God wants us to save ourselves. He wants His presence to be experienced in our communities. He wants our young men to know the good news about sanctified sex.

To a fifteen- or sixteen-year-old male, sex is very important. That is where he is biologically. All of his hormones are screaming for expression. His growth and his sexuality are always on his mind. Telling such a fifteen- or sixteen-year-old, "Don't get anybody pregnant—don't sleep around," is not good news to him. We must teach a so-called sexual gospel that features the benefits of sanctified sex.

Because we typically do not tell young men about sanctified sex, they listen to the world whose message is, "If you want it, go and get it." The Christian message of the body as the temple of the Holy Spirit pales in comparison. We need an army of Christian men who will discreetly sit down and describe to these impressionable young minds what sanctified sex is really all about. We need men who will say, as I said to my son, "Sanctified sex is awesome. Your dad may be up in age, but he still enjoys it." If you describe the sexual experience in these terms, a young man would be a fool to choose otherwise. Even if he has already engaged in premarital sex, you can tell him how God will do a new thing in his life. He can believe this and practice this renewed life by faith.

To remove sex from Satan's hand, we need to understand and pursue sanctified sex. This will involve some of us married brothers getting it together in our own bedrooms. We must set our sexuality apart and allow God to show us how special it can be. We must learn about enjoying this blessing from God's perspective because He designed this gift and He has a purpose for it. The Bible lists at least ten purposes or ways to use sexual energy creatively. These are presented below.

TEN PURPOSES FOR SEX

Procreation

The first purpose for sex is procreation. The sexual act can lead to the creation of life.

Recreation

The second purpose for sex is recreation. The sexual act can be fun.

Education

The third purpose for sex is education. Through the sexual act, one can discover how wonderfully God has designed your mate's body. First Peter 3 tells husbands to dwell with their wives according to knowledge. This means to live with her and sleep with her in a knowledgeable way. Learning all about her erogenous zones will result in your inheriting a blessing. My wife and I now occasionally make love for purely educational purposes. We discover: "What happens when . . . ?" Young men who experiment with young ladies before marriage will have problems in their marriage. What worked with one person may not work with your wife. She is unique.

Sanctification

The fourth purpose for sex is sanctification. God has created a vehicle to keep you set apart. As the apostle Paul says in 1 Corinthians 7, "It is better to marry than to burn." Making love to your *own* wife will keep you pure. One of the reasons I have not committed adultery is because of the presence of God in my sexual life. Of course the Bible and the Holy Ghost have done wonders for me, but the beauty of sexual love with my wife is the icing on the cake. It keeps me set apart (sanctified).

Gratification

The fifth purpose for sex is gratification. Gratification has to do with satisfying sexual desires. It is not sinful or demonic to desire to make love, yet there are some who falsely believe that sex is from the devil. That is simply not true. Sex is too good to come from the devil. He is into destruction. God is into creation. With sanctified sex, He has created one means of giving you the desires of your heart. Our communities need to hear those who have had their sexuality redeemed say so.

In the Song of Solomon, the woman describes her husband's desire for her. This is the Genesis 3 curse reversed. Because of the Fall, a woman's desire for her husband was unhealthy. Because of Christ, it is healthy. It is a great feeling to have your wife desire your body and vice versa. This need to be desired sexually, to be wanted, comes from God. There is too much shame and guilt concerning sex in our communities. We need to take back what Satan has stolen from our bedrooms and get back into the book—the Bible.

Also in the Song of Solomon, the Shulammite woman brags about her mate's lovemaking ability. When was the last time your wife bragged about yours? Too many of us exaggerate about our sexual ability, but if you asked your wife, what would she say? She would probably say that in two minutes it is all over. For some, it may be twenty seconds. This ought not to be! When we go back to following God's script, we will be "greater than Solomon." I want my wife to brag not only on my preaching but also on my lovemaking. I want her to tell me, "There is none like you, Haman."

Many men have no honor in the bedroom. In such situations, the wife sees making love merely as a duty or obligation because she is not getting anything in the bargain. Due benevolence is her only motive for having sex. She does not like it. She does not desire it and you probably have to initiate every time. Because of this, you have no good news to tell young men who are involved with secular sex. If so, you have not taken your sexuality to God and allowed Him to sanctify it. Do not wait until you marry. Start now. Ask God to renew your mind about your sexuality. Nothing is too hard for Him. As He writes his law of lovemaking in your heart, you will begin to understand the purpose of sex.

Consolation

The sixth purpose for sex is consolation. In Genesis 24, Rebekah makes love to Isaac when his mother dies. Afterward, he feels better. This pain reliever is better and cheaper than any drug. Sanctified sex will alter your bad mood and put you in a better one, something that eating, drinking, shopping, and watching television cannot do.

Edification

The seventh purpose for sex is edification. Learning to be a good lover will enable you to build up (edify) your wife. You may ask her, "What's wrong? She may say, "I don't know." But after a little sanctified sex, she is walking around humming and singing. My son sees his mother in this great mood and teases, "Dad, you should be ashamed of yourself!" I joke, "Hey, a man's got to do what a man's got to do."

Becoming a good lover is a learning process. After seven years of marriage, my wife was ready to leave me. Because of my addiction to masturbation and pornography, I had become a terrible lover. I thought I had it together until my wife rolled over and said, "We won't be doing this again." We went one whole year, in the same house, in the same bed, without sex. God renewed my mind. By changing my thinking, I understood lovemaking from His perspective. Previous "garbage" regarding my sexuality and my wife's sexuality was dumped. The miraculous took place in my bedroom, and the same can happen for you.

Intoxication

The eighth purpose for sex is intoxication. Proverbs 5 talks about being drunk with your wife's breasts at all times. Fondling and caressing your wife's breasts will get you "high," much higher than drinking Bacardi and sniffing coke. As men we often get excited when we see a nipple or a little cleavage. There is no need to be ashamed about this. God designed us that way. There is nothing sinful or perverted because you get this "rush." Thank God that all the parts work. Just do not expect to get high all day, all the time. By using yourself up before marriage, however, you create a greater need for more excitement. That is Satan's plan. He wants to burn you out with secular sex. Then when you are supposed to get "drunk" with your wife—you cannot. You need something stronger, something "freaky," deviant. If Satan can get you to engage in secular sex and develop a tolerance for expressing your sexuality unbiblically, your wife's body will not do a thing for you.

It is important to realize that God had your pleasure in mind when He designed you. God designed sexuality with our good and His glory in mind. He does not want you to curse Him in your bedroom, but to worship Him.

Imagination

The ninth purpose for sex is imagination. Many of us have bad sexuality tapes playing in our minds, which hinder our sexual enjoyment, because of flashbacks of past relationships or sexual encounters. Such bad tapes keep your brain uninvolved in the sexual act and hence what you practice is physiological and biological sex without psychological sex. God wants us to enjoy the process of making love. In the Song of Solomon, the husband and wife imagine what making love will be like.

Our allowing junk-cluttered minds makes our fantasies a battleground. In such a state, one cannot distinguish a good thought from a bad one. Once you are married, your mind may become distracted. You become a spectator, which men are extremely guilty of being, watching and thinking about performance. While you are making love, you are wondering, "Did I touch the right spot, did I say the right words?" This takes away from the sexual experience because your body is with your wife, but your mind is elsewhere.

God wants our minds to be free, without guilt or shame when we engage in the sex act. He wants us to think about the prospect (before we make love), the process (being totally involved), and the product (thinking back and remembering all the details). By renewing your mind, you will think about sex from God's perspective. Instead of putting the wrong information in your brain, put in the right information. This will prepare you to enjoy this gift from God. This will also break your impulse-oriented habit—getting a thought and following through. Now, think about this impulse, "What should I do with this thought? Is it legitimate or illegitimate?" In time, you will develop legitimate fantasies concerning your mate.

Communication

The tenth purpose for sex is communication. When one says, "I love you," what kind of love is being referred to? The Bible describes five types, which in the context of marriage can be defined this way:

- *Agape*—unconditional love no matter what
- *Storge*—providing for your family
- *Philia*—being good friends with your spouse
- *Epithumea*—being attracted to one another, physical love
- *Eros*—wining-and-dining romantic love

Years ago I made a commitment to my wife to give her not only her needs but also her wants and her desires. This has cost me. She has tested me on this. There are things she desires—she does not *need* them, she does not necessarily *want* them—she simply *desires* them. My response has been: "If God gives me the grace, time, and money, and the desire or want is not contrary to Scripture, you got it. That is how God treats me."

BENEFITS OF SANCTIFIED SEXUAL ENERGY

If we do not sanctify our sexual energy, our biology will control us. God wants us to be creative with this sexual energy, not be a slave to our passions. When our sexual energy is under control, our aggression, ambition, and affirmation all benefit.

Aggression

Aggression is part of our nature that must be controlled. Testosterone, a hormone, contributes to the drive of aggression. What will we do with this aggressiveness? We could rape someone (God forbid), or we could create something legitimate. Learn how to handle this aggressiveness. When many of us feel the so-called urge to merge, we become locked into the mind-set of "I gotta have sex." If we cannot find someone, we get involved in solo sex (masturbation). This is a waste of creative sexual energy.

Using our aggressiveness in a healthy way gives us the ability to solve problems. Because of my schedule and my age, I need to conserve my energy. If not, I cannot be the lover my wife needs me to be. When I was younger, I could preach three or four times a day, play basketball, then come home and enjoy sex. Now I have to conserve my energy, which sometimes means that I take a nap. My body may be ready, but the look in my wife's eyes says she's expecting more than a quickie. That is why I sanctify my energy, setting it apart.

Ambition

Ambition is the God-created desire to do something. Using your sexual energy to accomplish something legitimate is very satisfying. Therefore we need to have goals and ambitions in the sexual area just as we do in the other aspects of our lives.

Affirmation

Sexual energy affirms that we are alive. It affirms that we are males who cannot control involuntary responses. Quit being embarrassed that you get erections. God has designed our bodies to have a daily erection. Do not be surprised when this happens, and do not conclude that with each erection you must relieve yourself. Rather thank God that your parts work and go on about your business.

God wants us to understand who we are and what we have. He does not want us preoccupied with our biological functions. He wants us using our sexual energy for legitimate reasons.

HABITS THAT WASTE SEXUAL ENERGY

The key to abstinence is not, "I won't do it," but rather our making a commitment to sanctified sex. This protects us from five destructive habits that waste our sexual energy.

The first destructive habit is pornography. This is simply a perverted depiction of sex. Violence, force, movies, multiple partners, dolls, and so forth cannot satisfy sexual desires.

The second destructive habit is perversion. Perversions, sexual behaviors that are inconsistent with Scripture, cannot satisfy sexual desires.

The third destructive habit is chronic masturbation. This unhealthy form of self-love gives relief whenever you want, and in your mind you become the perfect lover. But it is a means to avoiding reality.

The fourth destructive habit is fornication. Fornication is any sexual sin such as sleeping around or sleeping with the person you are dating, which breeds guilt, shame, and fear and is inconsistent with the Word of God.

The fifth destructive habit is denial. Denial is saying things like, "I don't have any sexual needs ... I don't think about it." God wants you to appreciate your sexuality, which is important. Ignoring this part of your life can make you a terrible lover later on, because you are repressing who you are. Do not let your sexuality control you, but thank God for who you are. He will show you how to manage your vessel. When temptation comes, and it will, God's grace will be sufficient.

When you repress your desires or your sexuality, however, temptation will force your back against the wall. This is because of the buildup you allowed. Daily we are exposed to lustful situations. Denying that these temptations bother us is destructive. Many married men will come home with a "snoop doggy dog" look in their eyes. Why? Because they have been "sniffing" at other women all day. You cannot take fire in your bosom and not be burned.

The opposite of denial is understanding the times you must avoid certain women. It does not matter how much Holy Spirit you have. Just looking at the strange woman will ensnare you.

AVOIDING TEMPTATIONS IN THE SEXUAL AREA

When I travel, I take my sexuality and shut it down. When I arrive back in Detroit, there is no denial. I may, however, have to wait a couple of days. I may have to say, "Lord, this is what I want, this is what I need, this is what I desire."

I do not push God out of my sexuality. I acknowledge Him in all my ways and He directs my paths. One of the things I do with God is describe in detail what I want. He has never struck me down for this. Rather, He renews my mind, saying, "Come now, Cross, let's reason together. I know you would like to do this, but look what it will lead to. The wages of sin is still death!" This sobers me. This truth brings my temperature down.

Do not try to handle temptation alone. Do not try to clean yourself up and then come to the Lord. Set your sexuality apart now. When your mind is running crazy, talk to God about it. Do not simply say, "O Lord, help me not to" but, "Lord, this is what I want to do." Remember the Scripture that says: "There hath no temptation taken you but such as is common to man; but God is faithful, who will not suffer you to be tempted above that which you are able, but will with the temptation also make the way to escape that you may be able to bear it" (1 Corinthians 10:13).

Talking to God about all these details when I am tempted enables me to talk to Him later on, saying, "Lord, this is what I want to do with my wife." Only now, I hear Him say, "Go, Cross! Go, Cross!" I am familiar with His voice so that when I have thought the wrong things, I have heard

Him say, "No, Cross ... No, Cross." As I sanctify myself, I preserve my sexuality for God's use. David poured his complaint before the Lord. Go and do likewise.

Sexual energy can build you up or burn you out, affecting your soul and spirit—your mind, will, and emotions. It can bind your soul by putting you in bondage. It can bind your mind, preoccupying your thoughts. It can bind your will, enslaving you to sexual addiction. It can also bind your emotions, determining your mood swings.

BECOMING A GOOD LOVER

One of the prerequisites for becoming a good lover is self-control. If your feelings control you, you will not laugh when you are making love. You will not be disciplined. If you have a bad day, you will carry it into your bedroom. You will be led by your feelings. Sexual energy can be a blessing or a burden. You must discover the gift, delight in the gift, discipline the gift, and dedicate the gift.

Why not try standing in front of the mirror, nude, and thank God for every inch of your body. Dedicate your penis to the Lord. Quit running from your image in the mirror, embarrassed to look at yourself. This is not "freaky." God does not want us to be embarrassed about this part of our body.

DEALING WITH SEXUAL ABUSE

Some of us have been abused. I was abused at seven years of age. My first imprint concerning sexuality put unhealthy images in my brain. I had to allow God to replace this imprint. I had lost my sexual innocence. Innocence means being without harm or danger. Yet, God has restored that innocence and sex is no longer painful or harmful. For additional information on sexual abuse, see Joan A. Ganns (1991). God wants to do the same for you. He wants you to delight in the gift of sex.

DEVELOPING THE GIFT OF SEXUALITY

God also wants us to develop the gift of sexuality. We need to be sexually mature. Paul said that his goal was to present every man perfect or mature in Christ. Many of us are sexually immature, however. We have not come to the place where we thank God for who we are, what we have, and what it does.

If we are to align the next generation's sexuality according to Scripture, we will have to dedicate our gift of sexuality to God as well. This involves the daily struggle of developing the correct mind-set and the correct habits.

CONCLUSION

The battle to regain sexuality has to be fought by all men of God. We as Black men have our special challenge. Our young men and boys cannot fight this alone. They need experienced warriors to lead the way. Many of us have never heard preaching or teaching in this area. We must correct this, however, because God wants us to control our reins—our glands. He wants our young men to be prepared to be good lovers when they become husbands.

Satan, however, has kept our communities in bondage. We are not enjoying sex in its fullness. Therefore, we have no good news, no message to tell our children. Secular sex has caused us to cheapen or defile the gift. It causes us to defraud one another. For some, the gift is damaged by sexual abuse and perversion. Some of us detest and hate this gift because we do not realize its power. Our wives would be happier if we learned how to be good lovers.

We cannot be a professional without being trained, so we must quit lying about our ability and get the education we need.

The gift can become demonized. For years this hindered my walk with the Lord. I would say to myself, "If I could just quit . . . I could really be used of the Lord." I was a Satanic stronghold.

We have brought many men into our churches because of their profession of a faith in Christ. Few have been taught how their sexuality can become liberated. This liberation does not mean free to do what we want to do but rather free to do what we are supposed to do.

If we are to win this battle, we have to take it to the streets. We have to allow God to change us. We have to come out of the closet and talk about the struggles and the problems that we are facing. Only then can we preach the gospel, the good news that God has saved the best sex, sanctified sex, for last.

REFERENCES

Cross, H., Jr., D. E. Scott, and E. Seals. 1992. *Wild thing: Let's talk about sex*. Farmington Hills, MI: Quality Publishing.

_____. 1991. *Sanctified sex*. Farmington Hills, MI: Quality Publishing.

Ganns, J. 1991. Sexual abuse: Its impact on the child and the family. In *The Black family: Past, present, and future*, edited by L. N. June. Grand Rapids: Zondervan.

The King James version of the Bible.

Penner, C., and J. Penner. 1981. *The gift of sex: A Christian guide to sexual fulfillment*. Waco, TX: Word.

Rodney S. Patterson

Male Bonding:
Men Relating
to Men

RODNEY S. PATTERSON, a native of Chicago, Illinois, is the Assistant to the Vice President for Student Affairs and Services and also the Multicultural Development Coordinator at Michigan State University. He is founder and pastor of the Ebenezer Baptist Church, Lansing, Michigan. Rodney established the first Black church in the state of Vermont, the New Alpha Missionary Baptist Church, in 1989. He received a bachelor of arts degree in theology from Valparaiso University in Indiana and a master of arts degree in higher education administration from Michigan State University. He is completing his doctorate in educational administration. Rodney is married to Dr. Charlene Patterson.

Chapter 5

Rodney S. Patterson

Male Bonding:
Men Relating to Men

T he subject of emotional bonds between and among males is such a vital issue that it has captured the attention of many writers (Caldwell & Peplau 1982; Devlin & Cowan 1985; Duck & Wright 1993; Elkins & Peterson 1993; Harris 1992; Lewis 1978; Reisman 1990; Wright & Scanlon 1991). Yet words such as *love,* when used to describe those bonds, create interesting reactions. The unfortunate result is that these reactions have only reduced the support, camaraderie, enrichment, and advocacy that men so desperately need and can benefit from.

This chapter will focus on the subject of men who experience and form intimate relationships with each other. I refer to this phenomenon as true male bonding and believe that the absence of such has contributed to African-American men's lessening effectiveness in our society. I share my personal experiences with male bonding in the hope that they have instructive value for the discussion that follows. Additionally, I review the literature on the subject and discuss male bonding from a biblical perspective.

PERSONAL EXPERIENCES

Early Experience: School Daze

Upon making the decision at thirteen years of age to attend a private, all-male Catholic institution, I received a barrage of teasing-like, derogatory comments from both men and women. I was told by women, "You're too cute to go to an all-boys school. You'll probably end up becoming a 'fag.'" I was taunted by my male friends, hearing comments like "only sissies go to all-boys schools." Despite the peer pressure, I decided to attend Hales-Franciscan High School, on the south side of Chicago.

One of the first experiences that I remember was the "showers." Overcome by paranoia upon entering for the first time the public shower stall used by all students after physical education classes or sporting events, I carefully watched the movements of each of my male classmates. As the year progressed, I became much more comfortable with the idea of showering with other boys in an open shower stall.

Little did I know at the time, but each instance during that four-year period of my life was enhancing my ability to bond with and relate to other men. By graduation, my classmates and I knew that we had become a close-knit group, spending nearly every moment in classes, on the athletic fields, and even socializing after school. I attribute my return to the church (which subsequently led to my receiving the call into ministry) to a close friend I met during my freshman year.

Graduation day revealed just how close we had become. We had entered as immature, unpolished, mischievous brats and were leaving those hallowed halls as young men, prepared to assume responsibility for bettering ourselves and aspiring to higher heights. We left that gymnasium, eyes filled with tears, when we realized for the first time that our daily interactions had come to an end. We embraced, sobbing uncontrollably as family and friends stood by dumbfounded by our emotional outburst. We had come to love each other as brothers as well as friends, and we were not ashamed to express how much it hurt to think that we would soon be separated. That day, we literally experienced our high-school motto—Unto Perfect Manhood—actualized by our ability to express our emotions with dignity and without shame. I consider that experience, in retrospect, one of my greatest lessons in male bonding.

Professional Conferences

In 1989, I had another bonding experience while attending a higher-education conference for administrators in Washington, D.C. As I stood conversing with several male colleagues in the foyer of the hotel lobby, one gentleman whom I had never previously met and who seemed to possess a magnetism, drew most of my attention. Our encounter was brief, but quite memorable because our kindred spirits connected. A power and chemistry were at work that neither of us was willing to openly acknowledge at the time but that both of us experienced.

As men, we seldom speak of our encounters in such terms for fear of being misunderstood or misperceived. We fall victim to our fears—fears impregnated by historical socialization processes that have placed vise grips on our emotional expressions. Consequently, some relationships never fully develop.

"Richard" (not his real name) and I exchanged business cards, a customary pattern within professional circles. Both of us committed to maintaining contact beyond our initial encounter, but neither of us kept our promise. One year later, Richard and I reconnected at the same annual conference and we were very apologetic for breaking our promises made the previous year. Vowing to do better, we subsequently visited each other in our respective hometowns the following year. During my visits with Richard, the seeds for writing a chapter on this subject were planted. Because Richard and I connected on a spiritual plane, we avoided waddling in the superficiality of typical relationships and quickly experienced dialogue about more germane issues. Richard passionately expressed his vision of also writing on the subject of men loving men and the need for us to experience, nurture, and encourage the formation of intimate relationships and networks. Relationships with women, he believed, were critical, yet some needs could only be met through male bonds. The need for such relationships was obvious to Richard.

As Richard spoke, I immediately comprehended. In fact, I felt exactly the way that Richard did, but never had I heard it articulated so poignantly and succinctly. Because of this experience, I began to question why men experience difficulty establishing intimate friendship relations or fail to acknowledge that intimate bonds can and do exist among men.

Million Man March

My most fascinating, captivating, and rewarding example of male bonding came unexpectedly after I thought I had finished writing this chapter—that of being "one in a million." The Million Man March on Washington on October 16, 1995, brought African and African-American men together in such an electrifying manner that the United States and the men involved will never be the same.

I experienced and saw what I never anticipated would occur during my lifetime. Reconciliation and bonding—the true orders of business—were indeed realized that day. As we (African and African-American men) gathered at the nation's front door, we were united by gender and ethnicity.

Economic status, educational attainment, and religious affiliation had no place that day on the Capitol mall. Bound together by a spirit of unity, we defied the stereotypical depictions. No crimes were committed, no gang warfare occurred, no "dope" was smoked, no foul language was uttered, and no crack pipes were lit. Rather, we were bonded and united in brotherhood.

If we never again demonstrate our capacity to do so in future years, on that day we as Black men proved to ourselves, the nation, and the world that we can bond and that we do love ourselves and each other. This magnificent and unique experience made me proud—truly proud—to be a Black man: "one in a million," yet "a million as one."

FATHERS AND SONS

Recently, while flying to California, I sat watching a young man about thirty to thirty-five years of age lead his son down the plane's aisle toward the restroom. As the two waited patiently in the single-file line that had formed before them, the father stretched his massive hand downward, placed it on his son's head and caressed it, gently stroking backward and forward. As I watched, I realized that male bonding begins within the father-son relationship. Immediately, I revisited my past. Most memories of my childhood relations with my father have grown faint, but a few intimate moments still remain crystal clear thirty years later.

I recall taking quiet walks along the Lake Michigan shore in the cool of the morning, just my dad and me. I remember accompanying my dad to his weekly softball games, watching from the sidelines as he actively participated. I replay the moments following his game, how he engaged me in a one-on-one version of pitch and hit. Most memorable were those rare occasions when I would awaken early in the morning, before my brother and sisters, finding my dad still asleep. I would slither into his bed, crawl up against him ever so closely until he would take his big, burly arm and wrap it around my petite frame, pulling me closer to him.

Although as a child I never heard my dad utter the words "I love you, son," I never questioned his affection for me. Most young boys miss those opportunities. Too many of our young African-American boys grow up without fathers to serve as prominent male models for their lives. Statistics show that nearly half of all children in our society reside in single-parent homes with mothers as the head of the household. As a consequence, if bonding relationships are formed within the lives of these young boys, they occur through other relationships, if at all. Unfortunately, some grow up without establishing solid, intimate relationships with male figures; hence they learn to get along without them.

A *U.S. News and World Report* article (1995) entitled "Honor Thy Children" reported that 38 percent of today's children live apart from their biological fathers. That figure has more than doubled since 1960. This means that nearly two out of every five children in the United States do not reside with their biological fathers. Even worse, over half of the nation's children can look forward to spending part of their childhood without their fathers present. The statistics are even more alarming for African-American youth, two-thirds of whom are born out of wedlock.

The absent father is believed to be directly connected to the problem of "boys with guns" and "girls with babies." "Social scientists have made similar links between a father's absence and a child's likelihood of being a dropout, jobless, a drug addict, a suicide victim, mentally ill, and a target of child sexual abuse" (Shapiro et al. 1995, p. 39). K. Wilkinson (1974) suggests that "father-absent" homes in which no other male models are present have also been associated with young males' greater reliance on peers rather than adults and family members. Additionally, S. M. Harris (1992) mentioned that for low-income male youth, peer alliances become important during their early development, and that low-income youth tend to align themselves with and become dependent on their peers for support and approval. Gang members also serve as role models for young males reared in low-income communities.

Young boys need their fathers in the home to model appropriate behavior, lest they fall victim to the culture of the streets. The presence of biological fathers has an even greater impact on determining the likelihood of success and happiness among children. This holds true for all children regardless of financial status or ethnic background (Shapiro et al. 1995).

RESEARCH ON FRIENDSHIP

Much research has been conducted on the subject of same-sex friendships, some dating back to the early 1970s. Unfortunately, not much has focused on cross-gender interactions (Wright & Scanlon 1991), nor on African-American masculinity (Harris 1992). The majority of research has examined relationships between White, middle-class adolescents and young adults (Harris 1992). A review of that literature, however, will uncover, first, what is meant by *friendship* and *intimacy* within same-sex relations; second, comparative differences between same-sex relations among men versus those among women; and third, barriers that prevent men from establishing true bonds.

Inconsistencies in defining the concept of friendship have caused much difficulty. For example, a friend has been described as "an acquaintance, a neighbor, a close friend, a best friend, or a confidant." Family members, at times, have even been considered as such (Caldwell & Peplau 1982). A study conducted in northern California included an effort to refine how friendships were measured by using predefined words such as *intimate, good,* and *casual* (Caldwell & Peplau 1982).

The word *intimacy* also suffers from similar ambiguity, yet most often it refers to the disclosure of personal problems or concerns. Feelings of affection and closeness might also be included as signs of intimacy (Reisman 1990). R. A. Lewis (1978, p. 108) speaks of "emotional intimacy in behavioral terms as mutual self-disclosure and other kinds of verbal sharing, as declarations of liking or loving the other, and as demonstrations of affection such as hugging and nongenital caressing."

Friendship, however defined, indeed has its value. For many people, friendships provide a sense of support, emotional exchange, assistance, and fun. It lets people be themselves (Suttles 1970). According to Roberto and Kimboko (1989, p. 10) friendships have been consistently found to positively impact the "morale and life satisfaction of older adults."

L. A. Baxter (1992) included playfulness and camaraderie as important aspects of friendship. Both genders considered them critical components. Men and women also shared similar values regarding other aspects of friendship. According to Caldwell and Peplau (1982), both sexes preferred spending intimate moments with small groups of friends rather than larger groups of less intimate people.

The literature, however, reveals a plethora of information that depicts differences in how men and women relate. On average, women are said to regard friendship more highly than do men. Findings suggest that women invest more in friendships and gain more from them in all respects (Duck & Wright 1993). Research also supports the notion that friendships among adult women are richer regardless of age (William 1959), that intimacy is more prevalent among women (Powers & Bultena 1976), and men are more likely to have intimate confidants (Booth 1972; Booth & Hess 1974; Lowenthal & Haven 1968). Additionally, Weiss and Lowenthal (1975) perceived women's friendships as stressing reciprocity, while J. M. Reisman (1981) considered men's friendships as more associate.

The earlier findings of R. M. William (1959) were expanded on by latter-day researchers who found that women's friendships were more complex and holistic, while men's relations with other men centered more around structured activities. Men's friendships were considered less holistic (Block 1980; Weiss & Lowenthal 1975; Wright 1982).

R. R. Bell (1979) proposes that friendships among women are more frequent, interpersonal, and significant than men's friendships, which commonly lack intimacy and emotional richness. Studies conducted by Olstad (1975) and Powers and Bultena (1976) support this notion, indicating that men, though reporting more same-sex friendships than women, lack intimacy and closeness. Caldwell and Peplau (1982, p. 723) believe that " men might have more casual friends than women, but women might have more intimate friends than men." They go on to discuss what might be considered the most significant difference between how men and women interact in same-sex friendships: self-disclosure. Researchers have suggested that men have difficulty with emotional intimacy (Lewis 1978; Pleck 1975b) and are less emotionally expressive (Balswick & Peek 1971; Komarovsky 1967). Compared to women, men disclose less personal information (Cozby 1973) and also receive less personal information from others (Jourard & Richman 1963; Komarovsky 1976). Reis (1984), Winstead (1986), Clark and Reis (1988), and Reisman (1990) concluded that women exhibit more intimacy and self-disclose much more in their same-sex relationships than do men. Women are also said to place more value on and desire relationships that emphasize intimacy and discussion of personal problems (Caldwell & Peplau 1982; Davidson 1978; Lyness 1978; Reisman 1990; Yoon 1978).

Caldwell and Peplau (1982, p. 728) also mentioned noticeable differences in how men and women spend time together in same-sex encounters by suggesting that "women showed a greater preference for 'just talking' with friends, were more likely to indicate ... talking was an important thing to do with a best friend and reported talking about more personal topics with a best friend. In contrast, men were more engaged in activities with their friend and more likely to talk to their best friend about activities."

Harris (1992, p. 75) introduces critical information specific to African-American males and their same-sex relations. Harris begins by addressing the issue of masculinity among men. The traditional attributes associated with maleness within the American society (e.g., independence, self-confidence, assertiveness, headship within the family structure), were denied African-American men during slavery. Harris states that

> the institution of slavery limited the actual and perceived independence, self-confidence, aggression, power and even sexual behavior of African American men and introduced a style of manhood which they were prevented from displaying but eventually aspired to emulate. Ironically, after slavery was abolished, African American men were confronted with expectations from Euro-Americans and the African American community to behave, feel and think according to traditional masculine norms. Conflicting values and expectations regarding masculinity engendered a conflict with African American males that continues today.

Furthermore, Harris (1992) notes how slavery was a period of "demasculinization" for African-American males, and as such, assertiveness and the role of provider and protector of one's family were discouraged or prevented. In fact, in many instances, African-American men were forbidden to live in familial arrangements.

Even today, society has witnessed what Harris (1992, p. 75) described as "alternative styles of masculinity" developing among young African-American youth. That alternative style has served youth in coping with "social and interpersonal pressures, similar to but fundamentally different from traditional masculinity." One fundamental difference Harris mentioned is depicted in the perspective that youth share about being considered smart. For many young Euro-Americans, being smart is encouraged and is, in fact, highly regarded among men. However, among many African-Americans, being smart places youth among the outcasts within their own community. Being smart is considered socially acceptable for girls or Euro-Americans but not for young African-American males. For them, it represents conformity to authority figures and their values (Harris 1992).

Skills in other areas are perceived as critical by African-American youth. Harris (1992, p. 77) mentions that "skills in physical, verbal and emotional areas are especially encouraged as demonstrations of maleness." As early as the third grade, success in fighting, athletics, and risk-taking are perceived as "manly." The ability to outwit peers and authority figures—

to "play the dozens" (that is, the ability to accept and give taunts) is an aspect of masculinity.

Because many African-American youth experience difficulty in finding acceptance in mainstream society and its traditional framework, many youth opt for gang relations. This is particularly true for youth lacking male role models and/or living within low-income communities. Harris (1992, p. 78) elaborated further that African-American males join gangs to seek to remedy both interpersonal and intrapersonal needs that are not met in more socially acceptable ways. Their tendency is to seek "superficial bonds with several friends" rather than encounters that "promote communication, affection and acceptance."

Harris further noted that African-American men often struggle, not only from traditional issues of masculinity but also from deeper, more suppressed issues of oppression. As a consequence, we must not only address traditional barriers as experienced by mainstream society, but we must also address those issues specific and unique to us as African-Americans.

MOUNTAINS AND MOLEHILLS

Lewis (1978, p. 115) discusses four barriers that he perceived as roadblocks that keep men from exhibiting emotional intimacy within their relationships. Three of the four stemmed "directly from the traditional roles into which most men of our society have been socialized." The first of the barriers deals specially with norms traditionally prescribed to men by society. According to tradition, men were generally not supposed to be self-revealing, sensitive, or emotionally expressive (Pleck 1981; Devlin & Cowan 1985). Men have been socialized not to report feelings, nor experience feelings that could be perceived as signs of weakness (Harris 1992).

Robert Brannon (1976) suggests that traditional roles have limited men's abilities to develop meaningful relationships. He characterized the American men's socialization patterns using four themes: "no sissy stuff," "be the sturdy oak," "be a big wheel," and "give 'em hell". Two other writers also discussed the difficulties that men experience in attempting to establish relationships with other men due to the pressures and demands associated with male sex roles (Fasteau 1974; Pleck 1974). These pressures have greatly impacted same-sex relationships among men.

Second on the list of barriers is self-disclosure. As stated earlier, men self-disclose at lower rates than do women and reveal much less personal information about themselves to others (Jourard 1971; Jourard & Lasakow 1958; Jourard & Landsman 1969; Jourard & Richman 1963; Lewis 1978). Results from a survey of men attending Ivy League colleges revealed that men disclosed more to their closest female friend than to their closest male friend (Komarovsky 1974, 1976). Numerous reasons, no doubt, account for why men tend to self-disclose at lower rates; only one, however, will serve as the focus of attention. J. Pleck (1976) attributes men's inhibited affections to society's stress on competition. He (p. 111) suggests that, since many "powertrips" are directed toward other men, in order to win more approval, wealth, and status, it is very difficult for male friends to mutually disclose themselves, since disclosure amounts to increased vulnerability in a competitive milieu.

The preoccupation with competition and winning keeps us from revealing our most intimate feelings to one another, thus, protecting us from vulnerability. When we view each other as competitors, reaching out to another beyond levels of superficiality becomes quite difficult (Komarovsky 1974; Lewis 1978). Lewis (p. 110) renders a critical statement in this regard: "If disclosure of liking one another is so difficult, it is little wonder that hugging, holding hands, caressing and kissing, which are allowed between close friends in some cultures, are not observed in our culture." The fear of disclosure limits communication among men not only concerning problems that men experience but also concerning affections men can neither openly acknowledge nor embrace. Further discussion of this fear leads us to our third barrier—limits on love.

Americans have difficulty expressing love due partly to constraints imposed on them by the limits of the English language. One word used to describe the many facets of love can only lead to confusion and misinterpretations. Greek linguists escaped the dangers of such perils by simply creating more than one word to capture the multifaceted aspects of love.

Dr. Martin Luther King Jr. makes mention of this concept in his work "The Power of Nonviolence" (see Washington 1986). Endeavoring to make clear the notion of *agape*, Dr. King discusses it and two of the other Greek words for love and the meaning associated with each. *Eros* refers to aesthetic or romantic love. *Agape* is the love God exhibits for humanity, and it is unconditional, understanding, creative, and redemptive. *Philia* is love reciprocated between and among friends.

It is love in the last sense (*philia*) of which I speak when referring to "true" male bonding. Too often, there is an assumption that love referenced in relationships among men relates to *eros*—erotic tendencies. Thus, relationships are either denied or delayed due to distancing created by external or internal assumptions. When men find themselves attracted to one another (as Richard and I were), most fear *eros*, never even considering the possibility that *philia* is the bond drawing them together. Instead of investigating feelings, men typically choose to ignore them, potentially missing opportunities to form strong brotherhoods.

Research supports the notion that homophobia (fear of homosexuality) greatly impacts men and their ability to form intimate relationships (Brannon 1976; Devlin & Cowan 1985; Lewis 1978; Morin & Garfinkle 1978). Men tend to even fear touching each other, unless done roughly as in contact sports. This too derives from strong cultural prohibitions. If men are to ever experience true male bonding, we must become more comfortable within same-sex friendships.

The fourth barrier mentioned by Lewis (1978) relates to the lack of models who can provide examples of "affection-giving" between males. Between 1975 and 1977 Lewis conducted a series of intimacy workshops for men during which he discovered that more than half of the participants reported not remembering their fathers hugging them even after they were somewhat older. It is not uncommon to hear men express that they experienced little or no physical affection from their fathers during childhood or later in life. Although the father's role represents only one component of the perpetuated cultural norms present in modern society, when fathers begin to model fewer restrictions and more affection for their sons, we are likely to see positive changes in same-sex relationships.

WHAT'S THE BEEF?

Researchers show that many men have never experienced having a close male friend. Neither have they loved and cared for a male friend without feeling a sense of guilt, or feeling that they might be ridiculed (Komarovsky 1974; Pleck 1975a; Goldberg 1976; Lewis 1978). Those who have experienced close relationships have suffered within their relationships from lack of trust, personal sharing, and limited emotional investment because of so-called norms (Jourard 1971; Fasteau 1974; Steinmann & Fox 1974; Pleck 1974, 1975a; Goldberg 1976; Lewis 1978).

Some writers assert that the absence of intimacy among men is leading to many social problems (Lewis 1978) while others argue that the

absence of deep relationships among men correlates with the rise in suicide rates (Goldberg 1976). Harris (1992, p. 79) even believes that

> limited emotional expressions, low self-disclosure, indirect expression
> of anger, sexism, homophobia and roughness generalize to situations
> in which behavior and performance are evaluated according to more
> conventional standards. This type of personal style produces several
> problems for African-American males: including restricting their abil-
> ities to relate emotionally and behaviorally within intimate relation-
> ships; reducing employment opportunities; decreasing the favorability
> of college attendance and progression; and increasing the attractive-
> ness of activities that can lead to incarceration.

There is no question that men would benefit from heightened levels of
intimacy within their relationships.

As one might imagine, there are some drawbacks as well as positive
results for men who are willing to form true bonds with each other.
Reisman (1978, p. 118) discusses both negative and positive aspects in his
work. He suggests that some men have related their having been hurt by

> (a) being openly rejected by one who was formerly their friend; (b)
> being open to negative labeling by friends and others who either mis-
> understand one's motivation or are threatened by them; (c) being sus-
> ceptive to easy manipulation by those one has attempted to trust and
> with whom one has risked some deeper interaction; and (d) having to
> define themselves as persons who are dependent to some degree on
> other men for emotional support.

The positive outcomes also described by Reisman (1978, p. 119), include

> (a) discovering new parts of the personality through learning to share
> and care for other males, (b) opening oneself to a novel range of previ-
> ously unknown feelings and experiences, and (c) the growth of very sat-
> isfying and meaningful relationships with other men.

WHAT DOES THE BIBLE SAY?

According to the book of Genesis, chapter 1, the first bond that man
formed was between himself and God, his creator. Later, we read of man's
forming a bond with nature and with woman. If men are to be successful
in relating to others in life, like Adam, men must first bond with God.

When men sufficiently bond with God, they come to realize how they relate to themselves as well as to those around them.

The Bible is filled with countless examples of bonding relationships, both successful and unsuccessful, between men. The first sibling relationship in the Bible ended in a tragic travesty. However, several relationships following the demise of Cain and Abel serve as a reminder for us that we can dwell together in love and unity. Abraham's relationship with Isaac epitomized the sanctity of the father-son relationship. Enoch's relationship with God epitomized the sanctity of man's relationship to God. David's relationship with Jonathan epitomized the sanctity of man's relationship with men. The books of the Old Testament hold a plethora of examples of men who sought to live in proper relationship with man.

Such is also the case of the New Testament. Of all the same-sex relations depicted in the New Testament, the model for male bonding is most solidly demonstrated by Jesus Christ. As in all things, Christ provided men with the perfect example, even in forming bonds among men. Christ chose twelve men to be intimately involved in His ministry, each representing much diversity. During their three-year affiliation, those men became quite close to Jesus and one another. Christ modeled bonding behavior constantly: brotherhood; servanthood; love for God, Himself, and one's fellowman; and personal sacrifice. Within the bond that Christ created between Himself and each of His followers, we find no fear of physical contact and no lack of self-disclosure. This truth is most apparent in Jesus' washing the feet of the disciples (John 13), the intimate meal in the upper room (Matthew 26), and the ultimate sacrifice made at Calvary (Luke 23).

Accepting Christ on a personal level begins with self-disclosure. When we confess our sins, we expose our vulnerability before Christ, yet before Christ we are not in danger. As we enter into relationship with Him, He provides us with a perfect model of relating with all others. Jesus knows what being a true friend is really about, and of true love in friendship. "Greater love hath no man than this, that a man lay down his life for his friends" (John 15:13). When men begin to acquaint themselves with Christ and strive to model Him in every aspect of living, including how men relate with one another, they will find much success. Men will experience stronger bonds devoid of the fears and barriers society has erected.

REFERENCES

Ames, C. 1993. Restoring the Black man's lethal weapon: Race and sexuality in contemporary cop films. *Journal of Popular Film and Television* 20: 52–60.

Balswick, J., and C. Peek. 1971. The inexpressive male: A tragedy of American society. *Family Coordinator* 20: 363–68.

Baxter, L. A. 1992. Forms and functions of intimate play in personal relationships. *Human Communication Research* 18: 336–63.

Bell, R. R. 1979. *Marriage and family interaction.* 5th ed. Homewood, IL: Dorsey Press.

Block, J. D. 1980. *Friendship: How to give it, how to get it.* New York: Macmillan.

Booth, A. 1972. Sex and social participation. *American Sociological Review* 37: 183–92.

Booth, A., and E. Hess. 1974. Cross-sex friendship. *Journal of Marriage and the Family* 36: 38–47.

Brannon, R. 1976. The male sex role: Our culture's blueprint of manhood, and what it's done for us lately. In *The forty-nine percent majority: The male sex role,* edited by D. David and R. Brannon. Reading, MA: Addison-Wesley. 1–45.

Caldwell, Mayta A., and L. A. Peplau. 1982. Sex differences in same-sex friendships. *Sex Roles* 8: 721–32.

Clark, M. S., and H. T. Reis. 1988. Interpersonal processes in close relationships. *Annual Review of Psychology* 39: 609–72.

Cozby, P. C. 1973. Self-disclosure: A literature review. *Psychological Bulletin* 79: 73–91.

Davidson, S. L. 1978. The therapeutic dimensions of friendship between women. *Dissertation Abstracts* 39 (1-A): 192.

Devlin, P. K., and G. A. Cowan. 1985. Homophobia, perceived fathering, and male intimate relationships. *Journal of Personality Assessment* 49: 467–73.

Duck, S., and P. H. Wright. 1993. Reexamining gender differences in same-gender friendships: A close look at two kinds of data. *Sex Roles* 28: 709–27.

Elkins, L. E., and C. Peterson. 1993. Gender differences in best friendships. *Sex Roles* 29: 497–508.

Farrell, M. P. 1986. Friendship between men. *Marriage and Family Review* 9: 163–97.

Fasteau, M. F. 1974. *The male machine*. New York: McGraw-Hill.

Goldberg, H. 1976. *The hazards of being male: Surviving the myth of masculine privilege*. New York: Nash.

Harris, S. M. 1992. Black male masculinity and same-sex friendships. *Western Journal of Black Studies* 16: 74–81.

Jourard, S. 1971. *The transparent self*. New York: Van Nostrand Reinhold.

Jourard, S., and M. Landsman. 1969. Cognition, cathexis, and the "dyadic effect" in men's self-disclosing behavior. *Merrill-Palmer Quarterly* 6: 178–86.

Jourard, S., and P. Lasakow. 1958. Some factors in self-disclosure. *Journal of Abnormal and Social Psychology* 56: 91–98.

Jourard, S., and P. Richman. 1963. Disclosure output and input in college students. *Merrill-Palmer Quarterly* 9: 141–48.

Komarovsky, M. 1976. *Dilemmas of masculinity: A study of college youth*. New York: Norton.

_____. 1974. Patterns of self-disclosure of male undergraduates. *Journal of Marriage and the Family* 36: 677–86.

_____. 1967. *Blue-collar marriage*. New York: Vintage.

Lewis, R. A. 1978. Emotional intimacy among men. *Journal of Social Issues* 34: 108–21.

Lowenthal, M. F., and C. Haven. 1968. Interaction and adaptation: Intimacy as a critical variable. *American Sociological Review* 33: 20–30.

Lyness, J. F. 1978. Styles of relationships among unmarried men and women. *Sociological Abstracts* 26: 1249.

Morin, S., and E. M. Garfinkle. 1978. Male homophobia. *Journal of Social Issues* 34: 29–47.

Olstad, K. 1975. Brave new men: A basis for discussion. In *Sex/male—Gender/masculine*, edited by J. Petras. Port Washington, NY: Alfred Publishing Co.

Pleck, J. 1981. *The myth of masculinity*. Cambridge, MA: MIT Press.

_____. 1976. The male sex role: Definitions, problems, and sources of change. *Journal of Social Issues* 32: 155–64.

_____. 1975a. Male-male friendship: Is brotherhood possible? In *Old family-new family: Interpersonal relationships*, edited by M. Glazer. New York: Van Nostrand Reinhold.

_____. 1975b. Masculinity-femininity: Current and alternative paradigms. *Sex Roles* 1: 161–77.

_____. 1974. My male sex role—and ours. *Win* 10: 8–12.

Powers, E., and G. Bultena. 1976. Sex differences in intimate friendships of old age. *Journal of Marriage and the Family* 38: 739–47.

Reis, H. T. 1984. Social interaction and well-being. In *Repairing personal relationships*, edited by S. Duck. London: Academic Press.

Reisman, J. M. 1990. Intimacy in same-sex friendships. *Sex Roles* 23: 65–82.

_____. 1978. Adult friendships. In *Developing personal relationships*, edited by S. Duck and R. Gilmour. London: Academic Press.

Roberto, K. A., and P. J. Kimboko. 1989. Friendships in later life: Definitions and maintenance patterns. *International Journal of Aging and Human Development* 28: 9–19.

Shapiro, J., J. M. Schrof, Mike Tharp, and Dorian Friedman. 1995. Honor thy children. *U.S. News and World Report* 118: 38–49.

Steinmann, A., and D. Fox. 1974. *The male dilemma*. New York: Jason Aronson.

Suttles, G. D. 1970. Friendship as a social institution. In *Social relationships*, edited by G. McCall et al. Chicago: Aldine.

Washington, J. M. 1986. *A testament of hope: The essential writings of Martin Luther King Jr.* New York: Harper and Row.

Weiss, L., and M. Lowenthal. 1975. Life course perspectives on friendships. In *Four stages of life*, edited by M. Lowenthal, M. Thurnher, and D. D. Chirboga. San Francisco: Jossey-Bass.

Wilkinson, K. 1974. The broken family and juvenile delinquency: Scientific explanation or ideology. *Social Problems* 21: 726–39.

William, R. M. 1959. Friendship and social values in a suburban community: An exploratory study. *Pacific Sociological Review* 2: 3–10.

Winstead, B. A. 1986. Sex differences in same sex friendships. In *Friendship and social interaction*, edited by V. J. Derlega and B. A. Winstead. New York: Springer-Verlag.

Wright, P. H. 1982. Men's friendships, women's friendships, and the alleged inferiority of the latter. *Sex Roles* 8: 1–20.

Wright, P. H., and M. B. Scanlon. 1991. Gender role orientations and friendship: Some attenuation, but gender differences abound. *Sex Roles* 24: 51–66.

Yoon, G. H. 1978. The natural history of friendship: Sex differences in best friendship patterns. *Dissertation Abstracts* 39: 1553.

PART 2

STRENGTHENING RELATIONSHIPS WITHIN FAMILIES

Lloyd C. Blue

How to Romance Your Wife

LLOYD C. BLUE is chief executive officer of Church Growth Unlimited, headquartered in Mendenhall, Mississippi, and is the former pastor of North Oakland Missionary Baptist Church in Oakland, California. He is nationally acclaimed for his lectures in the areas of personal evangelism, ministry of the Holy Spirit, abundant Christian living, building disciples, church growth, family enrichment, pastoral management and counseling, the mechanics of expository preaching, and methods for city- or state-wide revival meetings. Lloyd attended California Baptist College, received his bachelor of theology degree from the Institutional Baptist Theological Center, Houston, Texas, a master of arts degree from Union University in Los Angeles, California, and a doctor of ministry degree from the University of Central America. A native of North Carolina, Lloyd is married to Tressie Blue. They have one son, Lloyd II, and two adopted daughters, Kay and Robbin.

Chapter 6

Lloyd C. Blue

How to Romance Your Wife

INTRODUCTION

Very few couples seem to be experiencing this thing we call romance—that uncontrollable sensation or feeling often caused by just a glance, a word, a greeting, or a smile. This feeling is usually very strong during courtship. After the wedding, however, the romance starts to fade. We stop planning dates. We stop saying all those romantic words. We begin to take each other for granted, and it becomes easier to compliment others rather than our own mate.

WHAT IS ROMANCE?

Some people think romance is a myth, something that is entertaining in the movies, but not the way people live in real life. Some sincere Christians think that romance is just not necessary in marriage. They love each other in the Lord and feel that that is what really counts. Some people try to suppress romance because they are not interested in it. Some even rationalize that because they do not have it, it must not exist. Some people think that in their marriage, romance is just not possible. Nevertheless, the question remains, "What is romance?"

Romance is a thrilling love relationship involving oneness. It is a deep intimacy with another person that is filled with joy and excitement. This wonderful, almost indescribable sensation is known as "being in love." Some people call it being on "cloud nine." They feel energized and motivated, and when they are apart from one another, they can hardly wait to be together again.

There is a song that puts it this way: "I'm having day dreams about night things in the middle of the afternoon. While my hands make a living, my mind's on loving you." The person in the song wanted five o'clock to hurry and come so he could be home with her by six!

I believe that when God created Adam, He put in him the need for romantic love. The Bible says in Genesis 2:18–25:

> The LORD God said, "It is not good for the man to be alone. I will make a helper suitable for him." Now the LORD God had formed out of the ground all the beasts of the field and all the birds of the air. He brought them to the man to see what he would name them; and whatever the man called each living creature, that was its name. So the man gave names to all the livestock, the birds of the air and all the beasts of the field.
>
> But for Adam no suitable helper was found. So the LORD God caused the man to fall into a deep sleep; and while he was sleeping, he took one of the man's ribs and closed up the place with flesh. Then the LORD God made a woman from the rib he had taken out of the man, and he brought her to the man. The man said, "This is now bone of my bones and flesh of my flesh; she shall be called woman, for she was taken out of man." For this reason a man will leave his father and mother and be united to his wife, and they will become one flesh. The man and his wife were both naked, and they felt no shame. (NIV)

Of all the creatures God made, not one was suitable for Adam. In other words, the need in Adam for romantic love could not be fulfilled by any of these creatures; Adam was still lonely. So God performed the first surgery and took a rib from Adam's side and made Eve. When God brought Eve to Adam he took one look at her and knew that his lonely days were over. Now, if you will allow me to use my sanctified imagination, I think that romantic love soared through Adam's total being and he said, "Wow, this is it! This is now bone of my bone and flesh of my flesh. Wow!"

Gregory Godek (1993, p. 197), in his book *Romance 101: Lessons in Love*, makes this statement:

> It's just plain unrealistic to expect romance to last no more than a few years. Romance inevitably fades in the face of everyday life. Romance— it's just a passing phase we grow out of. I hear it in the Romance Class. I hear it in casual conversations. It drives me crazy every time. At least

in the Romance Class I have the opportunity, if not the responsibility, to point out to people that they're strangling their own relationships with this kind of thinking. You see, romance isn't about flowers and candy and cute little notes. Romance is the expression of love. Without romance, love becomes just an empty concept. I love you becomes a meaningless, automatic phrase. Romance is not a thing separate from love. It's not something that you grow out of as you mature. If anything, one's love grows deeper as one matures, and the romance—the expression, the action of love—stays vibrant and creatively alive.

Because romance is the expression of love, we must not allow it to die.

WHY ROMANCE YOUR WIFE?

In Ephesians 5:25, the Bible states: "Husbands, love your wives, just as Christ loved the church and gave himself up for her." Thus, we are to romance the woman we vowed to love and to cherish until separated by death. I believe there is a misconception about the true nature of romance and its relationship to love. What happens is that people remove the concept of romance from love, where it belongs, and connect it to other things—things like being single, being infatuated, being immature and irresponsible, being forever moving and searching and unsettled. When this happens the surface expressions of romance—passion, intensity, excitement—become linked with those states of being. One then begins to believe, for example, that being single is exciting and being married is boring. Nothing could be further from the truth.

If you want a dull, boring marriage, however, you do not have to do anything to create one. The problem is that some people believe that all marriages are this way. Not so—your marriage does not have to be that way—you can change your relationship by changing your beliefs. I know many couples who have been married for twenty-five years and even some over forty years who "still have it going on." They have exciting "affairs" with their mates. They still date each other. These individuals all have one thing in common: they understand that they have control over whether or not their lives are filled with romance on an everyday basis. A romantic marriage is not something that is reserved for a few privileged couples, but is available to anyone who believes that it is possible and is willing to work at it. Paul wrote in Romans 12:2: "Do not conform any longer to the pattern of this world, but be transformed by the renewing of your mind.

Then you will be able to test and approve what God's will is—his good, pleasing and perfect will" (NIV). Proverbs 23:17 states, "Do not let your heart envy sinners, but always be zealous for the fear of the LORD (NIV)."

The questions that we must ask ourselves at this point are these:

1. Do I believe that marriage has to be dull, boring, and routine?
2. Do I believe that marriage, yes, even mine, can be filled with romance—hot—passionate romance?

If your answer to question 1 is yes, I trust that before you finish this chapter you will change your mind. If your answer to question 2 is yes, then you are ready to face what is yet to come.

WAYS TO BE ROMANTIC

Godek (1993, p. 198) says, "Romance is a state of mind. Romance is a state of being. Romance is the expression of love." I totally agree with Godek. While romance often starts as a "state of mind," it must move beyond mere thoughts and intentions and be communicated to your wife, through words, actions, gifts, gestures, or sometimes just a tender look.

As men, we tend to think of romance as an event, when in fact, romance is a process. It is not a one-time thing that is accomplished and then forgotten. In order to work, it has to be an ongoing thing, a part of the fabric of our daily life, because women are motivated and empowered when they feel cherished. Let me suggest that you put your thinking cap on and come up with some ways you can make her feel cherished.

There are countless ways to do this and I will list some that I trust you will find helpful.

Activity 1: Sending Romantic Cards

Buy a card that expresses the way you feel, mail it to her, and when she thanks you for the card, take her in your arms for a moment and tell her, "Baby, I love you and I mean everything that card says." If you really want to get her going, send her a card every day for a week. Check with your post office to see if you can get next-day delivery, and if so, mail the first card on Saturday, then another on Monday, and so on. Make the Friday card a sexy one. She will love it and you are going to have a weekend to remember!

Activity 2: Giving Her Roses

Bring or send her roses. If she has a job outside the home, send her eleven roses at her place of work. It does not have to be a special day. On the card write, "If you want to see what a dozen roses look like, take these and stand in front of the mirror." You will make her the envy of all her fellow workers. I know because I did it.

Activity 3: Saturday Night at a Hotel

First, make sure she can be available. Tell her that you are taking her on an overnight date a week before the event. This is very important if you have children, and it will give her time to anticipate the date, which can be as much fun as the date itself. If she asks for more information, tell her, "It's a surprise. Just dress as if you were going out to dinner and be sure to bring your overnight kit." Second, make reservations at a four-star hotel and, if possible, reserve a suite. You are not going to do this every weekend so make the most of it, even if you have to save up for it. Third, on Saturday morning pick up the key and make sure you put romantic music (tape recorder, if necessary) and roses with a romantic card in the room.

Timing is important. If need be, you may want to secure the help of the hotel staff to turn on the music at just the right time. If your car has a tape deck or CD player, select the song that says what you want to say, and when you start up the car, turn the music on. When she looks in your direction give her the most seductive look you can muster and tell her, "I love you, Honey, and I sure hope you enjoy your day." When you arrive at the hotel, say to her, "I picked up the key when I went out this morning, I didn't want you to have to stand around waiting for me to register." When you open the door to your suite with the music and the aroma of the roses flowing around the room, well, you can pucker up and get ready for a "mess" of kissing, and while you are kissing be sure to do some slow dancing across the room with your queen. About that time, there should be a knock at the door—room service with your favorite beverage and snacks that you ordered when you were at the hotel earlier.

Now it's time to relax, relate, and enjoy the music and one another. This would be an excellent time to bring out the lotion and give her a foot massage. Then lie across the bed and touch and talk. Tell her all the ways you love her and how much you need her—tell her, "Baby, I wouldn't last a day without you." About 7:00 P.M. there should be another knock at the door—room service again. In the parlor, in the dim glow of candlelight, she enjoys with you her favorite meal.

Well partner, I'm going to stop now. I cannot stand anymore of this. You will have to let your feelings take you the rest of the way.

Activity 4: Playing Love Songs

The market is filled with love songs. Think about what your wife wants to hear and find a love song that will express it. For example, I went away for a week of preaching, and heard a song by Vince Gil called "Look at Us." I bought the cassette and set the tape on that particular song so when my wife picked me up at the airport, I could play it for her on the way home. These are the words of that song:

> If they want to see what true love should be
> They can look at us.
> Look at you still pretty as a picture,
> Look at me still crazy over you,
> Look at us still believing in forever,
> And if they want to see what true love can be they can look at us.

When it was over she told me how much she loved it, but the look on her face had already said it.

Activity 5: Valentine's Day

I plan to send my wife a written invitation to dinner and a private concert (with tapes) to hear her favorite love songs sung by their original recording artist. Some of her favorites are "Through the Years" and "Lady" by Kenny Rogers; "Unforgettable" by Nat King Cole; "Have I Told You Lately That I Love You?" by Rod Stewart; "Look at Us" by Vince Gil; and "Wind Beneath My Wings" by Lou Rawls as well as some Luther Vandross and Barry White.

But first, I plan to take her to her favorite restaurant for dinner and then to a hotel suite for the concert and evening just for the two of us— you get the idea, right?

Activity 6: Getting Ideas

One way to generate romantic ideas is to focus on your wife. If you focus your attention on her, just think of her a little more often, then romantic ideas will simply pop up all around you! I guarantee it. Romantic gifts will jump off store shelves into your hands, and romantic opportunities will present themselves to you over and over again.

Activity 7: Taking Action

Add these ingredients in any combination or measure to your next romantic gift or gesture: anticipation, intrigue, and surprise. Mix well, do not half-bake it, and serve with a flourish.

Activity 8: Little Things Mean a Lot

Do not just hand her a soda—open it first. Do not just hand her a stick of gum—pull back the wrapper for her. Pull out the chair for her, even at home. Open the car door for her and close it after she is seated.

Activity 9: Wrapping a Gift

Get her a bottle of perfume and put it in a paper bag, twist the top and tie it with a ribbon. Then put it in a larger bag and then repeat the process until you have about ten bags. When you present the gift, be sure to tell her, "Don't mash the bag, you may damage the goods." Now you can enjoy yourself watching her carefully open each bag. In the bag with the perfume make sure there is a card expressing your love for her. This also works well with four or five boxes. Make sure each box is gift-wrapped. She will feel good about herself, and she will love you for it.

Activity 10: Verbal Expression

No matter how many things you do, it will not take the place of verbal expression. Your wife needs to hear you say how you feel about her. She needs to hear you say, "I love you," with your mouth, not just with things. Say it often, daily even. This can be done when you leave for work or when you come home. Sometime in the middle of the day call her and say, "Honey, I just called to tell you that I love you, see you later. Good-bye," and hang up the telephone before she can say anything. She also needs to hear you say, "I need you like the river needs the water," "I need you," or "I wouldn't last a day without you." She needs to hear you say she is beautiful in your eyes. When she asks, "How do you like my dress?" Tell her, "It's great, and I am sure it would not look that good on any other woman on earth." She wants to know how she looks to you.

Let me call your attention to the master when it comes to telling a woman how she looks:

"How beautiful are your feet in sandals,
O prince's daughter!
The curves of your hips are like jewels,
The work of the hands of an artist.
Your navel is like a round goblet
Which never lacks mixed wine;
Your belly is like a heap of wheat
Fenced about with lilies.
Your two breasts are like two fawns,
Twins of a gazelle.
Your neck is like a tower of ivory,
Your eyes like the pools of Heshbon
By the gate of Bath-rabbim;
Your nose is like the tower of Lebanon,
Which faces toward Damascus.
Your head crowns you like Carmel,
And the flowing locks of your head are like purple threads;
The king is captivated by your tresses.
How beautiful and how delightful you are,
My love, with all your charms!
Your stature is like a palm tree,
And your breasts are like its clusters."
I said, 'I will climb the palm tree,
I will take hold of its fruit stalks.'
Oh, may your breasts be like clusters of the vine,
And the fragrance of your breath like apples,
And your mouth like the best wine!"

"It goes down smoothly for my beloved,
Flowing gently through the lips of those who fall asleep."
    (Song of Solomon 7:1–9 NASB)

Notice that he describes his wife in many different ways. Give some thought to how you might describe these areas of your wife to her and watch her melt into your arms. Also, notice that Solomon selected the most beautiful and attractive objects of his time to describe his wife's body. You do not have to describe her whole body at the same time, you might just tell her how beautiful her eyes are and at some other time, tell her how beautiful some other part of her body is to you.

Activity 11: A Date with Your Wife

You should date your wife often. Do it weekly or monthly. You cannot overdo it and it does not have to be expensive. The idea is to be alone with her, to talk about the things she wants to talk about. When you take the time to date your wife, it helps her to feel special, and she needs to feel special.

Personally, I like to date my wife on Friday night, because we usually sleep in on Saturday morning. Sometimes we go to dinner, sometimes a movie, sometimes both. Sometimes we go to a mall and just walk and talk and window shop. There have been times when we have gone out for a cheeseburger. Other times we have driven to a spot with a special view and just sat and talked. This is a good time for you to encourage your wife to talk about those things she has been wanting to talk about all week when you both were too busy. You might ask her some questions like, "How has it been going for you this week? or, "If you could, what is the one thing you would change about me?" This way you can learn what is on her mind and help her deal with any problems she might be facing.

WHY ROMANCE YOUR WIFE?

Ephesians 5:28–29 states: "In this same way, husbands ought to love their wives as their own bodies. He who loves his wife loves himself. After all, no one ever hated his own body, but he feeds and cares for it, just as Christ does the church" (NIV). We should romance our wives because romance is a part of what love is all about and we are commanded to love and cherish our wives as we love and cherish our own bodies. The apostle Paul believed that life was precious and that every care should be taken to preserve it. He also believed that a healthy husband believed as he did and would value his body, doing everything possible to preserve it. Because Paul believed this way, he commanded husbands to love their wives as their own bodies. Romance is not an option. We must do everything in our power to preserve a healthy relationship.

WISDOM IS REQUIRED TO ROMANCE YOUR WIFE

You are beautiful, my darling, as Tirzah,
lovely as Jerusalem,
majestic as troops with banners.
Turn your eyes from me;
they overwhelm me.

Your hair is like a flock of goats
  descending from Gilead.
Your teeth are like a flock of sheep
  coming up from the washing.
Each has its twin,
  not one of them is alone.
Your temples behind your veil
  are like the halves of a pomegranate.
Sixty queens there may be,
  and eighty concubines,
  and virgins beyond number;
but my dove, my perfect one, is unique,
  the only daughter of her mother,
  the favorite of the one who bore her.
The maidens saw her and called her blessed;
  the queens and concubines praised her.
(Song of Songs 6:4–9 NIV)

Solomon did and said it best. Briefly, let us consider how Solomon loved his wife. What were his "secrets"? A husband trying to follow New Testament admonitions in carrying out his role can find no better guidelines and examples of Ephesians 5 in action than those provided by Solomon in Song of Songs 6:4–9, where we note, first of all, that he praised her on her physical appearance and her great character. He totally refrained from criticizing her. It was as if she did not deserve any. Husband, your wife needs to hear similar praise from your lips. Every wife needs to be praised for her beauty by her husband. It is this that makes her beautiful. It also gives her confidence and builds her self-image.

You have perhaps heard the words "Not tonight" or "I have a headache." Well, do not feel alone, so did Solomon (see Song of Songs 5:3). Now I want to call your attention to how he handled this most delicate matter. He extravagantly spread the door handles with perfume (myrrh). He did this so she would know that he was not angry and that he loved her as much as ever. Becoming an irate husband at times like these will not help you or your wife. Always seek to turn your negatives into positives. Why not say something like, "That's all right, honey, get a good night's rest, you'll feel better tomorrow. Would you like to sleep in my arms? I love you very much. Good night."

Because Solomon behaved like a lover, his wife quickly realized that she should correct her mistake. As soon as they were together, instead of rebuking her, Solomon reassured her of his love for her. Your wife should know that even if you do get a little angry sometimes, the one thing she can count on is your love for her. As Solomon, the lover and king did, exercise wisdom in romancing your wife.

WELCOME ROMANCE FROM YOUR WIFE

In Song of Songs 7:10; 8:3, the Shulammite woman does the talking and the initiating. After all, Solomon has been describing her physical attractiveness and sexual delights. He is ready, and according to the verses just preceding this section, so is she. She is ready to celebrate with him. Notice that in chapter 7:1–12, this is sex from God's point of view— explicit and intimate. It is filled with pleasure and enjoyment and there has never been a more beautiful description nor a more complete picture of romantic love. The words, "There I will give you my love," in verse 12 emphasize that the Shulammite is looking for a romantic and secluded place to enjoy their lovemaking. She feels the need for privacy, for a change of environment, for renewal, and for romance that will be remembered.

Take it from me, a man who has been married to the same woman for forty years, no matter how much you enjoy sex at home, there is a need for romantic getaways with your wife. This does not have to be expensive or for a long period of time, it can be just one or two days at some romantic place. Or it can be just one night at a hotel, away from the children, away from the phone, away from the same environment. Believe me, it will do you good.

There is so much more to be gleaned from this passage, but what I want to do is stress the point that in this case it is the wife who is planning this getaway and the husband welcomes the idea. Therefore, as men we must welcome romance from our wife.

WILL TO ROMANCE YOUR WIFE

After this there was a feast of the Jews; and Jesus went up to Jerusalem.

Now there is at Jerusalem by the sheep market a pool, which is called in the Hebrew tongue Bethesda, having five porches.

In these lay a great multitude of impotent folk, of blind, halt, withered, waiting for the moving of the water.

For an angel went down at a certain season into the pool, and troubled the water: whosoever then first after the troubling of the water stepped in was made whole of whatsoever disease he had.

And a certain man was there, which had an infirmity thirty and eight years.

When Jesus saw him lie, and knew that he had been now a long time in that case, he saith unto him, Wilt thou be made whole?

The impotent man answered him, Sir, I have no man, when the water is troubled, to put me into the pool: but while I am coming, another steppeth down before me.

Jesus saith unto him, Rise, take up thy bed, and walk.

And immediately the man was made whole, and took up his bed, and walked: and on the same day was the Sabbath. (John 5:1–9 KJV)

God is love and He created man to love Him back. Love cannot be compelled, it must be freely given by an act of the will. Therefore, we must will to romance our wives and when we do, the Lord, who lives in us in the person of the Holy Spirit, will empower us to do so.

We can see this so clearly in the above passages. Notice particularly verse 6, where Jesus asked the man, "Do you will to be made whole?" In verse 7, this man did two things that we must be careful about. First, he focused on the past instead of the present. Focusing on the past is dangerous, because it detracts us from what is available to us in the present. Second, he focused on the problem instead of the possibility (see v. 7b). Focusing on the problem can create in us the fear of failure and it is hard to see possibility in this state of mind.

Jesus then said to the man, "Take up your bed and walk" (v. 8). The man did the only thing he could do—"he willed to obey"—and at that moment all he needed to obey was provided by the Lord Jesus. Verse 9 says that the man was made whole by the act of his will to obey the Lord's command. Likewise, you have been commanded to love your wife. "In this same way, husbands ought to love their wives as their own bodies. He who loves his wife loves himself. After all, no one ever hated his own body, but he feeds and cares for it, just as Christ does the church" (Ephesians 5:28–29 NIV).

Notice that you are to nourish and cherish your wife as your own body. This means that just as you provide for the needs of your body, you must provide for the needs of your wife, and romance is a need.

Because loving your wife is a command, you can by faith will to love your wife romantically and, according to 1 John 5:14–15, trust God to provide the power to get it done. Notice what it says: "This is the confidence we have in approaching God: that if we ask anything according to his will, he hears us. And if we know that he hears us, whatever we ask, we know that we have what we asked of him" (NIV).

CONCLUSION

Now here it is in a nutshell. By faith, will to love, act lovingly, and romantic love will come.

It is so important that we understand this. As husbands we must view romantic love as a calling from God on our life and, as Paul writes: "The one who calls you is faithful and he will do it" (1 Thessalonians 5:24 NIV). Paul also writes: "For it is God who works in you to will and to act according to his good purpose" (Philippians 2:13 NIV). We have a faithful God who is at work in us, both to will and to do what He has called us to do. For this reason we are without excuse. *Romance your wife.*

REFERENCES

Dillow, J. C. 1977. *Solomon on sex*. Nashville: Thomas Nelson.

Ferguson, D., et al. 1994. *Intimate encounters*. Nashville: Thomas Nelson.

Godek, G. J. P. 1993a. *Romance 101: Lessons in love*. Weymouth, MA: Casablanca Press.

_____. 1993b. *1001 more ways to be romantic*. Weymouth, MA: Casablanca Press.

Gray, J. 1993. *Men, women, and relationships*. Hillsboro, OR: Beyond Words Publishing.

Hocking, D., and C. Hocking. 1986. *Romantic lovers*. Eugene, OR: Harvest House.

1984. *The holy Bible: New international version*. Grand Rapids: Zondervan.

The King James version of the Bible.

1978. *New American standard Bible*. Chicago: Moody Press.

Rainey, D., and B. Rainey. 1986. *Building your mate's self-esteem*. San Bernardino, CA: Here's Life Publishers.

Wheat, E., and G. O. Perkins. 1980. *Love life for every married couple*. Grand Rapids: Zondervan.

Michael R. Lyles and Larry Purvis

Building Powerful Families

MICHAEL R. LYLES is the medical director of the Rapha Inpatient Adult Unit at Charter Peachford Hospital in Atlanta, Georgia, and has a private practice in psychiatry with the Atlanta Counseling Center. He received his bachelor of science and doctor of medicine degrees from the University of Michigan and completed his psychiatric residency at Duke University. Michael is a member of the Zion Baptist Church in Roswell, Georgia, and is currently a Sunday school teacher. He also works with the children's church program. Born in Chicago, Illinois, and raised in Spartanburg, South Carolina, he moved to Detroit, Michigan, as a teenager. He is married to Marsha Washington Lyles and they have one son, Michael, and two daughters, Morgann and Mallory.

LARRY PURVIS is a case manager with Project New Hope of the Salvation Army in Atlanta. He earned a bachelor's degree in business administration from the University of Northern Colorado and is studying for a master's degree in theology from Guinnett Hall Baptist College in Lawrenceville, Georgia. Larry spent almost twenty years with IBM in various positions. He was the founder and president of the Community Outreach and Development Center and the Adolescent Support and Advocacy Program. An ordained minister at Zion Baptist Church in Roswell, Georgia, he works with a parent support team and assists with pastoral counseling and school consulting. He is married to Alva Dickerson Purvis, and they have one daughter, Kelli Malisa.

Chapter 7

Michael R. Lyles and Larry Purvis

Building Powerful Families

Men can't be trusted—they are all pond scum. They lie and manipulate to get what they want from you and give nothing in return but pain. I can't speak for White men and never will—but Black men are all dogs! As a Black woman, my lot is loneliness because Black men don't know how to act. It's bad enough when I feel used by a White person at work, but what the brothers give me at home is more painful! It made me want to drink to escape—but even alcohol couldn't numb my loneliness.

Linda K., a middle-aged African-American female

My father used to live large. He had the fine job, nice house, big car—I mean everything. Then he started hitting that rock [crack cocaine]. He started staying out, yelling at my mom, and never had any money. They finally divorced and he is now on the street—hustling and homeless. I see him and I see myself— what I am supposed to be—a loser, a junkie, a hustler. It scares me because I don't want to do it, but I don't know how not to do it. It's like destiny.

Tony B., a teen-age African-American male

A television commercial in the Atlanta, Georgia, area begins with an African-American woman holding her four-year-old son whom she calls "an endangered species" due to urban violence. Indeed the image of African-American males as perpetrators and victims of violence, drug abuse, sexual looseness, and family abandonment is widely circulated by the media. Our music is of lust and passion but little of respect and relationship building. According to *USA Today,* 15 September 1994, with one-third of Black children living with a never-married parent (usually female) and 64 percent having an absent parent (usually male), the negative stereotypes of African-American males take on such power that the comments of Linda K. are not unusual. In fact, if the statements of Linda K. and Tony B. had been made by Caucasians about African-American males, there would be an outcry of racism. The fact that these statements were made by us about us is more telling and more tragic—symptomatic of a sense of hopelessness and despair that is destroying individuals and families.

In contrast to this sense of negative destiny, the authors of these chapters feel that African-American men can be lovers and leaders of their families. We feel that there are principles that are essential to the life of any healthy family—be they a family of color or not.

In this chapter we will highlight the characteristics of strong families and the skills that any man, regardless of ethnicity, must have in giving proper leadership to that family. Before talking about these general principles, which apply to all successful families, however, we must deal with the factor that complicates the task for African-American men in leading, and African-American women and children in following—racism.

RACISM AND AFRICAN-AMERICAN MEN

In psychology, we learn that the experiences of the past influence and mold our perceptions of the present. Pain and loss as well as happiness and joy weave together to leave both healthy and not-so-healthy imprints in our self-esteem and on our ability to form relationships in the present. As African-American men, we cannot forget that we got our start in this country as mere chattel—only three-fifths human. Men debated about whether we had souls and whether we had the capacity for more than manual labor and breeding. The debate about the equality of African-Americans with Whites raged through periods of segregation, Jim Crow laws, White flight, and the more recent discussions of racial differences.

Whereas how we started out over 370 years ago does not and should not dictate our plight today, some of the techniques and images that were used to make African-Americans, male and female, feel inferior, stigmatized, and self-hating are still present today. For example, part of a man's responsibility in building a strong family is providing for them economically. A man of color who cannot find meaningful employment or who is penalized for advancement because of the color of his skin alone has a much greater task in building a strong family.

African-American men are constantly striving to achieve some source of success in an economic system that was not designed to benefit them. The only institution controlled historically by us has been the Black church, a few schools, and a few businesses. Even though some African-American men have achieved phenomenal success against great odds, most of us continue to operate in economic systems where race is still a factor.

Ron J.'s story illustrates how the combination of racial exclusion and frustration provided real and perceived obstacles to his asserting his role in leading and loving his family. Ron J. was a forty-year-old African-American married male who was "raised in church" and was a college graduate. While in college, he began to drink and "party" a great deal. He met his wife, settled down, left the party scene and decided to become "the Black businessman with the three-piece suit." In his new career with a large firm, he quickly became aware that he was not invited to play golf and tennis and was never invited to the impromptu social gatherings at his White co-workers' homes. He then began to feel that he was being passed over for promotion, which left him in his entry-level position despite his having better productivity than his White peers who were promoted.

> I became angry and irritable. Nothing that I could do seemed enough for them. I wanted to do more for my wife and new baby but I was not calling the shots and the person who was didn't seem to play fair. I started drinking after work before going home. I became irritable and short with my wife. I began to drink more and had an affair. I then began to snort cocaine and basically didn't care anymore. I was a failure at work but a success at the bar. I didn't care whether I played with my child. I didn't care whether I spent time with my wife. I was so depressed. On the outside, I appeared together and arrogant but on the inside I was unhappy, drifting, empty, and angry.

THE PSYCHOLOGY OF SELF-HATRED

In our work with survivors of sexual abuse, we often find that the survivors develop patterns of self-abuse that rival or exceed the negative impact of the initial trauma. Racial stigmatization can be just as painful and shame inducing as any form of abuse—sexual, emotional, or physical. In like fashion, the person who is abused racially can respond, as other abuse survivors, with self-hatred and "us-hating" behavior.

In the book *Black Rage*, Grier and Cobbs (1968) wrote of the price that racism can extol from its victims. They found that hopelessness, anger, despair, and shame are common responses to racism. In addition, a sense of false pride can hide much insecurity but not deal with it. Anger can be taken out on spouses, children, or each other in acts of verbal or physical violence or neglect. Strong feelings of shame can be turned into self-destructive actions through drugs, sexual indiscretion, or financial irresponsibility.

The bottom line is that it is very difficult to love someone when you hate yourself. African-American men who are interested in leading and loving their families must learn how to feel good about themselves and their capabilities. We must have a sense of direction and hope instead of despair and hopelessness. Otherwise we have little to offer our families that they could not get outside the family—i.e., rejection, anger, sadness, and loneliness. Ron J.'s and Linda K.'s stories did not end as described above and therein lies the beginning of the answers and the promises of hope.

TRANSFORMING THE MIND

I never thought that I could respect a *Black* man again. I had given up. Then I met Jesus and He was unlike any man I had known. He loved me without strings attached. He filled the empty place in my soul. I was no longer desperate for a relationship. I now saw things differently. I even believe that God could have a man for me. I could even respond to the man who treated me like Jesus does. I could learn to really respond to that! —Linda K.

I finally hit bottom. I messed up our money. I couldn't repair the car. I was so mad with myself. But I couldn't change. I was stuck. Then someone reminded me that Jesus came for people who couldn't help themselves—people who were stuck. After much struggle with my pride, I turned my life over to Jesus and gradually things have changed. I am not depressed anymore. I've been drug free for six months, wanting to spend time with my wife and daughter and am even more productive at work. I still haven't been promoted and probably will not. I've been told that the company appreciates my work but I still don't get any invites. But now I am thinking of inviting them—taking the initiative to love them—because they are as messed up as I was. God has a plan for me and no one can stop God. —Ron J.

For African-American men to build better families, we must lead a godly life. Both Linda and Ron were stuck in hopelessness, self-hatred, and despair but had their lives changed, their minds transformed, and their hearts empowered by an encounter with the living Christ. Romans 12:1 speaks of us having our minds transformed by God. Second Corinthians 5:17 speaks of the total change that God can perform in the hearts of those who are "in Christ."

Ron J. had been in the church, but the church did not give him what he needed to build a family. Linda K. had been religious, but religious dogma did not move her beyond despair and hate. Just as Jesus taught Peter to learn a different way than the sword (John 18:10–11), He has taught a different way to African-American men.

Many African-American men are building better families because we are stronger, wiser, and seeking to please God in all that we do. The humility and control to respond properly and appropriately in relationships in and outside the home comes from God. The example of leadership that Christ set must be the example for us if we are going to build better families. Christ was interested in doing the will of the Father. We must be willing to live a life before our families that is pleasing to God. With the Word of God as our standard, we can withstand the usual attacks on marriage and family life from business, boredom, neglect, and personality conflicts (Rosenau 1991), in addition to the negative stereotypes, racial stigmas, and economic stress.

In order to build better families, African-American men must communicate standards, expectations, and His genuine love. This is not conditional love but rather godly or unconditional love as described by Paul in Ephesians 5:25–30:

Husbands, love your wives, just as Christ also loved the church and gave Himself up for her; that He might sanctify her, having cleansed her by the washing of water with the word, that He might present to Himself the church in all her glory, having no spot or wrinkle or any such thing; but that she should be holy

and blameless. So husbands ought also to love their own wives
as their own bodies. He who loves his own wife loves himself; for
no one ever hated his own flesh, but nourishes and cherishes it,
just as Christ also does the church, because we are members of
His body.

Likewise a man must love the members of his family unconditionally. Only unconditional love will allow us to make the sacrifices that lead us to build better families. Unconditional love is required of us if we are to stand up against all the pressures that confront us without compromising or giving up.

Whether married or divorced, we must still accept our responsibility as fathers. If we cease to be a responsible parent in divorce situations, the children can grow up not knowing that they are loved by both parents. The likelihood of perpetuating broken or dysfunctional families in these cases is significantly increased. The importance of communicating godly standards, expectations, and unconditional love cannot be overemphasized. Generally speaking, practically all members within a family would like to be accepted and approved of, and when we care about ourselves, then we care about others. It is the conveying of godly standards, expectations, and unconditional love through the example of Jesus Christ that makes the difference.

Standards and expectations for a family must be conveyed and communicated in a clear and effective manner. The father's role in setting these standards and expectations cannot be overemphasized. It is essential to the proper development of the young Black male. Many times when young Black boys are in trouble it is because of the lack of male leadership and guidance in the home. Male leadership and guidance are equally essential for the young Black female if she is to grow up experiencing a positive relationship with a male and feeling loved. Both young boys and girls will stand a highly probable chance of not developing strong positive self-images and high self-esteem if they are abandoned, ignored, or misunderstood. If we as Black men are to build better families, we must clearly communicate godly standards and high expectations and, most important, we must practice unconditional love.

QUALITIES OF STRONG FAMILIES

If we are to set standards for what God expects of our families, we should have an idea of what makes families successful. This is something that most men, be they persons of color or not, have to learn since few of our families of origin were without faults.

As to the strengths of Black families, R. B. Hill (1972) presents the following positive characteristics:

1. Strong kinship bonds
2. Strong achievement orientation
3. Adaptability of family roles
4. Strong religious orientation
5. Strong work orientation

Some of the characteristics as described by Money (1978) include the following:

1. *The ability to express appreciation to each other* (as contrasted with the verbal degrading of one another—i.e., the "dozens") *and communicate.* Strong families can speak truthfully with each other, express feelings safely and appropriately, listen to each other, and are able to work out differences. (Ephesians 4:15, 25, 29; 1 Thessalonians 5:11; 1 Corinthians 13:6)
2. *The commitment to spend time together.* Strong families learn to enjoy each other and respect each other. They are students of each other. They are committed to each other. (Deuteronomy 6:4–9; Exodus 20:12; Matthew 19:6; Mark 7:9–13; 1 Timothy 5:3–5)
3. *A high degree of religious orientation.* Strong families have shared values and beliefs and a sense of submission to God that gives purpose and meaning to what they do. (Matthew 28:20)
4. *The ability to deal with crises in a positive manner.* Strong families draw together in times of stress and support each other rather than attack each other. (1 Peter 3:8–12; 4:7–11)

QUALITIES OF WEAK FAMILIES

In contrast to healthy families, dysfunctional families are characterized by the following:

1. *The focus is on criticizing each other and blaming each other.* Appreciation is seldom expressed because "we don't want him or her to get a big head." However, there are not any limits on criticism.

2. *Communication about real issues like family problems and conflicts do not occur.* Much talk may occur about trivial issues or other families' issues, but major issues like alcoholism, affairs, and marital disputes are seldom discussed in a calm, helpful manner.

3. *Time spent together is negative* due to ongoing family crises that are overwhelming or the simple fact that the members of the family barely know each other or do not like each other.

4. *Commitment is violated* due to affairs, incest, or marital neglect.

5. *Religious life is absent or without meaning.* The family may go to church as a ritual—but just that—as a tradition or ritual that does not hold meaning.

GETTING REAL—ATTITUDES THAT BUILD

Many men of color want to do the right thing by their families but don't know how. How do I start to change? How do I start to gain their respect? How do I start to grow spiritually? How do I move beyond the past mistakes to starting anew? The answer is in the word *HOW*—with Honesty, Openness, and Willingness.

The greatest problem that anyone faces in making a change in a problem area is getting honest. Most of us like to minimize how bad a situation is. We like to minimize how powerless and frustrated we are at changing it. We are reluctant as proud men to admit our failures and mistakes. As "strong" men, we do not like to admit that we are weak. In fact, the greatest problem that we face in counseling men is convincing them that they need counsel—i.e., that they do not have all the answers.

Honesty is about putting away the pride, putting away the arrogance, putting away the toughness. Honesty is about admitting that we do not know how to love our families. We do not have the ability to forgive as we should. We do not have the ability to control our emotions all the time. Honesty is about telling it like it is to God and one other person to whom we can be accountable. Honesty teaches us that we need help and do not have all the answers. Honesty teaches us that we are accountable for what goes on in "my house" because it is ultimately God's house. In summary, honesty teaches us what we can and cannot do ourselves.

Openness is an attitude of being teachable. Too many men are not teachable. Too many men do not take responsibility for improving their family's situation, tending instead to blame others for the problems.

Openness is an attitude of humility that leaves defending oneself at home and takes responsibility for what we have done to hurt this family. Openness follows on honesty in that it suggests that we need to learn something. We need to become students of our wives and children in a humble, godly manner so that He can wise us up. Openness is ultimately about recognizing that God is our source. The attitude of openness is one of listening to God through His Word and prayer—becoming available to His leading and influence. Openness looks for direction and in the Word of God finds it.

Willingness is where the rubber hits the word. The willing man not only recognizes that he needs help (honesty) but also recognizes that he needs help from God (openness). Willingness is about surrendering to the Lordship of Christ so that He can work in our lives. Talk is cheap; it takes willingness to obey, willingness to submit, willingness to live by God's standards instead of our own. The willing attitude hungers and thirsts after God and seeks God and His way, by whatever means necessary. It may involve changing friends and having new playmates and playgrounds. It may involve getting into an accountability relationship with other men. It may involve making a commitment to read everything that you can find on being a godly man in your home (Farrah 1994; Lewis 1994; McCartney 1994; McClung 1994). Willing, surrendered attitudes do not focus on blaming others or making excuses but rather focus on seeking answers and on reconciliation. The willing man, walking in God's power, learns how to love with *agape* love (1 Corinthians 13).

CONCLUSION

It is the premise of this chapter that African-American men, like all men, can build strong families—with God's help. We need His help to be the men of character that our families need and the men of righteousness that our communities need. We need to become associated with holiness and success—not failure and carnality. We must change our perception of ourselves and our priorities before we can influence others. Many of our families are in dire need of help. Just like a man addicted to crack, we have become too comfortable with moral failure, self-hatred, and hopelessness. Our communities have become associated with sin, not righteousness, thus mirroring a general decline in family life throughout our society. However, we must take responsibility for us—for each of our families and do whatever is necessary to restore values, righteousness, and holiness to our communities.

As a closing summary, we have taken many of the points of this chapter and adapted them to the twelve-step model for Christian recovery for addictive behavior (McGee et al. 1990). It is our hope that each reader will explore the area of his or her family life that is in need of recovery and healing.

TWELVE STEPS TO BETTER FAMILY LIVING

1. We admit that by ourselves we are powerless to lead and love our families as we should (see Romans 7:18).
2. We come to believe that God, through Jesus Christ, can give us the power and motivation to be leaders and lovers of our families (see Philippians 2:13).
3. We make a decision to turn our lives over to God and receive His love, forgiveness, power, and instruction regarding our families (see Romans 12:1).
4. We make a searching and fearless inventory of ourselves and our families and take responsibility for what we as men have done wrong to our families (see Lamentations 3:40).
5. We admit to God and to another human being the exact nature of our wrongs as leaders and lovers of our families (see James 5:16a).
6. We commit ourselves to obedience to God through personal discipleship and spiritual growth, desiring that He remove patterns of sin from our family relationships through the power of the Holy Spirit (see James 4:10).
7. We humbly ask God to renew our minds so that our attitudes about our marriage and family can change (see Romans 12:2).
8. We make a list of all the family members that we have harmed and become willing to make amends to them and minister to their needs (see Luke 6:31).
9. We make direct amends to and ask forgiveness of such family members where possible, except when doing so will injure them or others (see Matthew 5:23–24).
10. We continue to take personal inventory, and when we are wrong, promptly admit it (see 1 Corinthians 10:12; Psalm 139:23–24).

11. We seek to grow in our relationship with Jesus Christ and our families through corporate prayer, Bible study, worship, meditation, and obedience (see James 1:5–6).
12. Having had a spiritual awakening regarding the priority of family, we try to carry the message of Christ's grace and restoration power in families to others, and to practice these principles in all of our affairs (see Ephesians 5:25–33; 2 Timothy 3:1–5).

REFERENCES

Farrar, S. 1994. *Standing tall*. Sisters, OR: Multnomah Books.

Grier W. H., and P. M. Cobbs. 1968. *Black rage*. New York: Basic Books.

Hill, R. B. 1972. *The strengths of Black families*. New York: Emerson Hall.

Lewis, P. 1994. *The five key habits of smart dads*. Grand Rapids: Zondervan.

McCartney, B. 1994. *What makes a man*. Colorado Springs, CO: NavPress.

McClung, F. 1994. *God's man in the family*. Eugene, OR: Harvest House.

McGee, R. S., et. al. 1990. *Rapha's 12-step program for overcoming chemical dependency*. Houston: Rapha/Word.

Money, R. 1978. *Building stronger families*. Wheaton, IL: Victor Books.

1978. *New American standard Bible*. Chicago: Moody Press.

Rosenau, D. 1991. *Slaying the marriage dragons*. Wheaton, IL: Victor Books.

1994. *USA Today*. September 15.

Claude L. Dallas Jr.

The Meaning of Fatherhood

CLAUDE L. DALLAS JR. is administrator for Martin Pollak Projects in Baltimore, Maryland (a therapeutic foster-care program for children and youth). He is formerly executive vice president of Ecclesia, Inc., a church-planting ministry. Prior to Ecclesia, Claude served with World Vision, Inc., as a national program manager, with Liberty University as the Director of Urban Outreach, with Israel Baptist Church as the Minister of Christian Education and Development, with Minnesota Mining and Manufacturing as a sales representative, and with Pfizer, Inc., as a sales representative. Claude has a bachelor of science degree from Ohio State University, a master of science degree from the University of Cincinnati and a master of arts in religion from Liberty University. He has completed some graduate work toward a doctor of philosophy degree in higher education from Nova University. Born and raised in Cincinnati, Ohio, Claude is married to Sheilah Ferebee Dallas and they have four children: Renay, Robyn, Sheila, and Claude III.

Chapter 8

Claude L. Dallas Jr.

The Meaning of Fatherhood

Be ye therefore followers of God, as dear children; and walk in love, as Christ also hath loved us, and hath given himself for us an offering and a sacrifice to God for a sweet smelling savour.

(Ephesians 5:1–2 KJV)

INTRODUCTION

This chapter will focus on what makes parenting by African-American males unique in regard to our role as fathers and as Christians. Specifically, I will address the challenges, responsibilities and rewards of Black fatherhood. This will be accomplished by referring to written works and to my experiences as a father of four and as one who has been single, married, divorced, and remarried to the same woman during the past twenty-six years.

Having been exposed to all of the negative facts about African-American fathers, I remain hopeful in our Lord's ability to increase the number of men who are rightly related to Him and are serving as effective fathers.

Much has been written on fatherhood. In regard to African-American fatherhood, one of the most prolific writers is Earl O. Hutchinson (1990, 1992, 1994a, 1994b, 1995). In *Black Fatherhood II: Black Women Talk About Their Men*, Hutchinson (1994) explodes the popular, media-driven stereotypes of Black men as criminals and drug addicts by featuring Black fathers who are taking on the challenge not only of raising a family but also succeeding. Although not writing from a Christian perspective, he shows that despite prevailing misconceptions, the male presence is still strong in many African-American homes. Such misconceptions form the core of many of the challenges facing Black fathers. Other research on this subject has been undertaken by Thompson (1994) and Bozett and Hanson (1991). This research focuses on intact, economically stable families and has served to paint a different picture of the contemporary African-American family and the role of the father.

I believe the challenges that we as Black fathers face can be placed into three broad categories: (1) external, (2) internal, and (3) personal. The biblical remedies for coping with these challenges are (1) commitment to a God-centered life, (2) commitment to a stable and fulfilled Christian marriage, and (3) commitment to spiritual leadership (see also Sears 1990). Each of these remedies will be discussed later in this chapter.

There are many ways in which we, as Black men, conduct ourselves as fathers. Some of us are more involved in raising the income to provide for the family than with the nurturing and development of our children. Fatherhood is acted out in a seemingly endless variety of ways, fulfilling a number of different social responsibilities. The forces that generate a family culture suggest a finite number of major approaches to fatherhood (Bozett & Hanson 1991). In this chapter, however, I focus on the Christian perspective of Black fatherhood as the most appropriate model.

The rewards of fatherhood vary to a large degree depending on the expectations, perceptions, and experiences of the father. That section of the chapter will be treated from the perspective of the available literature along with some personal experiences and observations.

THE CHALLENGES OF BLACK FATHERHOOD

External factors that challenge fatherhood include racism, crime, under- or unemployment, poverty, economics, and political decisions. Internal factors that challenge fatherhood are such things as our psychological processes; our family-culture norms; our values, rules, and expectations.

Most of the research that has been undertaken in regard to Black fatherhood and Black families has assumed that the problems of such are a direct result of the Black male's failures and thus follow a pathological paradigm. Such a perspective reinforces the myth that Black men are the sole causative factors in the crisis facing Black Americans. Robert B. Hill (1993) insists that as Black men, we must be seen as distinct and relevant—not as a deficient White counterpart.

A complete list of challenges to fatherhood would vary depending upon one's age, socioeconomic status, and commitment to the Word of God. Such a list includes

- Having the contributions and values of Black males broadly disregarded (Pate 1994)
- Overcoming dominant societal stereotypes of an absent father (Bozett & Hanson 1991)
- Being a good father without having had a role model (Lloyd 1992)
- Teaching children ethnic values when their exposure to other Blacks is minimal
- Maintaining an individual identity in the context of one's culture
- Being assumed to be incompetent until proving otherwise
- Challenging racial issues in the business environment
- Being excluded from the decision-making process
- Addressing an absence of mentors, which leads to our improper acclimation to the social environment
- Questioning the so-called unwritten rules of behavior (Dickens & Dickens 1982)

EXTERNAL CHALLENGES

All of the aforementioned challenges directly impact our perception of ourselves and our performance as fathers. Dickens and Dickens (1982) do an excellent job of assisting Black males in the corporate environment understand the ways in which other Black professionals have overcome their frustrations and anger. In fatherhood we must learn to deal with the frustration, hurt, pain, and anger often associated with discrimination and prejudice. It is sometimes easy to feel victimized when trying to deal with the hand that we have been dealt—the burden of racism and prejudice—and the result of the social pressure that comes with being Black. As fathers we must learn to cope with life's situations as well as be able to instruct our children about what they can expect.

I am reminded of Adam and Eve's conversation with God shortly after the Fall. Adam wanted to remind God that the central issue of sin had come into being as a result of the woman whom He, God, had given to him. God knows our problems and dilemmas without being reminded and can use them to make us become more like His Son, Jesus Christ. Knowing this fact may seem like little comfort during our trials, but this truth can sustain us and provide the strength to endure the circumstances.

Errol Smith (1991) relates that his father told him to control anger by realizing that there are many things in life that one can do nothing to change and that there will always be people who will prejudge you. Hence we must not allow others to upset us lest we become victims of anger. Smith further suggests that we shrug our shoulders and move forward. In addition to Smith's advice, I suggest that we pray and let God's strength sustain us. Remember, people without hope and faith are watching our lives to see whether being a Christian actually has an impact on our lives. While Smith's principles are good from the secular perspective, having a relationship with God provides other alternatives to handling feelings of anger, frustration, and so forth. It is necessary for Christian fathers to see the relevance of the gospel in their lives, for it can speak in every situation if we are open and desire to understand the truth. Thus, a Christian father can be the agent for teaching his family members to exhibit faith, hope, love, self-confidence, self-respect, self-esteem, self-pride, honesty, trust, and a fear (reverential trust) of God. Shirley Spencer June (1991, p. 105) speaks about the unique challenges to parents of Black youngsters. She states:

> To counter these negative forces, parents can focus on helping their children anticipate and interpret accurately and honestly the experiences they will face. Further, children can be helped to respond to these experiences in a way that fosters their positive development. This, however, is no small task because many of the problems Black families and children face in America today are the result of discriminatory practices that have been entrenched in American culture for many years.

BIBLICAL SOLUTION: A COMMITMENT TO A GOD-CENTERED LIFE

I recall Crawford Loritts, a staff member of Campus Crusade for Christ and a nationally recognized speaker, making the statement that "circumstances do not make us who we are, they reveal who we are." We cannot always control our external or environmental circumstances, but we can control the way in which we respond to them. Recall Job, Joseph, and Daniel who, respectively, were stripped of their earthly possessions, mistreated by their own brothers, and taken into captivity despite royal heritage. Also consider the long list of witnesses of the faith who endured hardship (Hebrews 11). Let us never forget that God demonstrated His love for us by sending His only Son as a sacrifice to endure the shame and ridicule of men. When our life is centered on God, the opinions of others have less effect.

The responses of these saints to their situations stand as great testimonies to the way in which we, as men of God, should respond to the injustices of this world. Commitment to God is the key! Our responses to circumstances and relationships can serve as indicators of our commitment to God Himself.

INTERNAL CHALLENGES

Internal forces that affect our role as Black fathers include the dynamics of the community, the family, the individual, and how each of these subsystems impress and prevail upon each other. Hill (1993) indicates that these three factors can have reciprocal effects.

On the one hand, Hill treats in detail the negative internal factors such as teenage delinquency, homicide, alcohol abuse, drug abuse, and crime. He reports that many of our youth need to work to assist with the income of our families. Additionally, Hill states that eight out of ten Blacks think that Black churches have helped the condition of Black Americans. On the other hand, D. E. Mosley (1994) reviews many of the positive aspects of Black families in a changing Black community.

The incidence of divorce in this country has increasingly placed stresses on our marriages and our role as fathers. Christians almost equal the percentage of nonbelievers in securing divorces.

BIBLICAL RESPONSE: COMMITMENT TO A STABLE AND FULFILLED CHRISTIAN MARRIAGE

It is critical that both husband and wife see the Word of God as central in their marriage in order to maximize fatherhood. Also important for a stable and fulfilled Christian marriage and fatherhood is the practice of worshiping together. This can be a challenge if the pattern set by our parents differs from this perspective. My wife and I made the decision to always worship together, regardless of where we locate. This commitment was particularly significant since my wife had been raised in a household where each parent attended a different church. This had also been practiced by her maternal grandparents.

Central to the stability of the family is that the Word of God be seen as the authority for solving all disputes and problems and as a source for wisdom and guidance. In our family, when my wife and I discuss a situation, we pray about it together, and then we share our individual opinions. If we disagree, she will ask me, "Is this what you believe, after prayer, is God's will for our family?" If I give an affirmative response, my wife will throw her full support behind the decision. To our children and the world, we are united on that particular decision. This places a big responsibility on me, the husband, to insure that I am rightly related to God on a moment-by-moment basis. However, this is powerful role modeling for our children.

PERSONAL CHALLENGES

There are many differences that we men quickly discover after we are married—differences in backgrounds and concept of family, love, culture, home traditions, values, and views on economics. For example, my wife, raised as an only child by college-educated parents, had a very different set of experiences and expectations than I, the last of five children and one who was raised by parents who did not complete high school. The Word of God is central in handling these differences.

The involvement of fathers in the day-to-day household responsibilities is very important and adds adaptability. Often we feel that if our wives are able to stay at home with our young children, then we need not be involved with the household labor since she "is not working." Z. Hossain (1993) examined the division of household labor and child care in sixty-three middle- to lower-middle income, dual-earner, African-American families with infants. According to the study, father involvement in child care and household activities did not vary whether mothers worked full-time or part-time. This suggests that there are some of us who are not taking into consideration the added responsibilities of working mothers as they relate to household duties. Hill (1972, p. 17) shares an appropriate statement: "It is a strength when family members can 'fill in' and assume each other's roles as needed. For example, a father can function as a 'mother' and children can temporarily be 'parents' to their father and mother."

As Blacks, those of us who have reached the status of middle and upper-middle class often find that there are some "perils." G. E. Ziegenhals (1991, p. 509) refers to comments Blacks made at a 1991 Black Family Ministries Conference in Chicago. He stated: "The peril of 'middle class-lessness' was a dominant theme throughout the conference, though this condition was never defined beyond the implication that it is 'materialistic' and 'Eurocentric.'" The increasing incidence of both parents working has implications on the family as well. A. C. Crouter (1994) summarizes the changing American workplace and the resulting implications for both individuals and families.

Two of these perils or challenges that I personally have observed are that of dispersion and distance. Dispersion is the physical separation from other Blacks in various neighborhoods in which we live. It is difficult (but not impossible) to teach our children Black culture and their responsibility to the poor when we live in upscale, predominately White communities. Distance is just that. We have often moved great distances away from our nuclear families in pursuit of career goals. The support system has subsequently been weakened.

BIBLICAL RESPONSE: COMMITMENT TO SPIRITUAL LEADERSHIP

Being a father who is also a spiritual leader is a challenge. The type of self-control and self-denial called for in the Word of God goes acutely against the self-fulfillment that so pervades our media and our homes.

Fathers commanded a high position in the family during Old Testament times. The Hebrew word translated into English as husband actually means "lord," "master," "owner," or "possessor" (Genesis 18:12; Hosea 2:16). Because of his position, shared to some degree with his wife, a man expected to be treated as royalty by the rest of his family. The fifth commandment carries this idea of the importance of the parents one step further when it states, "honor your father and your mother" (Exodus 20:12). The word *honor* often refers to one's response to God. In other words, this commandment suggests that the parents should receive recognition similar to that given to God. With such a position, one would have to assume that the challenges for men who want to fulfill the role as a father must be great—particularly after the Fall.

When we become children of God, we are changed with a new paradigm. No longer are we alienated from Christ, but we become joint heirs with Him. Because of God's commitment to transform us into the image of His Son, changes are inevitable. The issue is: To what degree does our Father have to apply pressure to effect the changes?

After God created Adam, He declared, "It is not good that the man should be alone" (Genesis 2:18). Subsequently, God created woman and united the couple; and they became "one flesh" (Genesis 2:24). Thus, the family was designed by God to provide companionship for the various members. In addition, the institution of marriage was approved and sanctioned by the Lord (Matthew 19:4–6). For an excellent treatment on the subject of Black male-female relationships, see Sherrill Burwell (1991).

Although there have been many challenges for which I have been trained and educated, there has been no greater challenge than my role as a father. There are varying degrees of challenge in being a father both through the different stages of each child's life as well as through our own.

THE RESPONSIBILITIES OF FATHERHOOD

The responsibilities of Black fatherhood will be discussed in three categories: (1) spiritual, (2) social, and (3) economic.

Spiritual

In Scripture, the father was responsible for the spiritual well-being of the family. He functioned as the "priest," sacrificing on the family's behalf (Genesis 12:8; Job 1:5). Later, when a priesthood was established in Israel and the layman no longer had to offer sacrifices, the father's spiritual role was redefined. He continued, however, to be the religious leader in the home and was involved in the training of the children (Exodus 12:3, 26–27; Proverbs 22:6; Ephesians 6:4). Black men have historically provided spiritually for their families through teaching them the truths of God's Word. McKissic and Evans (1994) place great emphasis on the historic role of the church in the lives of Blacks. In Scripture, the abundant life results from (1) a life that is yielded to God as seen in Romans 6:12–13; (2) a life of service as seen in Romans 12:1–2; (3) a separated life as seen in 1 Corinthians 6:17–18; and (4) a Spirit-filled life as seen in Ephesians 5:18–20.

Some pastors are recognizing the fact that the church must set the standard for male leadership and influence in this society. An article in

Ebony (1993) entitled "Changing Church Confronts the Changing Black Family" addresses such needs. The church is now doing more than ever before to instruct and to counsel Black families on their responsibilities and roles. With initiatives such as stress reduction workshops, financial planning workshops, and parenting workshops, the success of Black males is of the utmost concern. In this same *Ebony* article, Bishop Cousin is quoted as saying: "Our Church has focused on bringing the Black male into the mainstream of church life and getting the congregations and communities to understand that in order to have a fully functional family, one must have the Black male present" (p. 95).

Social

Socially, the biblical father's responsibility was to see that no one took advantage of any member of his family. Those who were not protected by a father were truly disadvantaged. The two most common categories of "fatherless" people were widows and orphans. Four specific duties of a father toward his son, as stated in the Jewish writings, were (1) to have the son circumcised; (2) to pass on his inheritance to his firstborn son; (3) to find his son a wife; and (4) to teach him a trade.

A. D. Pate (1994), in a memoir of appreciation of his father, highlights the invisibility of the African-American family man. By invisible he means the broad disregard for the contributions and value of Black males. Hope and the struggle to avoid disappointment in one's own life are qualities that sustain such men. K. Brodie (1994) reviews a book that suggests ten keys to successful coparenting in cases where the parents live apart. Socially, the fact of parents living apart will present the child with greater challenges, but they can be minimized by an actively involved father.

Economic

Economically, Scripture indicates that the father was to provide for the needs of the various members of his family. From time to time, however, a lazy person failed to provide for his family. Conscientious men sought to mock the lazy man, shaming him to do what was expected of him (Proverbs 6:6–11). The apostle Paul rebuked those who considered themselves Christian but who did not look after the needs of their families (1 Timothy 5:8).

One of the primary challenges for us as Black men in America has been to earn sufficient money to provide for our families. Many of us grew up in relatively poor homes and have now "made it economically." The vast majority of us, however, are in the lower-economic echelons. Insufficient discretionary income reduces the number of options for us to educate and expose our families to various experiences.

Black men are behind in education, economics, banking and finances, computer training, employment, and business ownership. Moreover, we are not the producers of the goods that we consume. It would seem that those of us who are earning good incomes should mentor and assist other men to reach the same levels of opportunity. The bridges between those who are at various economic levels are almost nonexistent. The church is a good place where the matching of two distinctly different people can be made, in the name of Christ. Volunteer programs and economic development programs abound in many churches. Organizations such as John Perkins's Christian Community Development Association offer a national network of Christian organizations that are having dramatic impact in their communities. Some churches have purchased closed hospitals and other businesses only to reopen them as a service and employer to the residents of their communities.

It is well known that children can best learn in an environment with both parents and where finances are adequate to provide for the basic human needs. G. J. Duncan (1994) investigated the effects of economic deprivation on child development by studying a group of children over an extended period of time. He found that both wealth and poverty are powerful correlates of the cognitive development and behavior of children. The greater the level of income, the higher the level of achievement by the children, according to Duncan.

With this background, one can more fully appreciate God as the believer's Father. He knows all about His children (us), even numbering the hairs on our head (Matthew 10:30). He protects us and rescues us when we get into trouble (Isaiah 63:15–16). He teaches us the way that we should go (Hosea 11:1–3) and He owns all things and supplies all of our needs (Matthew 6:33).

Given what God does for us as children, how then can we, as fathers, neglect the welfare of our children? Thus, as Black fathers we have a high calling.

The spiritual, social, and economic responsibilities of Black fathers are these:

To know our children in great detail. There is no way that we fathers can know our children with the same detail as God knows us. However, we must study them. Students in a school are responsible for attending class regularly, completing homework, being on time, making observations, listening, asking questions, taking notes, and participating in dialogue and activities that the instructor provides for their enrichment. Can a parent do anything less? Let us all make a plan to do this. Louise B. Ames (1992) gives a good general-development approach to discipline and raising good kids.

To protect and rescue our children. Physically protecting our children is becoming an ever more challenging task. Not only has violence become epidemic in the urban areas, but in the suburban areas as well. Crime, moral decay, and the constant mobility of families have all but eliminated the sense of community that was still in existence when I grew up in the 1950s. However, we must find ways to protect and rescue our children and rebuild community.

To teach our children. Taking the responsibility of being a teacher presupposes that we have the knowledge and the skills necessary to adequately teach. Each of us must ask: "Do I know the Word of God?" ("Study to show thyself approved unto God, a workman that needeth not to be ashamed, rightly dividing the word of truth"—2 Timothy 2:15.) What have I learned from the Word of God that I have allowed to change my behavior? How can I teach my children about racism in America without making them discriminate against someone else because they are a different color? How can I be the spiritual leader in my home when my wife knows more of the Word of God than I do and she has been teaching them?

These are all valid questions for Black fathers. Children will know whether the Word of God has impacted our lives through the way that we live at home. The church members might be fooled, our employer deceived, but our family really knows us. They are students of us, as husbands and fathers. It is therefore our responsibility to let the Word of God so change us that our children will have a biblical value system based on that which they have seen and experienced in our lives. Difficult? You bet, but certainly possible and necessary in order to realize some important rewards later in life.

Not only must we teach our children to be godly citizens, we must particularly teach our sons in order that they will learn how to become good fathers and husbands. G. R. Lloyd (1992) reviewed the plight of Black males in America and noted that the fate of Black America, particularly the Black underclass, is inextricably linked to the fate of Black boys and Black men. Ronald B. Mincy (1994) discusses interventions that can rescue troubled Black male adolescents as well as provide excellent examples. It is also our responsibility as Black men to teach our children appropriate values associated with family and the church (Lofton 1991).

THE REWARDS OF FATHERHOOD

The greatest reward that I can imagine as a parent is having the opportunity to see my children and grandchildren grow up and experience the joys of being parents with the spiritual heritage of Christ as the head of their lives. It is possible for many Black parents now to witness four or five generations functioning healthily.

Taylor, Chatters, and Jackson (1993) discuss the effects of the increased longevity of Americans and the resulting increase in the number of living generations in families as well as there being fewer people in each generation. This work was based on a three-generation family study (the National Survey of Black Americans) at the University of Michigan. They note that the great-grandfather can still be a great influence on generations that will be in existence long after his departure from the earth. Taylor, et al., further state that Blacks are more likely than Whites to reside in three-generation and other types of extended-family households. Research on child care and grandparents suggests that, in comparison to Whites, Black grandparents take a more active role in the parenting of grandchildren and are more likely to participate in the administration of discipline.

SUGGESTIONS FOR STRENGTHENING FATHERHOOD

I offer here fifteen suggestions that we can use to strengthen our effectiveness as fathers and increase our bond with our families:

1. Initiate a father's fellowship group. Let the members determine the format, meeting times, and activities. Consider including non-Christian men.
2. Have a "family table time." Ask every member of the family to come to the dinner table on a specific day of the week if this is not routine. You could open with a Scripture and share your desire to see the family be more of what God would have it to be. The first time, ask each family member to share ways in which you can be a better parent. Write the suggestions down without criticizing or

commenting. Give each person a chance to share and thank them for their input.

3. Memorize Scripture as a family. Select a weekly or daily verse to be memorized. Write it down on 3 x 5 cards. Post them around the house in places such as on the refrigerator, bathroom mirror, and so forth. Set dates to review the Scriptures and a goal of so many verses over a set period of time.

4. Place your family on your calendar. Schedule time alone with each family member. In order to get to know them, you must spend time alone with each one. Ask the children how they would like to spend their time alone with you.

5. Maintain a diary or journal on each family member. Record their preferences, struggles, future goals, Scriptural victories, and so forth. Keep this private, but review it before your special times alone with them.

6. Become involved in school activities. Volunteer for a responsibility with the parent group. Drop by the school to take your child to lunch, or let the afternoon be a fun-time surprise.

7. "Date" your preteen daughter. Many fathers give their daughters a ring to remind them to live a chaste life before God.

8. Let your children often see you and your wife being openly affectionate in front of them. Surprise your wife with flowers at her office, prepare dinner, or prepare an escape weekend without her knowledge. Spontaneity can keep romance strong in marriage.

9. Keep the confidences of children private. Just as sharing something that your wife has told you in private before a group can be damaging, the same can be true for your children.

10. Think of your interactions with your family as a bank account. In accounting, you make deposits and withdrawals. Doing special, happy things are deposits; insults, cancellation of plans, and so forth are withdrawals. You can create your own concept of paying interest and dividends. Sometimes it takes a lot of deposits to make up for a large emotional withdrawal.

11. Discuss the pressures of being a Black man with your family. Let them pray for you as you discover ways in which to let God handle the anger and retribution for the injustice that you experience.

12. Share your future goals with the children, both long-range and short-term. Such planning will lay the foundation for them to

incorporate the same process into their lives. Create a family "strategic plan." That is, just as your church and business have a mission and vision statement, create one with your family. Post it on the wall. As different opportunities arise, evaluate them against the mission statement and vision statement for the family. You will not have to eliminate certain activities, the entire family will do it.

13. Share together the *Ten Secrets to a Happy Marriage* (Norment 1993). These secrets are: make your mate your best friend; talk, talk, talk; listen, listen, listen; never forget that marriage is a partnership between equals; have fun together; be romantic and take your sex life seriously; maintain your attractive appearance; learn to change and to accept change; do not be afraid to argue but do so constructively; respect your partner as an individual.

14. Take the family on a trip to an African country, or any other location where Blacks are in power, which may give them a better perspective on the capabilities of people of color.

15. Attend a marriage-enrichment seminar.

CONCLUSION

The challenges of being a Christian Black father in America are great. In a world where selfish ambition and indulgence are the accepted norm, those of us who take parenting seriously according to the Word of God will shine forth like a light. Children of godly homes often do not understand the constraints that living a godly life places on them. But feedback from them later will more than justify the frustrations. It might be rather uncomfortable to reassess our career goals in light of the amount of time that we need to invest in our families, but we need to do so.

Is it any wonder that God said, "For if a man know not how to rule his own house, how shall he take care of the church of God?" (1 Timothy 3:5). Our home is our spiritual proving ground, and our family knows us very well. The survival of our family rests to a great extent on our willingness to make a commitment to the Word of God. Future generations will be affected by the actions that we take during our generation.

The responsibilities associated with being a Christian Black father can seem overwhelming, particularly for those who are not accustomed to planning, setting goals, leading in their homes, and trusting God. Bozett and Hanson (1991, p. 230) note that "fathers inculcate attitudes and behaviors their children need for educational and vocational attainment. They make important contributions to the child's socially appropriate gender-role identity, academic performance, and moral development."

God can give us the strength and the courage to change our behavior, to strive to improve our lives with the knowledge that we may fail and have setbacks, but we will be much further ahead than if we never began these changes. The church is taking an ever-increasing role in teaching us how to be good fathers as well as in holding us accountable in the process. Particular attention must be given to the quality and character of those of us who serve in leadership positions within the church.

The rewards for those of us who would live as godly Black fathers are many, but leaving a spiritual legacy for untold future generations seems to be the greatest reward. Watching our oldest daughter begin a family with similar values has been a great reward. It certainly has helped me to feel freer to spend time with the three teenagers who remain in our home.

Our children may grow up to be God-fearing, well-adjusted parents. There is also a possibility that this might not happen. In any case, we can feel content in knowing that we have done all that we can and have demonstrated the love of God to them in spite of the way that they may respond to our love. Is that not the way that God has loved us?

REFERENCES

Ames, L. B. 1992. *Raising good kids: A developmental approach to discipline*. Rosemont, NJ: Modern Learning Press.

Bozett, F. W., and S. M. H. Hanson. 1991. *Fatherhood and families in cultural context*. New York: Springer-Verlag.

Brodie, K. 1994. Families apart: Ten keys to successful coparenting. *Library Journal* 119 (1): 144.

Burwell, S. 1991. Strengthening and improving Black male-female relationships. In *The Black family: Past, present, and future,* edited by L. N. June. Grand Rapids: Zondervan.

Crouter, A. C. 1994. The changing American workplace: Implications for individuals and families. 1994. *Family Relations* 43 (2): 117–24.

Dickens, F., Jr., and J. B. Dickens. 1982. *The Black manager: Making it in the corporate world*. New York: AMACOM Books.

Duncan, G. J. 1994. Economic deprivation and early childhood development. *Child Development* 65 (2): 296–318.

1992. Present and accounted for: The other side of the Black father myth. *Ebony* 67 (8): 54–59.

1993. Changing church confronts the changing Black family. *Ebony* 68 (10): 94–100.

Hill, R. B. 1993. *Research on the African-American family: A holistic perspective*. Westport, CT: Auburn House.

_____. 1972. *The strengths of Black families*. New York: Emerson Hall.

Hossain, Z. 1993. Sex roles. *Journal of Research* 29 (9–10): 571–83.

Hutchinson, E. O. 1995. *Black fatherhood: The guide to male parenting*. Los Angeles: Middle Passage Press.

_____. 1994a. *Black fatherhood II: Black women talk about their men*. Los Angeles: Middle Passage Press.

_____. 1994b. *The assassination of the Black male image*. Los Angeles: Middle Passage Press.

_____. 1992. *Black fatherhood: The guide to male parenting*. Inglewood, CA: IMPACT.

_____. 1990. *The mugging of Black America*. Chicago: African-American Images.

June, S. 1991. The role of the home in the spiritual development of Black children. In *The Black family: Past, present, and future*, edited by L. N. June. Grand Rapids: Zondervan.

The King James version of the Bible.

Lloyd, G. R. 1992. The plight of Black males in America: The agony and the ecstasy—a summary comment. *Negro Educational Review* 43 (1–2): 41–44.

Lofton, F. C. 1991. Teaching Christian values within the Black family. In *The Black family: Past, present, and future*, edited by L. N. June. Grand Rapids: Zondervan.

Lorrits, C. Staff member of Campus Crusade for Christ. Personal communication.

McKissic, W. D., Sr., and A. T. Evans. 1994. *Beyond* Roots II: *If anybody ask you who I am*. Wenonah, NJ: Renaissance.

Mincy, R. B. 1994. *Nurturing young Black males*. Washington, DC: Urban Institute Press.

Mosley, D. E. 1994. The Black family in a changing Black community. *Contemporary Sociology* 23 (3).

Norment, L. 1993. Ten secrets to a happy marriage. *Ebony* 68 (10): 32–36.

Pate, A. D. 1994. The invisible Black family man. *Journal of Blacks in Higher Education* 4:76.

Sears, W. 1990. *Christian parenting and child care*. Nashville: Thomas Nelson.

Smith, E. 1991. *Thirty-seven things every Black man needs to know*. Valencia, CA: St. Clair Rene Publishing.

Taylor, R. J., L. M. Chatters, and J. S. Jackson. 1993. A profile of familial relations among three-generation Black families. *Family Relations* 42: 332–41.

Thompson, A. 1994. Review of *Research on the African-American family: A holistic perspective,* by R. B. Hill. *Journal of Marriage and the Family* 56 (1): 240–41.

Ziegenhals, G. E. 1991. Black values, families, and churches. *Christian Century* 108 (16): 509–11.

Kenneth B. Staley

Balancing
Career
and Family

KENNETH B. STALEY was born and raised in Philadelphia, Pennsylvania. He received a bachelor of science degree in civil engineering from Villanova University, a master of divinity degree and a doctor of divinity degree from Miller Theological Seminary. He is a professional engineer and is president of Nehemiah Corporation, a projects-managing and consulting firm. He is married to Sheila R. Staley and they are the parents of three children: Tabbatha, Christina, and Harrison.

Ken is a member of the Christian Stronghold Baptist Church in Philadelphia, where he serves as associate pastor and treasurer. He frequently speaks and leads workshops at family conferences and seminars.

Chapter 9

Kenneth B. Staley

Balancing Career and Family

Now it is required that those who have been given a trust must prove faithful. (1 Corinthians 4:2 NIV)

INTRODUCTION

Over the past thirty years as the African-American male has gained greater access to the so-called American dream, there has been added pressure for him to assume greater responsibilities in the home, community, and workplace. The African-American male has been asked to assume leadership in meeting the economic, social, emotional, spiritual, and physical needs of not just his immediate family but also of those in the extended family and community.

As males, we need to control these demands, which can become a continual pressure in one's life, leaving an individual overwhelmed. God commands us to have a balanced life. This involves establishing biblically sound priorities that show forth faithfulness with what He has entrusted to each individual as His steward.

Balancing career and family does not require extensive management training, but it does require the utilization of clear biblical principles. These biblical principles will help in time management, in solving problems, in delegating responsibilities, and in communication. Bible study, devotions, and prayer time will also benefit from a biblically balanced life. A balanced life requires you to become proactive rather than reactive. A proactive man is motivated and empowered to get things done. He is not just responding to situations; he is managing them.

Most importantly, however, in order for a man to have a biblically balanced life, a personal relationship with Christ and the empowerment of His Spirit to give clarity, direction, and wisdom is required. The critical principles of who is in control of our life, integrity, discipline, execution, listening, patience, planning, goal setting, family life, and prayer must be seen from God's perspective.

Men struggle with these issues because intertwined with them is the importance of our setting priorities. Operating a business, teaching, lecturing, pastoring, serving on organizational boards, having three children, and being married for twenty years has caused me not only to seek to reinforce these critical principles in my life but also to change my behavior. Applying biblical principles to my life has given balance to my relationship with my wife and children. It has enabled me to significantly remove stress from the workplace and establish discipline in all my activities. Above all, it has brought me into a closer walk with the Lord.

As men, balancing our lives will allow us to rebuild bridges that we did not realize had been torn down. Our communication will improve in all areas of life. Our prayer and devotional life will deepen. A balanced life will also have a significant impact on our marriage, family life, interpersonal relationships, employment, and ministry. Developing a balanced life is one step in being proven faithful. Take time to address each principle that will be discussed, and apply it to your life. Take hold of it. Bind it to you so that you will no longer conform to this world but will be transformed by God's will.

PURPOSE

As noted in the introduction, balancing career and family principles is a process that has many components. The principles presented in this chapter are to be used as building blocks or counterweights to bring conviction and change in the life of the reader.

This chapter will cover the topical areas of time management, priorities, and principles for a balanced career and family.

Time Management

There is a time for everything. (Ecclesiastes 3:1 NIV)

And the evening and the morning were the first day. (Genesis 1:5 KJV)

And God blessed the seventh day, and sanctified it: because that in it he had rested from all his work which God created and made. (Genesis 2:3 KJV)

There are twenty-four hours in a day, one hundred sixty-eight hours in a week. Forty hours on average are given to work (employment); fifty-six hours are given to the rest of the body; fourteen hours per week to prayer, Bible study, and devotions. That leaves forty-two hours per week for other activities because, remember, the sixteen waking hours of the Lord's day are for worshiping the Lord.

Can we be good stewards of forty-two hours? Yes we can. For example, I only need five hours of sleep to be well rested. This allows me to add eighteen additional hours to my forty-two, giving me sixty hours per week for other activities. Whatever your personal activity hours are, the goal is to control those activities or events that make up both work and activity hours.

The writer of Ecclesiastes notes that there is time for prayer—in fact a set time for every activity. God the Father demonstrated this divine time management in Genesis 1 through the process of creation and rest. God created the world in six days and rested on the seventh. He was productive. Our control of our time brings us greater productivity. Overcommitment, unnecessary interruptions, and not being able to say no are all signs of being out of control and of being a poor steward of the time that God has given you. In Ephesians 5:15–16 we are warned, "Be very careful, then, how you live—not as unwise but as wise, making the most of every opportunity because the days are evil" (NIV). You must plan your time. You must budget your time. You must set goals.

Planning is listing those items that must be accomplished in order of priority. Budgeting is determining the amount of time that you will spend on each item. Completing a specific task in a specific time frame is goal setting. We should plan for

- Husband and wife time
- Family time
- Time with each child, one on one
- Bible devotion time
- Prayer time
- Worship
- Physical well-being

- Individual family members' well-being
- Career
- Community activities
- Family financial needs

These tasks should involve short- and long-term planning as well as short- and long-term goals.

Priorities

In *Balancing Life's Demands* (1989), J. Grant Howard quotes Matthew 22:34–40 and notes that priority number one is to love God, and priority number two is to love my neighbor as myself. We have a responsibility to love God and our neighbor consistently and effectively. These two priorities go together. Many times the question is asked, "Who is my neighbor?" The answer is everyone. If you read Ephesians 5, you will see this commandment carried out to completion.

Priorities reflect our value system—what is important to us. Scripture tells us to "Seek first his kingdom and his righteousness, and all these things will be given to you as well" (Matthew 6:33 NIV). Seeking God should be the number-one priority in our life, and it involves your using your heart, strength, and mind. This requires spending quality time with Him in prayer, quiet time, study of His Word, and worship. Set aside time every day, either in the morning, afternoon, or evening. Find a quiet place where you can be alone and will not be disturbed. This must become a disciplined part of life—a "non-negotiable."

Along with a personal quiet time, if you are a husband and/or father, you must establish quality time with your wife and children. Ephesians 5:25 says, "Husbands, love your wives, just as Christ loved the church and gave himself up for her" (NIV). We read in Ephesians 6:4, "Fathers, do not exasperate your children; instead, bring them up in the training and instruction of the Lord" (NIV). It is your duty and priority to love your wife sacrificially and to demonstrate divine love toward your children—along with corrections and instruction.

Remember that being a workaholic is sin. So is burnout. We are to be good stewards of our bodies. In order to get a handle on your priorities, make a list of everything that you are presently doing. Include all your involvements and commitments. Now, list them according to priority. The first ten items should be weekly or daily priorities. All others should be weekly or monthly priorities. Next to each priority write down the amount of time per day, week, or month that is required in order for this priority to be performed in a manner that well pleases God. Remember, you only have forty-two hours of undesignated time per week.

Prioritizing will show you that you do not have enough hours in a week. Shorten your priority list, take control of your life, bring it into balance. In order to do this:

- Take a sheet of paper and divide it into seven columns. Label each column with a day of the week, beginning with Sunday.
- At the top of each column, under the day, write in the time that you wake up in the morning.
- Now list in each column your activities for that day, keeping them in order from the first activity to the last. This will become your plan.
- Now budget time for each activity.
- For the next twelve weeks, make up a schedule for each week. Try to live by this schedule.
- If you fail, write down the reasons and how you will correct the failure next week.
- After you have successfully completed your twelve weeks, continue with your weekly schedule. Build on this schedule to make it a quarterly schedule where you will note weekly goals, monthly goals, and appointments.
- Consider after twenty-four weeks using a Day-At-A-Glance Planner and a Month-At-A-Glance Planner (see Table 9.1).

Principles for a Balanced Career and Family

Discipline Yourself (Self-Control)

Disciplining yourself involves establishing plans and budgeting time as well as setting goals and completing them on time. The book of Proverbs was written "for attaining wisdom and discipline" as well as "for acquiring a disciplined and prudent life, doing what is right and just and fair" (Proverbs 1:2–3 NIV). We learn that "these commands are a lamp, this teaching is a light" (Proverbs 6:23 NIV). A man who makes God's commands and teaching a part of this life will become disciplined. From him will flow out wisdom and prudence, doing what is right and just and fair.

Proverbs 25:28 says that a man who lacks self-control is like a city whose walls are broken down. In other words, he is vulnerable. Discipline

Table 9.1

SCHEDULE FOR WEEK OF:

AM/PM	SUNDAY	MONDAY	TUESDAY	WEDNESDAY	THURSDAY	FRIDAY	SATURDAY
6							
7							
8							
9							
10							
11							
NOON							
1							
2							
3							
4							
5							
6							
7							
8							
9							
10							
11							
12							

means being in control—especially being in control of one's time. Being in control means training yourself to produce a specific pattern of behavior such as obedience and submission to rules and authority.

It is important that we plan our day, week, month, and year, keeping control of our tasks and commitments. Integrate your goals into your plan. Your goals should include husband-wife quality time, family-worship time, personal time, spiritual time, and work time. Budget your time to achieve your goals.

Integrity

Your word is your bond. Your word is an expression of your nature. Your word is a measure of your character. Each of us should want to be known as men who do what they commit to do.

You must have a nonnegotiable commitment to biblical consistency in your life. In short, you must be honest in all of your dealings and commitments. "Let your 'Yes' be 'Yes,' and your 'No,' 'No'" (Matthew 5:37 NIV). Do not overload yourself with commitments to the point that your honesty is questioned.

Patience

In our world of instant this and fast that, we have become a society that lacks patience. I was told about a man who became impatient when he was told that he would have to wait two minutes for his hamburger in a fast-food restaurant. Is this you?

As a Christian businessman and husband, one of the most difficult things in my life was to develop patience. It only happened when I balanced my life's concern with Scripture by making my request known unto the Lord and then waiting. "If we hope for what we do not yet have, we wait for it patiently" (Romans 8:25 NIV). When there were times of trial, I learned to "be patient in tribulation" (Romans 12:12 KJV). When I lacked patience with my wife and children, I learned that the "fruit of the Spirit is ... patience" (Galatians 5:22), because from patience comes understanding. "Through thy precepts I get understanding" (Psalm 119:104 KJV). Most of all, I learned that patience is a mark of biblical love (1 Corinthians 13:4).

Decisiveness

To be decisive means to be able to make decisions. As men called and ordained by God to lead, we must make decisions. If you make a mistake, evaluate and capitalize on it. In other words, learn from your mistakes.

Family Time

Scripture exhorts, "Love your wives, just as Christ loved the church" (Ephesians 5:25 NIV) as well as love her as you love yourself (v. 28). This takes time, effort, imagination, and planning. For some it will take a major overhaul of your priorities, which can be done if you

1. Write her into your schedule.
2. Plan monthly or quarterly evenings or weekends for one-on-one quality time.
3. Plan dates to send flowers or other small gifts.
4. Commit to saying, "I love you."
5. Always remember important days (anniversary, birthday, etc.).
6. Support her in her social activities.

Commit yourself to spend quality time with your children all together and one-on-one. Come to understand their individual temperaments, personalities, relationship with the Lord, life goals, and school concerns. Plan family devotional times and family evenings of fun.

Prayer

Become a man of prayer:

Give ear, O LORD, unto my prayer; and attend to the voice of my supplications. In the day of my trouble I will call upon thee: for thou wilt answer me. (Psalm 86:6–7 KJV)

The sacrifice of the wicked is an abomination to the LORD: but the prayer of the upright is his delight. (Proverbs 15:8 KJV)

And all things, whatsoever ye shall ask in prayer, believing, ye shall receive. (Matthew 21:22 KJV)

Rejoicing in hope: patient in tribulation: continuing instant in prayer. (Romans 12:12 KJV)

CONCLUSION

God has crowned man with honor and glory, blessed him with all spiritual gifts, and has given him access to His throne and His gift of eternal life. Through God's mercy and blessings, He has sustained man, not for man's selfish desires and worldly gain but for fellowship, one to another. "But seek first his kingdom and his righteousness, and all these things will be given to you as well" (Matthew 6:33 NIV).

REFERENCES

1984. *The holy Bible: New international version*. Grand Rapids: Zondervan.

Howard, J. G. 1989. *Balancing life's demands*. Sisters, OR: Multnomah Press.

Kastens, M. 1980. *Redefining the manager's job*. New York: American Management Association.

The King James version of the Bible.

Rush, M. 1987. *Management: A biblical approach*. Wheaton, IL: Victor Books.

Vine, W. E. 1985. *Vine's expository dictionary of Old and New Testament words,* edited by F. F. Bruce. Old Tappan, NJ: Revell.

Winwood, R. I. 1990. *Time management*. Salt Lake City: Franklin International Institute.

J. Derek McNeil

The Commitment to Marriage

J. DEREK McNEIL was formerly a therapist in private practice in Pasadena, California, and director of Ethnic Concerns at Fuller Theological Seminary. He has traveled nationally and internationally presenting workshops and seminars related to the *Black* family and marital issues. Derek was graduated from Eastern College with a bachelor of science degree in psychology and from Fuller Theological Seminary with a master of divinity degree concentrating in marriage and family therapy. Presently he is completing the final phase of his doctoral studies in counseling psychology at Northwestern University. He is married to Brenda Salter McNeil. They have a son, Omari Immanuel. Derek was born and raised in Philadelphia, Pennsylvania.

Chapter 10
J. Derek McNeil

The Commitment to Marriage

I was in the third year of graduate school when my wife painfully and angrily announced to me that I was doing a very poor job of being both a husband and a graduate student. I had to admit that I had become very invested in doing well in school and a great deal of my energies had gone to this end. I thought, *Hey, I'm pursuing my life's goal, my wife and family could certainly indulge me a little.*

As I listened to her opening statements I acknowledged that she had valid points, but I did not see how she could say that I was not committed to her. I was doing everything that I knew to function as well as I could, juggling both family and school. As I thought more about what she was saying, I started to get angry and annoyed with her, reacting quite defensively. I think I knew what she was trying to say, but I really did not believe that I had been that neglectful. The more she talked the more resistant I became. My acknowledging to her that she was right annoyed me even further. I had to eventually admit that my commitment to marriage had not really been a commitment to her. I was a duty-driven husband, but I had not invested the same energy in trying to establish an emotional closeness with my wife. I rationalized that since my family was clothed and housed I had adequately fulfilled my marital duty. It pained me to admit that I was wrong, and I left the conversation feeling injured and a little resentful.

I have come to think differently about commitment in marriage since this incident. In my clinical practice and in my personal life, commitments have taken on a new significance, particularly as they relate to relational quality and marital stability. This chapter focuses on marital commitment and issues that have made the maintenance of marital investment and fidelity more difficult for African-American men. I will spend most of this chapter looking at issues of commitment and intimacy, as well as of dependency. My hope is that by exploring the dynamics that occur for men in their relationships with women, we will produce an understanding that will allow us to strengthen our marriages and significant relationships.

After learning that I was going to write this chapter I sat down with a few of my very best friends, who are men, and asked them about their views of marital commitment and men. We spent an afternoon together just talking, and many of the ideas presented here were birthed in that session. I owe much of the insight of this chapter to these men and also to my wife, who has allowed me to explore and share our experience together for answers.

DEFINING COMMITMENT: HOW MEN AND WOMEN DIFFER

I believe the first task is to try to define what we mean when we use the word *commitment*. I have come to understand that men and women focus on different issues when they think of marital commitment. When women think of commitment they are often thinking of the emotional investment experienced in relationship with their partner. Commitment in this sense has an interactive relationship with intimacy and emotional closeness. Many women desire an emotionally invested partner who is preoccupied with her specialness. Commitment, therefore, is less a principle by which one acts than an emotion and attitude that one acts out. Certainly women are concerned with the fidelity of their partners, but the ideal relationship is symbolized by the specialness and value each partner feels for the other. Women say to themselves, If he loves me enough or if I'm lovable enough, he won't be interested in other women.

Men, though, tend to think of commitment as a principle of instrumental investment and sexual fidelity. Their notions of commitment are focused more on a sense of duty and integrity. Consequently, marital commitment is an investment of resources, the avoidance of an affair, and to a lesser degree, the expression of emotional closeness (outside of a sexual context). In my father's generation if a man "brought home the bacon," then he was faithful and committed to his family. He was primarily concerned about his family (wife and children as a unit) and providing for them. This is how he believed he could express his love. His commitment was not based in emotional closeness but in economic security and sexual exclusivity.

In fairness to my father's generation and ours, we have to briefly acknowledge how the expectations for marriage have changed. The present generation has been socialized to value marriage and sexual partnership a great deal more as a vehicle for emotional satisfaction. In this era of pop psychology, self-fulfillment, and self-improvement, both men and women are encouraged to seek out partners who can meet their emotional needs and make them happy. Couples are also encouraged to focus their hopes in the near future and alleviate their disappointments in the present, rather than focus on future generations. In the 1980s and early 1990s significantly fewer couples talked about staying together just for the sake of the kids. As the expectations increase and as the social sanctions for divorce decrease, emotionally unhappy people are more likely to end their relationship than they are to "stick it out."

Marital commitment is associated with many factors that are not considered by couples when they are in the heat of an interpersonal struggle. The complexity and stress of postmodern and postindustrial America have placed a tremendous strain on marital relations. The ability of a man to find work in a changing workforce; the societal attitudes about status, power, and race; and the social availability of extramarital partners all impact marital commitment. We must acknowledge that the relationship between a Black man and a Black woman cannot be adequately understood without considering their historical, social, political, and economic context (Cazenave 1983).

While considering the differences in male and female styles and acknowledging a historical perspective, we suggest that men and women have two different foci when they are speaking of marital commitment. It is very likely that many married men feel that they are committed to their family and are confused when their wives express discontent with the level of commitment that they experience from them. Conflict and confusion are inevitable if the meaning and purpose of the concept is different for each spouse. Hence, couples must first clarify what is meant when they talk to each other about commitment before they can struggle with what it means to be committed.

For a working definition, we will begin by stating that mature commitment is a promise to a course of action and a dedication to a long-term activity. Commitment is close to the virtue Erik Erikson calls fidelity; it refers to a definitive choice in the face of distracting and inviting alternatives (Marcia & Archer 1993). Within our definition we include both a sense of duty and a promise. Duty is the resilience of commitment, providing the "ought" of behavior and principles that guide situational choices. Commitment lacks teeth and the ability to fulfill its promise if it is solely dependent on emotional reactions. However, it will also lack soul and purpose if it is simply a principle of action disconnected from an ultimate goal. Dutiful behavior cannot be the end goal in a marriage, but it can be the vehicle that supports and protects a growing intimacy. When dutiful people lose sight of the redemptive purpose and promise of duty, tasks will become burdensome, enslaving, and rigid. Duty and promise are essential elements of committed relating; the absence of one or the other will decrease the quality of the relationship and ultimately the commitment.

As a final characteristic of our definition, we suggest that commitment is a choice. The willingness and ability to invest oneself in a relationship requires agency and volition. If one does not have the will to be accountable, or if one does not have a sense of personal control (power), one cannot maintain commitments. If commitment is an investment in another that requires duty, promise, and agency, it calls for people to relinquish some of their personal control and power. People who feel that they have limited control over their own lives or their environment will feel too inadequate to relinquish personal power to maintain commitments. They may have the desire but not the endowment or the sense of entitlement to choose to act on behalf of the relationship. Overly dependent people may have strong attachments that are very powerful, but their relationships are built on neediness rather than on mature sharing. There is an intense fear of loss that creates a strong bond in such relationships.

DEPENDENCY: ITS DANGERS

I recently met with a couple whose relationship was tragically rooted in an extreme dependency that both partners chose to call love. They were sitting in my office for the first time after seven months of marriage, having lived together for only two of them. They stated that they had come to therapy to see if they could salvage their marriage. As they began to tell their story it was clear that they had very little to salvage. The husband had had numerous affairs and had never stopped dating other women, before or after the wedding. Having been caught in the act several times by his wife, he remained unrepentant and defensive, chastising his wife for not trusting him. He was very hostile toward her and was verbally and physically abusive, but she continued to give him money and remained available to grant his sexual requests. The wife was deeply pained but she could not admit to herself how destructive the relationship had been. She was unable to let go of the relationship or hold him accountable for his behavior. During the therapy session, each repeatedly said that they loved the other but it was clear that they were overly dependent and needed each other more than they loved each other. The wife was dependent and passive, fearful of her husband's violence and easily manipulated by his periodic charm. The husband stated that although he despised his wife, no other women could take care of him as well as she had. He was an emotional child in angry adult clothing, afraid she would abandon him and resentful that he needed her. This was a very pitiful marriage that had very little commitment, very little mature love, and a great deal of neediness. The relationship had very little hope of offering either partner intimate companionship or a healing context.

MARRIAGE DEFINED THROUGH THE EXAMPLE OF CHRIST AND THE CHURCH

In contrast, a very powerful model of commitment and the merging of duty, promise, and agency is found in Christ and His church. Marriage is the metaphor used to describe the relationship between Christ and the church. This model of marriage is designed to facilitate intimate partnership. Christ initiates the relationship and establishes an identity interdependent of the church and the relationship He has with it. He is fully committed to the degree that He suffers and relinquishes His life. Through this act Christ enables humanity to establish a new covenant with God, one that holds a promise of future glory. The covenant is dependent on the commitment of God and the sacrifice of His Son. Our three components—duty, promise, and agency—allow the growth of trust and fidelity and buffer those situational disruptions that strain the marital relationship. They also allow us to see how the committed space of the marital relationship can be a place of healing and restoration. Our definition of commitment and its elements are not exhaustive, but they allow us to begin to theorize and try to understand the difficulties that men may experience in establishing and maintaining marital commitments.

MALE RESISTANCE TO COMMITMENT

African-American men struggle with feelings of being on the outside and having few areas in their lives where they feel strong and powerful and at the same time included and essential. This state of disagreement has had an unfortunate consequence on Black marriages. As we defined it, commitment requires the agency or power to invest in a promise dutifully. If one has not the internal sense (locus) of control or a reservoir of personal power, the capacity to be maturely committed erodes. A very salient reason that men feel fearful and are at best ambivalent about commitment is the sense of power (influence and authority) that they lose when they yield to what feels like a more "feminine" definition of commitment. This is more than a communication conflict about the meaning of a word. The conflict with my wife that I earlier described was superficially one of definition and communication: What does commitment mean to her and how does that compare with what commitment means to me? A second deeper and more difficult issue to resolve was the level of resistance that I felt to giving in to my wife's desires. It felt like I was being asked to give up too much. My fear was that our relationship would be "her marriage" and "her relationship," only requiring my compliance with her wishes.

It is important to understand how this works itself out to diminished marital commitment. Men have particular difficulty committing to those things that do not offer them opportunities for mastery and esteem. When men feel alienated and unaffirmed, they can become very resistant to relinquishing whatever emotional resources and power they feel that they do have. Self-esteem losses related to employment and instrumental inadequacy degrade the commitment level of men. Those men unable to fulfill their roles as providers will be more sensitive to the loss of respect from their wives and family. If a man feels that he cannot please his wife or that he will not gain a respected position in his household, he will eventually withdraw and assume a peripheral position in the family and marriage. The withdrawal serves to protect these men from the anger and disappointment of their wives and from their own loss of status within the family. In addition to this strategy of withdrawal, men may also try to control their sense of loss by overpowering their spouses or becoming engaged in power stalemates.

Some men will use the power of their anger maladaptively to make a space for themselves within their families, but this usually causes the family members to avoid them, which alienates them even further. When men are felt to be "too strong," they limit the ability of their family to connect with them and feel safe. To gain power and status within the family they sacrifice intimate connections and contact. Typically their so-called strength is an overcompensation for feelings of inadequacy and is utilized to avoid emotional vulnerability and dependency.

Other men feel that they cannot win significant battles, so they fall into a strategy of avoiding loss. They thwart their partners by becoming entrenched in stalemates for control and power. When these patterns become entrenched in the characteristic style of their relating, each spouse will look to avoid the conflicts or seek to avoid the losses. I have seen at least two different forms of the stalemate themes. The styles of relating are different but both are stalemated relationships. There are couples who avoid fighting but who also avoid intimate interactions. They appear to peacefully coexist, yet they sacrifice intimacy for safety. Their relationships are power struggles of resistance, a continual test of who will hold out the longest and remain the least vulnerable. The second type of couple tussles constantly—living to fight. But neither spouse can tolerate the shame of losing a point, consequently their battles take on a never-ending quality. They do not know when they began or what they are really arguing about—they are just trying to avoid losing the present skirmish. When partners choose to adopt postures meant to resist or control in order to avoid some degree of emotional neediness, they increase their defensiveness and decrease the possibilities of emotional intimacy. All of these struggles erode trust and indicate that a couple is unable to get their needs met in the relationship.

Essentially both partners must feel that they can gain enough power to have their needs met in the marriage. The power sharing and the quality of the commitment shape the atmosphere of the relationship and determine if trust will grow and nurture the individual partners. When commitment is devoid of a promise to grow as both a couple and as individuals, stagnancy and decline in the relationship are inevitable. The decision to stay married may not be significantly altered, but the possibility of a nurturing mature marriage will becoming a diminishing hope.

As we close this section I want to review its main point. When men feel that they have lost or that they will lose emotional resources and power, inside or outside the family, they are less likely to be central in the family and intimately committed to it.

MEN, WOMEN, AND POWER

If men perceive marriage as a power struggle between the sexes, they will assume a posture of resistance, while avoiding giving in too much to the wishes of their wives. Most men continue to be ambivalent about women and power. The larger culture continues to socialize us as men to believe that we must be strong at all times and that it is preferable that we be more powerful than women. In addition, Black men receive a second socialization message that communicates that they must not be too aggressive or too dominant, in deference to the power of White society, or they risk social censure. This creates insecurity and ambiguity in the minds of Black men about power and status. To decrease this ambiguity some men hold rigidly to the notion that manhood is the capacity to dominate and control; therefore, to be strong is to control one's woman and children. This remains a pervasive traditional message. Even today, if a man is unable to "control his woman," he will experience at least some disapproval from other men. For Black men, the struggle to maintain a sense of status and power has been complex and tenuous. Black men have attempted to maintain some power or status by accommodation, seduction, intimidation, and resistance while at the same time avoiding feelings of dependence or submission in order to feel in control. Hence, the interaction of feeling powerless in the society and powerless in the home with one's wife is difficult for most Black men to handle. When women are perceived to be "too powerful" they awaken male fears that they will be reduced to the status of little boys once again—dependent and powerless.

For many men this perception of powerlessness is intolerable, and it stimulates a historical shame. Men who have experienced early-life trauma or low self-esteem have an even greater vulnerability to this shame. A man often responds to shame with rage and aggression, allowing him to escape his injury and restore a feeling of powerfulness. Most men who abuse suffer from a deep sense of depression, shame, and inadequacy. Their abusive rages are often stimulated by feelings of powerlessness or their unconscious feeling of needing to control a spouse by keeping her feeling as dependent on him as he feels on her.

Powerlessness and shame are heightened if, throughout childhood and adolescent development, there are not mature male models to help in identity formation and separation from the mother. Developmentally, boys learn to become men by identifying with male models. Typically, throughout childhood and adolescence they gradually separate from their mothers and identify more heavily with the available male culture. If a male model or male culture is not intimately accessible, boys and young men pioneer their own resistance toward their mothers. They may not have a model for what they can become, but they know what they do not want to be. Mothers and women are experienced as powerful and must be resisted if one is to become a "man." Men grow up believing that they must resist women to forge and stabilize their own identities as men. Since most of us as men have been raised primarily by women, much of our identity has been defined by women. Consequently, when a man struggles with his identity and feels powerless, he might assume that a woman in his life has taken his power from him (Pittman 1993) because his identity and power base are fragile and dependent on the reaffirmation of a woman. Paradoxically men must get women to affirm their strength, their seductive powers, their prowess, and their independence but at the same time try to avoid feeling too dependent on them.

We can now understand that women may be feeding a deep-seated resentment when they request that their men become more sensitive and committed to them. Eventually, resentment and anger will surface in men who feel inadequate and are pressured to become more vulnerable and dependent. Men whose identities are solely based in *not* being like women or maintaining control will have struggles being both strong and intimate. If they lose control or feel dependent they are likely to withdraw.

Most men resist the power of their wives the same way they learned to resist the power of their mothers. The initial hunger for a nurturing woman is tempered by the fear of the emotional engulfing power of that woman. Only feeling comfortable with so much closeness, men distance themselves to avoid feeling engulfed by feminine power. Some men avoid the threat by entering into affairs, which act to lessen their dependence on their wives. The extramarital affair serves to lower a man's powerlessness in the marital relationship while at the same time allowing him to satisfy some of his need for nurturing and emotional dependence without relinquishing too much control. Another variation on this theme is the philanderer. Philanderers repetitively seduce and charm women but avoid deeper relationships. With each so-called conquest they feel renewed strength and vigor, but they quickly become bored with the deeper possibilities of intimacy or commitment to one woman. Philanderers have learned to avoid both dependency and power loss by avoiding the duty of commitments.

Too much of male culture has validated these maladaptive strategies by which men meet their needs for emotional intimacy. The other option validated by men is to remain "cool," resisting any expression of emotional vulnerability or intimate commitment. Fathers and father figures who do not express and validate emotional closeness with their sons increase the susceptibility of their utilizing noncommitment to consolidate power. Sons need to see fathers and male mentors express dependency and validate intimacy as part of male culture. Power and real strength need to be redefined and placed in the context of a generational commitment. The expression of love and commitment in one generation entitles and empowers the next generation to express it. Most men have had very few models of emotionally committed fathers who remained strong, respected figures in their marriages, yet responsive to the needs of their wives.

The underinvolvement of fathers within family life has been evident throughout society and has proven to be particularly detrimental to young African-American men. Because of this, at least two liabilities are created relating to commitment: (1) the lack of a clear and interactive adult male who can model what commitment requires, and (2) the emotional defect experienced by the male child because he does not have a significant parent available to respond to identity and emotional needs. Absent fathers are not the only underinvolved fathers. Others may have had fathers at home who proved to be ineffective images, modeling either passive-aggressive behavior or angry-aggressive strategies to offset the power of their spouses. Fathers who have not explored their own feelings of dependency and powerlessness will transmit this ambivalence to their sons.

Commitment must have been modeled for men by their fathers and/or other male mentors with whom they can identify. A legacy of noncommitment can often be seen in previous generations of one's extended family. One's father or mother can introduce noncommittal relationship patterns into their present family from their family of origin. It is very difficult for a young man to demonstrate emotional openness that has not been modeled for him or expressed to him. This is also true of commitment. It is difficult for him to maintain commitments and be trustworthy if none have been trustworthy for him. Commitment must first be experienced before it can become fully operational. Some men have never had anyone commit to them or invest meaningfully in their lives, which leaves them less skilled in committing to others. In some cases fathers have also modeled infidelity, which establishes a vulnerability within their sons to repeat the pattern. The significant woman in a man's life may help him reach adulthood and may teach him about commitment but she is unable to model for him how to be a man committed to a woman in marriage. This is not to say that men cannot or have not learned a great deal from women. It is simply to say that men also need other men to mentor them and teach them what mature commitment means.

When being with a woman becomes the only place where a man can experience emotional vulnerability and nurturing, he is likely to be overly dependent on her. A married man will remain very vulnerable to extra-marital affairs if his only emotional connections are with women. In addition, male emptiness cannot be solely filled by nurturing women without producing a conflict between the need to express dependence and the need to feel autonomously strong. This conflict of the dependency and counterdependency modes may be evident in the marital relationship and may impact the degree of commitment (duty and promise) that a man is able to share with his wife.

COMMITMENT MAINTENANCE: HOW TO ACHIEVE IT

This chapter, in part, has tried to build a case for the fact that men need other men to help them become men who can make choices and live with their commitments. There is an essential need in our community for men to strengthen the commitments we make to our wives and to our children. Many of the growing number of children who live in poverty are there because their fathers could not make the choice to stay with them or support them. Many of these men could not find a sense of competence in being fathers or husbands because they lacked the skills or they lacked the will. This suggests that we must make a serious investment in African-American men to teach the necessary skills and provide us with a community of men who will call us to a higher vision and purpose.

African-American men are sensitive to the lack of power they may experience in their spousal relationships and the effect of the structural powerlessness they experience in the larger society. Feeling frustration due to social powerlessness and lower social status can lead to undue anger and resentment being redirected toward Black women. Therefore we must also advocate and support men in becoming more competent in their provider roles. The inability to hold a job will diminish esteem and erode commitment. The marital role cannot be realistically separated from the role of father and provider. Men who feel good about themselves as providers have more emotional resources to build upon in their marital relationships. Likewise men who have strong marital relationships are likely to have stronger commitments to their children and greater resilience in their role as providers.

Men will have to acquire additional strengths if they are to develop resilience that will enable them to weather external and internal strain and remain faithful to their commitments. We must learn to use our dependent feelings to foster interdependence with women and receive nurturing and support from men. Denial of dependency creates other difficulties for marriages and the interactions between men and women in relationships. Klimek (1979) states that the degree of awareness and acceptance of one's dependency needs, as opposed to their denial, avoidance, or compensation, separate the emotionally mature from the immature. Committed marriages need men who can reconcile the dependent feelings they are experiencing and avoid counterdependent withdrawal.

Men who feel dependent are not pathological or "effeminate"; the problem is that there is limited validation for dependency in male culture and the general society. All men experience dependency and need to rely on others for emotional support. The message that dependence is nonmanly and an indication of weakness causes men to struggle to find other ways to express dependent feelings. If men are unable to tolerate some dependence, they will be unable to tolerate intimate expression that is voluntarily vulnerable. Men who deny dependency (counterdependence) will experience emotional intimacy as threatening since intimacy also creates a feeling of vulnerability and powerlessness. The counterdependent man may maintain his commitment to the marriage but may struggle with intimate commitment to his spouse. For a marital commitment to maintain its integrity and fidelity men must invest in both the institution of marriage and in the women whom they marry.

In Ephesians 5:25–27 husbands are called on to sacrifice for their wives the way Christ sacrificed himself for the church, for the intention of helping her become all that she can become. Christ states that He is only able to do this because of His dependence on the Father (John 5:19). I suggest it would be difficult for any man to fulfill this mandate without a faith and dependence in God and without a community of men for support. It is our faith and connectedness with God that can provide us with new insight and the power by which we can invest ourselves in our wives. Commitment itself is born out of a faith and a hope in a future promise. For whatever reasons one commits himself to a worthy endeavor, the investment is indicative of the hopefulness of its outcome. Humans must live with a consciousness and hope in something beyond the immediate and beyond themselves. The marital commitment is based in the faith of its participants—their faith in each other and in God as a covenant partner. Faithfulness, however, does not encourage foolishness. It is also necessary to be cautious and use wisdom when one chooses to commit oneself to marriage or any other relationship. An immature or displaced faith will produce a commitment unable to endure situational difficulties. Even faith rooted only in one's spouse is insufficient to hold all the hopes of the marriage in the present social climate.

The community of male support can help us remain accountable to those things we have committed ourselves to. Without a deep intimate faith and without a community of support, commitments are possible but certainly not optimal, and they may lack resilience. There are seven behaviors that I believe can increase the capacity to commit and strengthen the marital commitment:

1. Develop a habit of making and holding to commitments.
2. Develop realistic expectations about your spouse and marriage.
3. Join a community of men who can support each other in their marital commitments.
4. Work to develop emotional resilience, the capacity to endure in difficult times.
5. Make a commitment to the person (spouse) in marriage as well as to the institution of marriage.
6. Continue to pursue emotional *in*dependence, to choose *inter*dependence.
7. Seek out older, mature men who have walked and talked commitment.

COMMITMENT AS HEALING: WHY

The final section is important because it attempts to answer the Why question. Why should we attempt to strengthen commitments or address our overdependency and counterdependency? I stated earlier that it is essential for the African-American community. I have also implied that it is for the sake of the most important opportunities in a committed relationship and intimate partnership to heal the hurts and injuries of the past. Mutual commitment to a covenant allows each party the safety, the relational space, and the time to work on the emotional reinjuries stimulated by the relationship over time. Unfortunately, some marital partners cannot form the trust in each other or in the marriage that is necessary to nurture its healing potential. If one cannot trust the commitments of one's marital partner, the reinjuries serve to create a despairing disappointment, relieved only by the options of withdrawal, extramarital relationships, or divorce. These same reinjuries could be opportunities to reevaluate our own neediness and dependence as we attempt to heal and grow to be more whole, but this requires a context of safety and fidelity.

We all enter relationships with some pull to reshape the past and rewrite a new chapter in our new relationships. We are all drawn to partners who will allow us to relate to them in ways that have personal historical significance. We bring our old issues, hurts, and mistrusts to the new relationship in the hope that it will provide a greater fidelity than did previous relationships. Trust develops when what we experience is what we desired or felt was promised to us. Conversely, mistrust develops when we feel that those things that we needed or that marriage promised are not delivered. Because no one can meet all of their partner's expectations or fulfill all of one's trusts, disappointment and emptiness results. If the partners are unable to manage these feelings, they will relinquish their ties to the present relationship to pursue another that appears more likely to meet their needs. Marriage, then, can be thought of as a search for trust and fidelity as well as the offering of trustworthiness and commitment.

The astute or the romantic reader will recognize that we have talked very little about love. This is not to devalue its power but to suggest that if it lacks fidelity or commitment, it is of questionable maturity or ability to endure. The attraction and selection of one's potential spouse or companion is often accompanied by intense physiological and emotional pulls, but the maturing of these early intense feelings requires fidelity, trust, and commitment. Amorous love must develop and evolve into a love that requires less immediate gratification—a love that is anchored in a willfulness that can endure emotional disappointments and that can offer healing opportunities. Committed space is the context in which this transition takes place. If two people are unable to move their early loving experiences beyond the feeling level to a committed partnership, they lack what it takes to have an enduring love relationship.

Two persons who can vow a vow to each other and honor their promises provide a space for love to mature and intimacy to grow. Commitment offers a safe space to continue a dynamic dialogue, re-adjusting and redefining the relationship to meet developmental needs and situational realities. A trustworthy environment and relationship in turn nurtures each individual and allows compassion, respect, and good-will to thrive. Conversely, mistrustful situations and contexts perpetuate the necessity for our defensive styles and relational patterns. If one can-not trust someone that he is attempting to be in relationship with, it is very difficult to move away from focusing on security and defense. Relationships have little chance of maturing beyond childlike hungers if one feels one's partner is not stable, responsible, available, and relatively consistent. It is not that other volatile relational styles are not stimulat-ing or appealing, but the depth of the relationship and the maturity of the relating is not likely to develop. Fidelity earns trust and a trusting envi-ronment allows for a mature love to develop. The erosion of trust will inevitably lead to a withdrawal and numbing of love or to an unhealthy relationship that is unbalanced (underfunctioning/overfunctioning) and based in neediness rather than a mature love.

CONCLUSION

Commitment promises to create the emotional safety to nurture a mature love and the dutifulness to hang on when situations are disheart-ening. Committed men must develop the skill and discipline to choose among various possibilities and refuse other immediate options that may appear attractive but not consistent with their long-term purpose. Committed men must prove to be able to be "faithful" or have fidelity between their actions and their stated future intentions. Finally, commit-ted men must also be flexible enough to change course and respond to sit-uational imperatives, yet maintain the integrity of their original chosen direction. As I look at the skills and the maturity required, I realize that most men have some but not all of these skills. All of us need to engage with other men of integrity and support each other in our commitments to family and marriage.

The Incarnation is God's great statement of commitment to human-ity. There is no greater statement of promise than God's gift of His Son

Jesus. With Christ, we have the eternal attention of God and an eternally committed investment in human affairs. This commitment comes as an invitation with no guarantee of reciprocal human partnership. It is clear in God's interaction with humanity that one partner in the relationship must provide fidelity for the relationship to grow and for the other partner to mature. It is God's commitment to covenant promises that we are encouraged to rely on in order to endure and flourish. God bids us to trust that the commitment that He made to us is constant, thereby allowing us the opportunity to grow in its safety and security. The marriage metaphor challenges us with the same question. Can we provide the safety of commitment to our partners that they may grow and mature?

REFERENCES

Cazenave, N. A. 1983. Black male—Black female relationships: The perceptions of 155 middle-class Black men. *Family Relations* 32: 34–50.

Dandeneau, M., and S. Johnson. 1994. Facilitating intimacy: Interventions and effects. *Journal of Marital and Family Therapy* 20: 17–33.

Doherty, W. 1991. Beyond reactivity and the deficit model of manhood: A commentary on articles by Napier, Pittman, and Gottman. *Journal of Marital and Family Therapy* 17: 29–32.

Kimmel, M., and M. Messner. 1989. *Men's lives*. New York: Macmillan.

Klimek, D. 1979. *Beneath mate selection and marriage: The unconscious motives in human pairing*. New York: Van Nostrand Reinhold.

McNeil, J. D. 1991. Effective marital counseling with Black couples. In *The Black family: Past, present, and future*, edited by L. N. June. Grand Rapids: Zondervan.

Parks, S. 1986. *The critical years: The young adult search for a faith to live by*. San Francisco: Harper and Row.

Paul, J., and M. Paul. 1984. *Do I have to give up me to be loved by you?* Minneapolis: CompCare Publications.

Pittman, F. S. 1993. *Man enough*. New York: Putnam's.

Sager, C. J. 1976. *Marriage contracts and couple therapy: Hidden forces in intimate relationships*. New York: Brunner-Mazel.

Willi, J. 1982. *Couples in collusion*. New York: Jason Aronson.

Willie Richardson

Male Leadership in the Home and Family

WILLIE RICHARDSON is the pastor of Christian Stronghold Baptist Church in Philadelphia, Pennsylvania, and is also the president of Christian Research and Development (CRD) of Philadelphia. Willie was a design engineer for twenty-five years. He is a graduate of Philadelphia College of the Bible and serves on numerous boards. Christian Research and Development was founded in 1977 and is involved in developing the Christian family and church through seminars, conferences, retreats, and workshops. Willie has authored several workbooks, book chapters, magazine articles, and is the author of the book *Reclaiming the Urban Family* (Zondervan, 1996). He is also the founder-director of Inner City Impact. Willie has a commitment to developing pastors as managers and has done so successfully with some one hundred pastors. He was born in Florence, South Carolina, and is married to Patricia Richardson. They have four children: Gregory, Garin, Gwendolyn, and Gerald.

Chapter 11
Willie Richardson

Male Leadership in the Home and Family

INTRODUCTION

Understanding that the African-American family is in trouble is the first step in changing the conditions it faces. Yet it may be argued that there are many healthy African-American families, and certainly I agree. I sound the alarm, however, along with many others, that there are too many poor families, too many divorces, and too many of our children and young people in prisons. The stability of our families is steadily eroding. There is too much hopelessness in our cities and among our poorest rural communities. We have lost our direction and too many families have lost their way. What we lack most is leadership for the family.

When there is leadership, there is someone taking the initiative to deal with the problems, hope is given to the people being led, and progress is being made. Leaders give guidance and direction, take on the burdens, and accept the pain of engagement along with the obstacles that stand in the way of success. In this chapter, I will present and discuss the key areas necessary for developing effective leadership in males and the family.

THE CHURCH'S ROLE IN DEVELOPING LEADERSHIP FOR THE HOME

It is no secret that the Black church is the strongest institution in our community, and help for families must come from our churches. Leadership development for the home begins with the pastor as leader of the church. To be effective, the pastor must have a burden to win men for our Lord Jesus Christ and to develop them as leaders of our churches and our families. (For how-tos on evangelizing and discipling men, see Richardson 1991.)

The pastor must realize that the church can face up to the deteriorating conditions of our families and can help save them, turn them around, and make them whole through the leading of the Holy Spirit, the power of God, and the love of Christ.

The church must also take Christian education seriously. The Sunday school is not just for children and a handful of adult Bible lovers. A biblical education for every member of the church should be a goal. God created the family (Genesis 2:20–24; 4:1–2) and has given His design for it (Ephesians 5:21–6:4) for His continual glory (1 Chronicles 16:28; Psalm 96:3). We must have trained Sunday school teachers who are knowledgeable of the Bible and how to teach. Sunday school is essential whether it is held at its traditional time or some other time like after Sunday morning worship service. In addition, weeknight Bible-study groups are also a way of educating families.

Having laypeople trained to do biblical counseling is yet another way of mentoring family Christian leadership. God does not intend that the pastor do all of the work. The church must be mobilized to minister to its own families and to reach out into the community. As I have stated in the book *Reclaiming the Urban Family* (1996, p. 32):

> The members of the church should do the training, supplemented by volunteers and professionals from the community. This activity should be led by the pastor who cares for the flock.

> God never intended the pastor to deal with every problem in the church. God, the Holy Spirit, has gifted each believer (Rom. 12:6; 1 Cor. 12:4–6), and the Bible makes it very clear that God's will is that the gifts be used for the common good of the members (1 Cor. 12:7). Gifts are not to be undiscovered or merely sitting on a pew.

> The Bible teaches that Christians should love each other deeply and be hospitable (1 Peter 4:8–9). Each person should use his or her gifts to serve others, faithfully administering God's grace. More members of the church must be mobilized into this type of service.

THE BIBLICAL MODEL OF LEADERSHIP IN THE HOME

There are five elements involved in a biblical model of leadership for the home. These are (1) the authority of God, (2) a loving servant-leader (the husband), (3) God's empowerment, (4) a love relationship, and (5) attitudes of cooperation.

The Authority of God

We are to live according to God's Word (Matthew 4:4). We are to surrender our lives to God through faith in Jesus Christ as our Lord and Savior (Ephesians 2:4–9), thereby being created in Christ to do God's will (Ephesians 2:10). Submitting ourselves to the authority of God means that we obey His command of being "filled with the Spirit" or being controlled by God, the Holy Spirit. God's model is that the husband, wife, and children submit to and be under the authority of God and His Word.

A Loving Servant-Leader—the Husband

God has designated the husband to be the leader of the family. This is explicitly stated in Scripture: "Wives, submit to your husbands as to the Lord. For the husband is the head of the wife as Christ is the head of the church, his body, of which he is the Savior" (Ephesians 5:22–23). The husband is to be a unique leader. He is to love his wife just "as Christ loved the church and gave himself up for her" (Ephesians 5:25). He is to be a sacrificial lover and leader. He is committed to his family for Christ's sake, and the so-called buck stops with him. Since he has faith in God and His Word, he is confident that he can lead in the home because God says so.

The Christian husband is not an autocratic dictator, but a servant-leader.

> *Jesus called them together and said, "You know that the rulers of the Gentiles lord it over them, and their high officials exercise authority over them. Not so with you. Instead, whoever wants to become great among you must be your servant, and whoever wants to be first must be your slave—just as the Son of Man did not come to be served, but to serve, and to give his life a ransom for many. The greatest among you will be your servant."* (Matthew 20:25–28; 23:11)

Paul and Richard Meier (1981, p. 107) state that

in his role as the husband, a leader delegates responsibility. A manager does not do everything himself; he has learned to utilize the gifts and abilities of other people. He needs to recognize the gifts and abilities of his wife and utilize her gifts in the operation of the home.

In the Old Testament Book of Proverbs we see a good example of this in the well-known chapter about the virtuous woman. Proverbs 31:10 [KJV] says, "Who can find a virtuous woman? for her price is far above rubies." The word *virtuous* means "a force with deep reserves." It carries the idea of a complex, resourceful woman with many gifts and abilities. The beautiful thing about the description in this passage is that it appears that the woman's husband has delegated to her many responsibilities according to her gifts. This makes him a good manager. He has recognized her abilities, and he has given her liberty and responsibility to exercise those gifts.

Our motivation is to serve God, meet the needs of our life partner (our wife), assume the responsibility to our children, and glorify Christ as Lord.

Leadership is not controlling the people you lead but influencing them through love and commitment to them. The husband as the loving servant-leader is a steward of the family that God has given him and surely will stand before God one day and give an account (Romans 14:12) for his leadership under the lordship of Christ since "the head of every man is Christ" (1 Corinthians 11:3).

John MacArthur Jr. (1994, pp. 32–33) states:

Authority and submission characterize not only all of creation, but the Creator as well. Paul says, "Christ is the head of every man, and the man is the head of a woman, and God is the head of Christ" (1 Corinthians 11:3). If Christ had not submitted to the will of God, redemption for mankind would have been impossible, and we would be lost forever. If individuals do not submit to Christ as Savior and Lord, they will be doomed for rejecting God's gracious provision. And if women do not submit to men, the family and society as a whole will be destroyed. Whether on a divine or human scale, submission and authority are indispensable elements in God's order and design.

Before instructing the Ephesians on how authority and submission should characterize their specific relationships (cf., Ephesians 5:22ff), Paul emphasized the general attitude when he said, "Be subject to one another in the fear of Christ" (v. 21). "Be subject" translates the Greek word *hupotasso,* originally a military term meaning "to arrange" or "to rank under." It expresses the relinquishing of one's rights to another. Paul counseled the Corinthian believers, for example, to be in subjection to their faithful ministers "and to everyone who helps in the work and labors" (1 Corinthians 16:16). Peter commands us to "submit [ourselves] for the Lord's sake to every human institution" (1 Peter 2:13). A nation cannot function without rulers, soldiers, police, and others in leadership. That's not to say they are inherently superior to other citizens, but leaders are necessary for maintaining law and order to prevent the nation from falling into a state of anarchy.

Likewise within the church we are to "obey [our] leaders, and submit to them; for they keep watch over [our] souls, as those who will give an account" (Hebrews 13:17). As is true with leaders in government, church leaders are not inherently superior to other Christians. But no institution—including the church—can function without a system of authority and submission.

In the home, the smallest unit of human society, the same principle applies. Even a small household cannot function if each member fully demands and expresses his own will. The system of authority God has ordained for the family is the headship of husbands over wives and of parents over children.

God's Empowerment

In this biblical leadership model, hope is guaranteed, for God, the Holy Spirit, and the Bible are the antidote to family hopelessness (Romans 15:4). The Spirit counsels, empowers, gives gifts, intercedes, regenerates, unites, directs, and gives wisdom. The Holy Spirit plays an integral role in the leadership in the home. Without the husband and the rest of the family allowing the Holy Spirit to have His way in the home, that home will be no different than any other home that is failing to meet the needs of families. The husband must submit to and be filled with the Holy Spirit to be effective in his leadership role.

A Love Relationship

The biblical leadership model is built on the love of God—*agape* love—unconditional love. The family must love God with all their heart, all their soul, all their strength, and all their mind (Luke 10:27). The wife must love her husband and support his leadership. The children must love their parents, obey them, and honor them.

Attitudes of Cooperation

A cooperative family is a submissive family. They submit to Jesus Christ as Lord and to each other as Christians (Ephesians 5:21). That is, the wife submits to her husband, the husband submits to his wife by loving her, and the parents submit to the children by caring for them and disciplining them fairly.

LEADERSHIP THAT SECURES THE BLESSINGS OF GOD

From a negative point of view, because of a lack of family leadership, homes are being destroyed by immorality, financial failure, alcohol and other drugs, juvenile offenders, mental illness, and divorce. These homes are "cursed"—cursed because Christ is not Lord. It is sad to say, but some such families are comprised of church members who are not receiving the blessings of God for their families.

A man who accepts his leadership role as the head of his family must be committed to God with the permanence of marriage—"until death separates." Leading a family is not easy. The Christian husband must have staying power. He cannot be a quitter. He must expect resistance to his leadership from time to time from his wife and children when they are "in the flesh" rather than in the Spirit. His objective must be to secure the blessings of God for his family, for he knows that "unless the LORD builds the house, its builders labor in vain" (Psalm 127:1). As leaders, we cannot forget that our wife is partner, lover, friend, and queen. Therefore, she is our number-one advisor.

There are nine areas of leadership that are necessary in order to secure the blessings of God:

1. Spiritual leadership
2. Problem solving
3. Family life goals
4. Put it on paper
5. Housing goals
6. Professional and career goals
7. Financial goals

8. Goals for family time
9. Health and physical goals

Spiritual Leadership

Before God called a priest, prophet, or a minister, He called husbands to be the spiritual leaders of the home. He is the resident pastor. Long ago, a husband and father by the name of Joshua, in modeling his leadership, said, "But as for me and my household, we will serve the LORD" (Joshua 24:15). If the husband is going to lead his family spiritually, there can be no doubt as to his allegiance to Jesus Christ as Lord. He must not only take his family to church but must also be involved in his church to advance the kingdom of Christ. He should monitor the progress of his family's spirituality along with his own. He must ask questions such as: Are all my family members Christians? Are they growing in the grace and knowledge of our Lord and Savior, Jesus Christ? Does our church have the ministry that will enable us to grow in Christ?

A loving servant-leader will lead his family in prayer and Bible sharing at home, being sure that every member is applying God's Word in their lives. Family life is intimate. Family members know each other's spiritual strengths and weaknesses. The husband, as the resident pastor, must guide family members to love and affirm one another and to be patient concerning each other's shortcomings.

Under his leadership, and in partnership with his wife, the servant-leader creates a spiritual atmosphere in the family with the goal of family members' maintaining a Christlike spirit. This kind of climate should make it easy to foster positive communication among family members. There should be family loyalty where sisters and brothers grow up supporting one another. Love must be understood spiritually and must grow and mature in the family in order for this to happen. Members of the family follow the loving servant-leader's example by continually showing appreciation for each member of the household.

Problem Solving

One of the most critical areas in family life where good, solid leadership is needed is in the area of problem solving. Too many men do not face up to problems. Rather, they run away from problems, are overwhelmed by them, and try to escape them through alcohol and other drugs. Through these methods they create new problems. As I have stated in *Reclaiming the Urban Family* (1996):

It is when we have problems, difficulties, troubles, or crises in the marriage or the family that some of us as Christians forget our faith, who we are, and who we belong to. As believers in the Lord Jesus Christ, we are told, "His divine power has given us everything we need for life and godliness through our knowledge of him who called us by his own glory and goodness" (2 Peter 1:3).

Since God has already given us "everything we need for life and godliness" and " ... in all things God works for the good of those who love him ..." (Romans 8:28), we as married people are never left alone to deal with problems without Christ. Remember, it takes three people to have a Christian marriage—the husband, the wife, and the Lord Jesus Christ. We must focus on Christ immediately when we face problems as individuals and as married couples.

The following must be exercised in family problem solving:

1. The presence of Christ must be practiced during times of crisis and problems. Invite Christ into the problem-solving process with prayer.
2. Each family member must be adaptable and flexible. Rigid, stubborn attitudes are disastrous.
3. Maintain emotional self-control.
4. Be Christ-centered rather than self-centered. The issue is not what I want, but what God wants.
5. Maintain an attitude conducive to problem solving. An attitude of indifference, coldness, callousness, alienation, or detachment closes off the ability to solve problems.
6. Calmly identify problems without accusing or blaming other family members. The idea is to focus on solving the problem, not placing blame.
7. Prioritize problems. If we do not sort out and prioritize problems, complex and multiple difficulties will overwhelm us.
8. Be committed to working through problems. This means that there should be open discussion between key family members who are affected by the problems or with the decision makers, who will be the husband and wife most of the time. Use your imagination—consider all possible solutions and the consequences of each solution. Get outside help if needed.
9. Offer thanksgiving to God when problems have been resolved or when God has given the grace to live with some of them.

Family Life Goals

In harnessing God's blessings for the family, dreaming and planning is in order. Ephesians 3:20 says, "Now to him who is able to do immeasurably more than all we ask or imagine, according to his power that is at work within us." Many nonbelievers have dared to dream, and the resulting accomplishments are astounding. As we learn and believe the promises of God, we must realize that God would have us to reach our full potential as individuals and as families. Certainly God is a resource for He is able to do immeasurably more than all we ask or imagine. He, however, has also made us a resource by his power that is at work within us. To reach our potential, we as husbands and wives must pray and dream, using our imagination.

As the leader of his family, a man cannot allow life just to happen to his family, leaving it to fate, but he must seek God's will, guidance, and direction for his family's course. God allows us to use our imaginations to dream of future accomplishments. As a matter of fact, it can be fun using your imagination, looking into the future with your mind and heart with no negative restrictions. I call this having a personal vision. We have attendees at our Don't Defeat Yourself Seminars go through an exercise using their imagination for looking into the future as to what they can become and what they can accomplish. Some of their lives have been radically changed in the area of being successful. Couples should free themselves and fly on the wings of faith in God to see where He will carry them.

Put It on Paper

As couples pray together, dream together, and plan together, also write your combined dream or vision for your family on paper. Begin planning by asking such questions as what would we like to accomplish in the next twelve months? What would we like to accomplish in the next three years? What characteristics would we like to build into our children as we raise them? What long-range plans should we begin preparing for?

In sum, in order to make your dreams come true, a couple must do the following:

- Pray together.
- Dream together.
- Write down your dream (the vision for your family).
- Plan together (including goals).

- Write down your plan. (It is not a plan if it is only in your head.).
- Take steps together in carrying out the plan.
- Thank God and give Him the glory for every accomplishment.

Housing Goals

Very few working-class African-Americans buy their dream house, because they cannot afford it. If, however, a young couple buy a start-up home that they can afford, build up equity in that home over a period of five years, and then sell it, they should use the profit from this home as the down payment on a better one. They should build up equity in this newer home until they are ready to purchase the next home or their dream home. It takes dreaming and planning to fulfill such a reality.

Professional and Career Goals

I mentioned earlier that God has made us a resource to Him and to others. Our natural gifts, intelligence, working skills, education, experience, and even some of our spiritual gifts make us valuable in the job market or give us potential to own businesses. Are you in your desired job? Consider the following:

> Then I realized that it is good and proper for a man to eat and drink, and to find satisfaction in his toilsome labor under the sun during the few days of life God has given him—for this is his lot. Moreover, when God gives any man wealth and possessions, and enables him to enjoy them, to accept his lot and be happy in his work—this is a gift of God. He seldom reflects on the days of his life, because God keeps him occupied with gladness of heart. (Ecclesiastes 5:18–20)

> A man can do nothing better than to eat and drink and find satisfaction in his work. This too, I see, is from the hand of God. (Ecclesiastes 2:24)

If God is able to give us the gift of a job that we are happy doing, then it follows that we must be out of His will if we are in a job that makes us miserable. If God is willing to give us a job that pays well, enabling us to purchase possessions that we can enjoy, I think we should be seeking God's guidance and direction for such.

Examine your current job situation. What goals should you strive for on your present job? One, for sure, should be "Whatever you do, work at it with all your heart, as working for the Lord, not for men" (Colossians 3:23). Perhaps there is a future position you may desire. Maybe you do not have a profession or trade at all. Your goal should be to acquire a trade or profession. Perhaps additional training is needed. Pray, dream, plan, and take action.

Financial Goals

What kind of steward is your family with the talents, gifts, and treasure God has given? Is the family's present income adequate? Will this income be adequate in the future? What is your desired income? How can you and your family be better wage earners?

If your family is going to harness God's blessings, they must honor God by their worship giving, preferably tithes and offerings. Some Christians say that they cannot give to God this way; they cannot afford to. According to God's promises in the Bible, they cannot afford not to give God His tithes and His grace offerings.

It is God's will for His followers to be debt-free, to be lending money, not borrowing money (Deuteronomy 28:12–13; Romans 13:8). Unpaid debt, bad credit, and overextended credit have stopped families from owning homes, starting businesses, and getting out of poverty. There should be planning in how to get out of debt, thus enabling the family to save and make investments.

Goals for Family Time

Studies have shown how little time fathers spend with their children, parents spend together with their children, and husbands and wives spend with each other. Trying to correct this can be very difficult for African-American families when the wife's and husband's income are needed to support the family. It can be almost impossible when one spouse has a day job and the other spouse has a night job.

However, that is one of the reasons that a family that prays together, dreams together, plans together, and takes action together has an advantage. God is an active member of such families. God can do the impossible. God does answer prayer. The problem of spending time together must be faced like any other family problem—with a commitment to resolve it.

Time spent together and family activities must be part of the plan. Royce Money's book *Building Stronger Families* (1984, pp. 50–51) is very helpful in dealing with the issue of families spending time together. His advice is to

Commit to regular family times together. I admire families who seem to have it all together when it comes to scheduling special times for them to be with one another. "Every Monday night we have family time, no matter what," a friend told me. Since I've promised you that I would be realistic and honest, I must say that this type of rigid routine is hard for me to sustain. My several attempts through the years to become more systematic with our family times are silent testimonies to my failure.

Yet, let me hasten to add that there is tremendous value in special times together that are planned ahead. I am convinced that they must be a part of a healthy Christian family life. The *way* those times are brought about, however, opens up several possibilities. For some families, the same night every week is workable. For others, the time will vary, perhaps being during the day on a weekend. Families with variable schedules may find it advantageous to sit down at the beginning of the month and determine their times together. Of course, the older the children, the more difficult the scheduling. But, it's not impossible, so don't give up.

. . . First, these times have to be planned. "Someday" or "as soon as" won't work. And don't get discouraged and give up when your plans are temporarily interrupted. Be flexible. Second, I firmly believe that in the dual parent family, the father should take the lead in working out the family times. A lot of Christian mothers do it by default, but it is much better for Dad to assume that responsibility.

Time should also be allocated for fellowship with friends and relatives. There should be time for doing housework and yard work to maintain the quality of our living conditions and the value of our property as home owners.

Health and Physical Goals

One of the areas that many families neglect is health issues. Usually, this area gets attention only when there is illness. If, however, we set goals that will make us good stewards of the life and health that God has given us, some illnesses and accidents can be avoided.

Every family should have a family physician. Family members should have regular physical checkups with the doctor advising how often. Family nutritional goals should be set. Time for exercise and relaxation should be planned. An understanding and practice of stress management benefits good health.

There should be a family program of accident prevention—removing toys and other objects from walkways inside and outside of your home, getting rid of dilapidated ladders and kitchen stools, avoiding overloading electrical systems, staying away from the use of extension cords, and not leaving young children unattended can help avoid accidents.

CONCLUSION

Establishing good family leadership in the home is crucial for the well-being of our families. Men must take the lead in ensuring such leadership. Husbands and wives working together must accept the wisdom of God in this area and look into His Word for guidance. They must be determined to receive the blessings of God for their family and be willing to be a family model that has godly leadership. When we do these things, our home, our family, our church, our nation, and our world will be a better place.

REFERENCES

1984. *The Holy Bible: New international version.* Grand Rapids: Zondervan.

MacArthur, J., Jr. 1994. *Different by design.* Wheaton, IL: Victor Books.

Meier, P., and R. Meier. 1981. *Family foundations. How to have a happy home.* Grand Rapids: Baker.

Money, R. 1984. *Building stronger families.* Wheaton, IL: Victor Books.

Richardson, W. 1991. Evangelizing Black males: Critical issues and how tos. In *The Black family: Past, present, and future,* edited by L. N. June. Grand Rapids: Zondervan.

Richardson, W. 1996. *Reclaiming the urban family.* Grand Rapids: Zondervan.

PART 3

DEALING WITH THE CRIMINAL JUSTICE SYSTEM

Kenneth McDaniel

Avoiding
Arrest
and Prison

KENNETH McDANIEL was born and raised in Asheville, North Carolina. He was graduated from North Carolina Central University with a bachelor of science degree in chemistry and physics. He received a doctor of law degree from North Carolina Central University. He is admitted to practice law in North Carolina and Pennsylvania. He is currently Assistant District Attorney in the Philadelphia District Attorney's Homicide Unit (a position he has held for nine-and-a-half years). He is married to Anila McDaniel, and they are the parents of seven children: Kenneth Jr., Peter, Luke, Psalm, Michael-David, Melissa, and Rasheeda.

Chapter 12

Kenneth McDaniel

Avoiding Arrest and Prison

INTRODUCTION

The purpose of this chapter is twofold. First, I will discuss what needs to be done in case of an arrest. Second, I will offer ideas on what can be done to avoid contact with the criminal justice system. Obviously, I would prefer not to have to discuss this first topic, but we need to because of the African-American's high incidence of contact with the criminal justice system.

Let us begin by assuming that on Monday morning you go to your doctor and the doctor looks at you and says, "You know you have a wart on your finger. In my personal opinion, we need to take you to the emergency room right now and amputate your arm." Because of your knowledge and experience, you are going to look at that doctor and calmly say, "Thank you, but I'm going to get a second opinion."

We must have the same attitude about the legal profession as we do about the medical profession.

WHAT TO DO IF YOU ARE ARRESTED

General Overview Regarding the Issue of Arrest

It is two o'clock in the morning and one of your friends calls to tell you (after watching the arrest) that John, a member of your family, has been arrested and taken away in handcuffs. What will happen next is that John will be taken into custody and processed. Within three-to-five days from the time of the processing there will be a preliminary hearing. After the preliminary hearing, if there is evidence to show that a crime was committed and that it is more than likely that John committed the crime, then he will be held over for trial. At that time, a bail request may be made. Weeks or months later, John (the defendant) will go to an arraignment where there is also the possibility of bail. At the arraignment, the defense attorney will be given evidence to show what the commonwealth or state has against John. Eventually there will be a trial. The trial may be a jury trial or an nonjury trial with only a judge. John will then be found either guilty or not guilty. If guilty, sentencing will occur. In sentencing the issue will be whether or not John goes to jail. If John goes to jail, the next procedure or step is the possibility of an appeal.

In the processing phase, your family member will be fingerprinted and photographs will be taken (height, full-face, and profile). There will also be other people at the police station who have been arrested. So if you go down to the police station immediately, you are not going to get much information. At the police administration building there is a public defender, an attorney, a district attorney, and a bail commissioner. Instead of going there, call either the public defender or the assistant district attorney and ask what happened. They will give you a summary of what your family member is there for, what the charge is, and what the bail is. You can also get this information from the sheriff's office.

If you call and say, "My name is Ken, my brother is in jail. What time are you bringing him up before the bail commissioner?" and it is 2 A.M., they will probably say, "He will be brought in before the bail commissioner at 12 P.M." There is no point in sitting there waiting for all those hours when you can be home thinking about other things you need to do.

When a person is incarcerated and while they are being processed, one of the things that is going to happen to them is that somebody from the service division of the court system is going to interview them in jail. Usually this person is the one who will allow your family member to call home. These are court officials who are neutral and who are pretty friendly and polite. They will talk to the person while he is in custody. They will ask some questions because they need to know certain things about the person in order to have bail set in their behalf. They will ask for name, address, employment status, and birthdate, which they will verify with a call to the home. If you are not there, they will not be able to verify the information and will not be sure what kind of bail to recommend.

Another critical factor when an arrest has been made is attitude. If you or some member of your family is arrested, you are naturally upset, but just because you are upset does not mean that you should lose your cool. For example, a neutral person comes to you saying, "I'm here because the court wants me to be here and I need to record some personal data on you because we need to report this to the bail commissioner so he can make a decision about your bail. What is your name?" Let's say, you replied, "I don't want to tell you." Then they say, "Where do you live?" You reply, "That is none of your business." Guess what? When the officials see on the form that you did not cooperate and that they cannot verify an address, you are definitely going to be in jail for a long time prior to a preliminary hearing. My point is that attitude does affect what may happen to you. When you go before the bail commissioner, attitude is important too. If you are very hostile and uncooperative, then they will set bail as high as they wish.

The Bail Process

Bail is the amount of money one must pay in order to secure the release of a person charged with a crime. Most offenses are bailable, with the exception of first-degree murder. If bail is set, the person can get out of jail. There is a window open twenty-four hours a day where you can pay the bail within the police-administration building. For the most part, you are required to pay ten percent of the amount of bail. For example, if bail is set at $100,000, then 10 percent of that is $10,000. When you post bail, and the case is over, the court system will take 30 percent of that bail which, in this example, will be $3,000 of the original 10 percent that you posted. Hence, you will get $7,000 back. One can also put up real-estate as bail. Using real estate is a bit different. With real estate, you must deal with the real value of your home. Say for example bail is $100,000. Your home must be worth $100,000 or you cannot use it for bail. If you live in a jurisdiction where you can post bail through the use of a bail bondsman, contact one as soon as possible.

Handling Being Arrested

The most important thing to remember is to be polite. Do not use profanity. Be the Christian you should be. Instruct your family and friends to be the same way. Have a cooperative attitude.

Sometimes people say that when they were arrested someone did not read them their rights. Let us say that the police caught you inside a safe. They brought you in and said, "You know, we don't have to read you your rights because we caught you." You are not there simply to give a statement because the police do not know who committed the crime—they know that you did it. Therefore, if no statement is given, or no statement is asked of you, then your rights usually are not read to you.

If you ask the officer, "Am I free to leave?" he or she might say, "No. You are under arrest. Is there a statement you want to make? If so, you have the right to remain silent. Anything you say can and may be used against you . . ." In this case, you have just been read your rights.

Faced with an arrest, you can do what you want in regard to giving a statement. I tell my children that under no circumstances should they give a statement until they talk to a lawyer. When have you read in the newspaper that police officers, public officials, and judicial officials who have been arrested have ever given a statement?

Finding a Good Lawyer

You should get a lawyer who knows his or her job—a specialist. I am not going to hire a dentist to do open-heart surgery on me. If I want a criminal lawyer, I am going to find criminal lawyers. This choosing starts with your asking around. It starts with your taking the time to look in the Yellow Pages.

Do not run to the first lawyer you hear about. Look around, ask questions. You can call a lawyer referral service and ask, "Can I get ten names of experienced trial lawyers?" Some churches and other organizations also have lists of attorneys. If available, use those resources. There are both excellent attorneys and poor attorneys. Therefore, it is important for you to ask questions when you go yourself or with that loved one to see an attorney.

Let me make a point about securing a lawyer by giving an example of buying a car. If you want to buy a car, you might go to someone and say, "Look I am too emotionally involved because I want this car so much, could you negotiate the price for me?" When you go to a lawyer's office, you may not be emotionally up to talking right then and there. So you may want someone else to assist you in taking care of this business—someone who will help you keep your mind clear because there are many questions that need to be asked. It is your life or your family member's life at stake. This arrest may result in jail and having a permanent record, and you need a clear head at this time.

One of the questions to ask a lawyer is: Do you try criminal cases? Other questions to ask are: What is your success rate? How are you doing? Do you win or lose? Do you negotiate? Are your clients getting good deals?

Can I check with your other clients? If you have anybody who went to jail, can I call them or find out about them? If there are people walking around free, can I talk to them? Do you have any news clippings about yourself and what you have done? Is there anybody else I can call to check up on you? You should ask these questions because you are hiring the lawyer. Treat your session with the lawyer as a job interview. You are paying the bill. It is your life. When you have found out about the lawyer's track record, say, "Okay, here are the facts of my case. What do you think you can do for me?"

Before you conclude your interview, ask if he or she practices appellate law. Let us be realistic about this. If you lose and go to jail, you are going to need an appellate lawyer.

In addition to questioning the lawyer about his or her record, ask about first-time-offender programs. Suppose you or your family member is charged with drunk driving or drug possession and it is a first offense. There are programs for people who have been charged with a felony but who have no criminal record. It is at the discretion of the district attorney's office whether you get into such programs, so ask about them. In the end, you may have to pay restitution or you may be placed on probation. If at the end of the probation time you have no violations, you will have no record.

These are things that you need to think about because if you have no prior record, chances are you will have no record when you finish—providing you do what they want you to do. If the lawyer does not know anything about such programs, please leave. You may be in the wrong place. Lawyers ought to be able to answer questions about first-time-offender programs for you, which will reduce your lawyer expenses because you would be diverted into a program and spared a trial and a lot of other things. So, it is critical to ask about such programs.

Negotiating a Lawyer's Fee

One of the critical questions to raise with a lawyer is the cost of his or her services. Throughout the United States there is the Canon of Professional Responsibility which lawyers who practice abide by, doing certain things that all lawyers have agreed on. One of those things that a lawyer cannot do is charge an excessive fee.

What is an excessive fee? A fee should be the customary charge for similar legal services in the locality in which you live. What does that mean? That means that you have to ask around. You need to know how much your lawyer charges for defending cases like yours. If you find out that the lawyer charged one person $2,000 and another $3,000 and wants to charge you $10,000 for the same thing, then you know that something is wrong. That wide a fee spread is not customary. You may like that lawyer and may want that person to represent you very much, but if the price does not seem right, you should check elsewhere.

Sometimes people pick an attorney after seeing a television advertisement. You often see TV commercials that say, "I represent so and so. I guarantee that if you come to me and we win, we all get paid. If we don't win, I don't get paid." While this may be true in injury cases, it is not true in a criminal case. In fact, the Canon of Professional Ethics says that lawyers cannot collect a contingent fee for representing a defendant in a criminal case because we cannot guarantee you a victory in a criminal case.

Besides a contingent fee, there are several other types of pay agreements. In criminal cases there are two basic types. One is a straight fee wherein the lawyer represents you on the charges of rape or murder or aggravated assault or whatever, from the preliminary trial through an appeal, and the total fee is $15,000. You pay the total amount. That type of fee, however, is not very smart for the client.

A second kind of fee is also a straight fee, but you enter into a negotiated written agreement and you pay as you go. For instance, you negotiate the fee for a preliminary hearing. After that, you negotiate a fee for the actual trial. Later you may want to negotiate a fee for an appeal. It is important to remember that in a straight-fee situation you are either paying a flat fee regardless of the process, or you are paying a so-called negotiated fee for each stage of the process.

Let us suppose that you go to the preliminary hearing and you discover that you do not like the way your lawyer asks questions. You do not feel that he or she is doing enough for you. You want to fire the lawyer, but you have already paid $10,000 to $15,000. How much do you get back when you fire the person? Only the amount that is in excess of a reasonable fee—in this situation the amount that he or she has not done any work for. But say you and the lawyer disagree about the value of the services performed up to the time of the preliminary hearing. You are stuck if you do not have a negotiated pay-as-you-go fee, and now you are going to have to go to the Fee Dispute Committee to discuss what the lawyer should receive. Further, say you are stuck with this dispute while a criminal case is going on. You are now sitting in court worrying about how much of that money you are going to get back so you can hire your next lawyer. Thus, it is not smart to go with the one lump-sum straight fee.

It is better to pay in stages. For example, if you pay $2,500 for a preliminary hearing and afterward you are not satisfied or the lawyer is not satisfied, that is it. You can get another lawyer. If you are satisfied, you keep going. At the trial stage, you will then have an opportunity to do that again. Once you get to the day of trial, however, judges are not going to let you fire your lawyer.

Perhaps an analogy will help. Suppose you are in the hospital for surgery and you were supposed to pay the doctor bill for that day. You did not do it and you are about to have the operation. Would you feel that the doctor will do his or her best work? That is the same thing with lawyers. It is a terrible feeling when you are sitting at the table fighting for your life and your lawyer is saying to the judge, "Judge, please, let me get out of this case. This guy didn't pay me." The judge then looks at the lawyer and says, "Sorry, Mr. Lawyer, you know better than that, you are stuck with this case. You're going to try this case, and you're going to have to represent him zealously." The point is, he or she probably will represent you zealously—I know a lot of lawyers who would. What I am trying to say to you is, why worry about money throughout the entire trial? It is a life we are talking about, so why go through this? Negotiate the fee up-front in an appropriate way.

Who Selects the Jury

In the event that a case goes to trial, how much influence does your attorney have in selecting the jury? The prosecutor and the defense attorney, with the assistance of the defendant, select the jury. If a juror is brought in, I, as the prosecutor, ask questions, and the defense attorney asks questions. The questions give you a feeling of what a prospective juror is like. Eventually, there is a meeting of the minds that this person would be a fair and impartial juror.

After the Trial

Let us assume that you or your loved one has been found guilty. You still may have another chance. For example, under Pennsylvania law the person who has been found guilty can have a postconviction hearing. At this hearing, the lawyer goes before the judge who tried the case and says, "I want a new trial for my client because of the following mistakes," which are listed in a petition. The judge looks at the petition, and your lawer as well as the prosecutor submit briefs. The judge may grant you a new trial.

The point is that the original trial may not be your last chance—there is sometimes another proceeding, and you need to be aware of it.

This postconviction proceeding is called a "postverdict motion." At this level you can use the same lawyer if you have been satisfied with him or her, or you can hire a new lawyer to look at everything your first lawyer did at the trial. Hiring a new lawyer is a precaution you may want to take in order to prepare yourself for what you have to do.

You should be prepared for one final procedure. If you are found not guilty, your lawyer can get the charges against you, which are printed, erased from your record as if they never existed.

Handling Disputes Between Lawyer and Client

There are times when you may want to fire your lawyer. If so, the lawyer has to give you back what he or she has not earned. If there is a written contract, and if you have given him or her $10,000 ($2,000 of which is for the preliminary hearing) and the firing occurs at the preliminary hearing, then it is clear that you get $8,000 back. You can then go to someone else. But if the issue is not as clear-cut (there is no negotiated pay-as-you-go fee plan), you can go to the Fee Dispute Committee of the Bar Association, submit a petition, submit to arbitration, and get your money back. The problem is that you might need the money right then and there. A better way is to set up a plan for payment in stages—the preliminary hearing, trial, appeal, and so forth. That way all your money is not tied up at one time. You can have definite dates when certain things are due to be paid. If not paid, the lawyer can walk away, or you can walk away.

By the way, you might want to tell the lawyer up-front, "I need a good lawyer, but I also need to get my son out of jail. I have a preliminary hearing he has to go to. What should I do?" A solution might be to ask the lawyer whether he or she will take an assignment of the bail as part of the fee. Here is how that works. Say your bail is $10,000, and you paid $1,000. At the end of the case, you get your $1,000 back minus 30 percent from the city, or $700. Now if the lawyer charges $700 for a preliminary hearing, and you assign that particular piece of paper over to the lawyer, you have paid your preliminary-hearing fee. Bail refund is as good as money in the bank, and some lawyers allow you to pay in this way.

After you have hired the attorney, you may want to ask, "Now, in the event we lose . . ." (I mention losing because you need to be prepared for it.) If you lose the case, there are a couple of things that may have occurred. First, the facts were totally against you and you were guilty. Second, the attorney made a mistake on something and you are disputing his or her competency. If the lawyer did not make a mistake, then let the same lawyer do the appeal. But if you feel that he or she made a mistake, you may need an appellate lawyer to look at the trial transcript. Appeal if you think you are entitled to a new trial.

If you have a public defender who is not representing you properly, ask to talk with the supervisor. Or ask the court to appoint someone else.

Client Guidelines

1. Respect your lawyer. After the preliminary hearing, your lawyer will receive a discovery package—a list of the witnesses, the facts, the statements, the lab reports, and other proof that the prosecution has against you or your loved one. At this time, the lawyer will sit down with you and go over everything that the state may have against you.

2. Be prepared for good news (that they may not be able to prove the case against you).

But also be prepared for bad news. Sometimes lawyers get information in the discovery package that points right at you. They have fingerprints on you, they have you on videotape, and they have eye witnesses.

3. Maintain a good attitude. Do not have the attitude that the lawyer must get you off the hook. This is the wrong attitude to have. You have to be prepared sometimes for the hard truth. Ask your lawyer what will happen if you do not get off. Ask how much time in prison you are going to get. Sometimes people do not do that. Then the trial comes, and they are shocked because nobody prepared them for the worst.

4. Pay your bill. Having a lawyer who is not happy because you have not paid your bill is a terrible situation to be in. A house divided cannot stand, and neither can a lawyer and client. A paid lawyer is a happy lawyer who will seek to develop a good relationship with you.

HOW TO STAY OUT OF TROUBLE

Tips on Avoiding the Criminal Justice System

While I have shared tips on how to prepare yourself or a family member in the event of an arrest, my ultimate hope is that you avoid the criminal justice system.

Realizing this, I now share what I believe can be done. I will speak particularly to young African-American males, who are most at risk for involvement with the criminal justice system.

I am not a criminologist or a sociologist. However, after twenty years as a prosecutor I can offer a few tips that if followed will lessen the chance of your arrest or death.

1. Avoid so-called friends who commit crimes. Sooner or later they will involve you.
2. If your friends in your presence commit crimes, make it clear to them and their victims that you are not involved.
3. Control your temper. Thousands of people are killed and injured because of anger.
4. Control your mouth in the presence of the police as well as your adversaries.
5. Sit in court to see the criminal justice system firsthand.
6. Tour a prison or morgue. Ask questions about why some of the people are there.
7. Avoid places where crimes occur. If you know that crimes occur in a particular place, why are you there?
8. Avoid alcohol and drugs. They will always control you. You will never control them.
9. Avoid drug houses. They will either be raided by the police or by others, resulting in your arrest or death.
10. If you get into a fight or argument with someone who tells you they will be back, do not stick around. They do come back.
11. If you are in school, stay in school. It is a rare thing to find people who attend school on a regular basis committing a crime.
12. If unemployed, seek some type of training or involve yourself in positive activities. Remember, without education, training, or employment, you have nothing to fall back on but crime.

Clifford E. Washington

Surviving
the Criminal
Justice System

CLIFFORD E. WASHINGTON is a human-resource administrator in the corporate offices of Family Bookstores, Inc., of Grand Rapids, Michigan. He holds a bachelor of arts degree in social science from Aquinas College and is pursuing a masters degree in organization development from Aquinas's Graduate School of Management. He attends Family Worship Center Church and is a member of Prison Fellowship. He resides in Grand Rapids, Michigan, with his wife, Denise, and their five children: Chris, Kymbirlee, Lanetta, Clifford II, and Jeshurun. His seventeen-year involvement with the criminal justice system included more than fourteen years of incarceration within the Michigan Department of Corrections.

Chapter 13
Clifford E. Washington

Surviving the Criminal Justice System

INTRODUCTION

In light of the nation's preoccupation with crime, the African-American male has become the one who fits most criminal profiles. If the American public were asked to define the typical criminal, or the characteristics of the person most likely to come into contact with the criminal justice system, most would undoubtedly agree that the resulting description would be that of an African-American male.

Such uncritical labeling threatens to make the term *African-American male* almost synonymous with the term *criminal*. Over and over the perception that the African-American male is prone to violence is reinforced by the media and often by self-defeating actions of our own design. However, it is not the purpose of this chapter to deal with the issue of how the African-American male is portrayed vis-à-vis the criminal justice system.

In this chapter, I will first define what the word *survive* means and how it is manifested in the Bible. Second, I will define and outline the elements of the criminal justice system. Third, I will share my personal involvement with the criminal justice system. Finally, I will suggest solutions that can be used to guide men in general, and the African-American male in particular, in how to survive the criminal justice system and become productive men of God. This will be done by my discussing what is necessary for treatment and recovery and by my sharing key ingredients that are necessary for preparing to live productively beyond the prison walls.

SURVIVAL DEFINED AND ITS BIBLICAL MANIFESTATIONS

Webster's Ninth New Collegiate Dictionary (1985) defines *survive* as (1) "to remain alive or in existence; to live on, and (2) to continue to function or prosper." From Genesis to Revelation there are numerous stories and parables, psalms, and other lessons of survival. Throughout history the desire to survive has led many God-fearing men to stray from the path that God intended for them. Yet God, who is infinite in love and gracious in mercy, knows how to correct and redirect us back into his presence to fulfill His purpose on this earth. Survival has not changed. It is as real to us today as it was in the Old Testament.

Biblical Abraham was to become the father of all nations, yet he was challenged with whether to trust God for his survival or tell a lie and say that Sarah, his wife, was his sister. His instinct to survive twice overruled his faith in God to deliver. Abraham, however, increased in faith and died believing that God would fulfill the promise He had made to him.

Job, a just and upright man, trusted wholeheartedly in God. Because of his will and need to survive physically, emotionally, and spiritually, he would not let any situation, problem, or even peer pressure separate him from God. Job was eventually restored to health and blessed beyond measure. He lived a long and noble life.

Saul had been a good king, but jealousy, wealth, and prestige, which he thought he needed to survive, overruled his obedience and faith in God. He plotted to take David's (the soon-to-be king of Israel) life. Saul, though, was blind to the things that God had already given him to enjoy. He was so obsessed with pursuing David that it proved fatal to him.

David was King of Israel and was called a man after God's own heart. Yet David had Uriah sent to war with the knowledge that he would be killed because David was in love with Uriah's wife. David's preoccupation with what he thought he needed to survive overruled his obedience to God. David later repented, however, and turned from his destructive past, was spared, and lived to be king.

We African-American men must turn back to our ancestors' hope of deliverance and first love—God himself. We must be willing to learn obedience, sacrifice, and waiting and relying on God to raise us up and allow us to be the men that He has called us to be. Scripture says that God is the one who raises one man up and brings another down. There is no quick way to get to the top. Make no doubt about it, our sin will find us out. We must be goal-oriented to succeed. The many lessons, stories, psalms and/or parables in the Scriptures provide answers and guidance to life's perplexing challenges and problems. It behooves us to take the wisdom and knowledge that Scripture gives and apply it to every aspect of our lives. This is true also of those who find themselves involved with the criminal justice system.

CRIMINAL JUSTICE SYSTEM DEFINED

The criminal justice system is defined as the structure, functions, and decision processes of those agencies that deal with the management of crime—the police, the courts, and corrections. This broad definition comes from the President's Commission on Law Enforcement and Administration of Justice, more commonly referred to as the President's Crime Commission. The commission, appointed by President Lyndon Johnson to study the structure of criminal justice administration and to make recommendations for change, has been in existence for over thirty years—since President Johnson in a message to the Eighty-ninth Congress (March 8, 1965) declared his so-called war on crime. Johnson commented that "crime had become a malignant enemy in America's midst" (Inciardi 1990, p. 22).

The evolution and transformation that the criminal justice system would undergo was no doubt beyond the scope of the imagination of the 1965 Johnson administration. Nor is it likely that they imagined the social variables that have accounted for the moral erosion that this nation has endured—such as rampant substance abuse, the emergence of hate groups, the availability of mass quantities of drugs, corrupt political leaders, civil unrest, violence, declining moral values, a gross preoccupation with sex, negative ethnocentrism, overcrowded courts and caseloads, negative law-enforcement tactics, all of which made for a shift in the general public away from God and Christianity. These variables also have had a devastating effect on African-American males, many of whom are made scapegoats or used as smoke screens to mask the sudden decline of the moral fabric of the entire nation.

The police, the courts, and corrections have distinct and varying functions that are nevertheless inherently connected and dependent. The first component of the criminal justice system is the police who represent the largest and most visible component and are the initial point of entry for anyone involved with the system. Police tasks and functions include the investigation of crimes, the enforcement of law, crime prevention, and protecting life and liberty. Their overall job or focus is to maintain law and order (Allen & Simonsen 1992).

The second component of the criminal justice system is the courts. The courts' major functions are the protecting of individual rights, the presiding over trials, the settling of disputes, the declaring of guilt or innocence, and the management of the sentence phase. The court also serves as a general forum for litigation. Because the courts are empowered to dismiss or render a verdict of not guilty, the court could be the end of the process for many. An example of the courts' protecting individual rights is the use of the jury. The right to a trial by an impartial jury is guaranteed to every citizen by the Sixth Amendment to the Constitution of the United States.

The Gospels relate the story of one of the oldest forms of trial by jury. Specifically, the book of John tells the story of a bound Jesus, wearing a crown of thorns and being led to Pilate by a cowardly mob to face a jury of high-ranking priests and officials. When asked of His guilt or innocence, the jury vehemently rendered their verdict by shouting, "Crucify him. Crucify him."

Despite the intentions of the framers of the Constitution, for those convicted, the Sixth Amendment offers little comfort in easing the feeling of their being "crucified." A conviction is as traumatic as the loss of a close family member through death. The individual in question experiences a deep sense of loss, shame, humiliation, isolation, and hopelessness. I know because I have experienced many of these things.

After the conviction lies the penalty or corrections phase of the sentence. Corrections is the third, most lasting, and most potentially devastating component of the criminal justice system. It is the prescribed incarceration time for one found duly convicted. Although a component, corrections represents a system all its own. For the purpose of this chapter, the term *corrections* will refer to state and federal correctional facilities.

The potential devastation inherent in this component is compounded for the African-American male because of the stigma that is attached to corrections. For many African-Americans who face lengthy sentences, the prison sentence is initially viewed as a badge of honor. For the majority of people, however, a prison sentence is a sure sign that one is a loser who cannot handle himself in a free society or does not care to distinguish between right or wrong. Consider the view from Scott, a fourteen-year-old corporate gang member from Detroit, Michigan, as described in Taylor (1990, pp. 52–53): "Prison is for mugs that make mistakes. . . . Prison is for clowns who can't handle the life."

The major function of corrections has been a continual source of debate among criminologists, politicians, social scientists, theologians, and law-enforcement officials. Those who represent the penalty phase of the criminal justice system are made up of two factions. First are those who believe that the sole purpose of corrections is for punishment, for retribution or repayment, or for protecting the public. This faction also believes that those who have been duly convicted should forfeit their right to any social standing or citizenship within the general community. To justify this belief, advocates of this view cite, as evidence of the necessity to "lock'em up and throw away the key," negatives such as the recidivism rate (the rate of those who return to correctional settings after being released) or some isolated, high-profile crime that shocked public sentiments. The second faction believes that the sole purpose of corrections is to offer those convicted the opportunity to reform or rehabilitate their lives in hopes of their eventually becoming a productive part of society.

For the African-American male, the need to survive the criminal justice system is compounded by the fact that we are constantly bombarded with negative media images of brothers. Social structures such as the very powerful media daily disseminate news that all too often equate the image of the African-American male with the criminal justice system. It is very rare that a success story concerning an individual who was once involved with the criminal justice system is published. Therefore, the uninformed or misinformed public is left with only negative impressions of those who have been affiliated with the criminal justice system.

PERSONAL INVOLVEMENT AND SURVIVAL

Prior to my eighteenth birthday, I came into contact with the third and most lasting component of the criminal justice system—corrections. Like many, my involvement with the first two components was very minimal. By minimal I mean that it only took a few minutes of gross indiscretion for me to make my initial contact with the police—I was arrested. In my case, however, this minimal affiliation resulted in a series of court appearances and hearings that led to a very lengthy prison sentence. The result was my serving over fourteen years as an inmate or "correctional client" with the Michigan Department of Corrections after having been convicted of armed robbery and assault with intent to do great bodily harm less than murder.

Originally, when asked how I survived the years that I was incarcerated I would reply: "By lying down at night and then getting up in the morning." It was only later, after giving my life to Christ, that I realized that it was only due to His goodness and mercy that I survived and was able to come out clothed, in my right mind, and with the use of all of my limbs.

Many, upon receiving a lengthy sentence, suffer severe psychological and emotional problems. They experience an inability to adjust, adapt, or assimilate into the general population of the correctional setting. I have seen an inordinate number of African-American males who suffer from this malady. These same individuals often enter the system with a dependency on alcohol or other drugs with most of their freedom having been centered on trying to obtain such. Successful treatment is often difficult. Such individuals often fall through the cracks or get lost on the paper trail and merely float around the system for years never taking part in any programming.

The correctional setting is a city within a city with a culture all its own. Because of the violence that surrounds the inmate population, many inmates become involved in the prison underworld, which is often just an extension of their activities carried over from the outside. Just as immigrants come to the United States bringing with them their own culture, customs, rites, and agendas, the same is true of the many different individuals who make up the prison setting. Stabbings with ice picks and other make-shift weapons have often left inmates severely injured. Violent deaths among prisoners have always been a fact of life. The homicide statistics in Michigan prisons, for example, for the years 1985 through my October 1990 release, were one homicide for the year 1990, four in 1989, six in 1988, six in 1987, seven in 1986, and four in 1985 (Michigan Department of Corrections 1994).

Because of the severity of the crimes of prisoners around me, I realized that I did not wish to continue such a life. I had no way, however, of knowing how drastically my sentence or involvement with the criminal justice system would impact my life. I credit a friend (now my wife) who was discipling me with helping me decide once and for all to turn from a life of crime. Her love for Christ and for others rekindled a burning need in me that constantly reminded me that I had to live a productive life.

At the beginning of my twelfth year of incarceration I gave my life to Christ and learned that in Him, I could be forgiven and that I could obtain a new lease on life. I did not realize the challenge that was facing me by declaring my new-found commitment in Christ within the correctional setting. Nor was I prepared for the loss of my status within the prison culture once I declared my faith. In retrospect, I am amazed at the thought of my having been confined in a prison with 950 other inmates where only an average of fifteen ever participated in weekly Bible studies.

Christianity was not and is not taken seriously by the inmate population or the majority of the correctional staff. Many inmates have been exposed to the Word of God in some form, yet for several reasons choose not to practice it. During a time of severe need, however, such as news of family death or disturbing news from the parole board, many can be seen seeking God's mercy and guidance. The inmate population typically views Christianity as a crutch or a cop-out; and those inmates who are born-again or profess to follow Christ are viewed as lacking both the strength and the mental and physical toughness that is necessary when incarcerated. The majority of the correctional staff view those who practice Christianity either as being involved in a master con designed to elicit sympathy or trying to paint one's situation in a positive light to ultimately gain freedom. Such individuals do not realize that Christianity complements and adds to our manhood; it does not subtract from it.

After everyone had recovered from the initial shock of my new-found Christianity, I was constantly questioned, and my sincerity and commitment to Christ became a source of debate among both inmates and staff. I believe that since the majority of inmates have at some time been exposed to Christ through a parent, a neighbor, or a significant relative, they are intimidated by a fellow inmate who has found Christ. Although they may have had a strong relationship with those who exposed them to Christ, they may not have understood or placed much value on what it means to follow Christ because this relative's Christianity came through only during selective times. Many, like myself, had not seen or known many African-American males of a similar age who had actively sought Christ. For the first time they see in a fellow prisoner what it means to follow Christ. They see someone with similar likes and dislikes, someone with whom they can identify.

Upon receiving my ten-to-forty-year sentence in August 1976 (which was lengthened twice before my eventual release), I can remember asking the judge whether or not he was sentencing me to years or to months. I am now convinced that the judge took that question as a sign of arrogance, although I was as serious as an eighteen-year-old could be. Not only was I serious, I was humiliated. I felt worthlessness, fear, pain, and loneliness. I clearly remember saying, "Oh Lord." Skinny, yet tough as nails, all I could think of was "Oh Lord." Little did I know, He was all I needed to be thinking of and "Oh Lord" was all that there was to be said. As I reflect back, that was not a strange request or statement for me because I had been raised in the Word of God. My dad was and is an associate pastor, and for as long as I can remember, he was constantly trying to impart the Word to me as well as to my siblings.

Proverbs 22:6 says: "Train up a child in the way he should go [and in keeping with his individual gift or bent], and when he is old he will not depart from it." Throughout my years of incarceration I was constantly reminded of this verse. This Scripture passage does not mean that once you instill the Word in children, they will automatically live for God. It does mean that as children and young people grow into adults and go through many changes and encounter circumstances that far exceed their capacity for understanding they will not depart from the Word. From the Word that was planted within us during our most impressionable years and when all else is said and done and the doubt, fear, loneliness, and mental anguish depart, a new creature emerges.

I am convinced that it was the prayers of others that kept me encouraged and able to get through all that I encountered. I was constantly reminded of the love that my family had for me, even though I felt their pain and fear in regard to my situation. I now realize that for the majority of those who are incarcerated, little consideration is given to those family members and friends who love us. They too are incarcerated along with us, so to speak. They often feel the loss of us as traumatically as we feel the loss of our freedom. Those of us who are incarcerated must learn that the consequences of our behavior or actions severely impact the lives of those who truly love and care for us. Those whose lives have been interrupted by a loved one's involvement with the criminal justice system are serving their own time in their own prison. They are counting the days just as the prisoner is counting the days. They too experience feelings of helplessness, worthlessness, loneliness, and pain. They cannot change the prisoner, they can only stand by and watch as the person makes poor decisions. They long for something good or positive to come out of this time of separation and waiting but have no control over the situation. The pain is eased when the prisoner finally realizes the choices he must make.

THE NEED FOR TREATMENT AND RECOVERY

Those currently housed in correctional settings must understand that they will have the opportunity of starting their lives all over again once they are released and that they must be responsible as to the direction their life will take. It does not matter what one has done in the past; one must take full advantage of every self-help and educational program that the system has to offer. Even the most antiquated prison systems have at least the most basic of educational programs available, which is the most logical place to start for treatment and recovery.

It is my belief that the most effective and lasting program is that of Christianity. By attending and becoming involved in the religious programs one will not be popular in the prison yard nor be an icon in the underworld, yet you will obtain the tools for a productive life of love, freedom, and prosperity. Accepting Christ makes for a stronger man. Romans 5:4, in part, states that trouble and sufferings produce patience and endurance that lead to maturity and strong character. What is needed most among the African-American males who are in the prison system is patience, endurance, and the proper frame of mind. The best source of these attributes is the Word of God.

The prison setting is fertile ground for a new life for those who have become disenfranchised and have been cast out. The prison system offers countless opportunities for the Word of God to come forth to be planted in the lives of those whom society has all too often written off. The Word of God constantly reminds us that we are to go out and impel others to come to Christ.

I encourage everyone to reach out in love to encourage those in prison who may reenter society. I say to prisoners: "Do not give up."

PREPARING FOR PRODUCTIVE LIVING BEYOND PRISON WALLS

There are four key ingredients in preparing to live productively beyond prison. First, accept responsibility for your criminal behavior. Accepting responsibility is a must if one is to grow from the experience— just as is asking God for forgiveness. I know and have heard all the reasons and situations that have led men to become entangled in the criminal justice web. Nevertheless, before you are released, please take full responsibility for *your* own actions. Only then will you be able to put prison behind you. Then get on with what it is that God has in store for you.

Much of what we as African-American men go through is brought on by impulsive behavior. In preparing for reentry into society, I recommend that each and every person, prior to the parole hearing, successfully complete group therapy for impulse control. Most prison systems offer this program and the majority make completing it a mandatory requirement prior to consideration for parole or any type of release. Learning to recognize impulses that can bring on destructive behavior is what this program is all about. Once you are able to recognize these impulses, you will be in a better position to effectively address them before they escalate into further self-defeating behaviors.

Second, have realistic expectations, especially as to employment opportunities. One of the biggest misconceptions that I experienced was that upon release from prison I would be able to immediately become gainfully employed. Although I was able to find employment, it was what I considered to be less than "gainful." I quickly learned, however, that I had an advantage over most of the other employees. It seemed that the positive work habits that I had developed by working for $2.50 a day on the public work crews the last five years of my sentence set me apart from the employees who had not benefited from the grueling training that I had endured.

Third, seek a mentor or someone who is able to disciple you. Seek out a career mentor or a mentor in general—preferably in a local church or possibly through the prison ministry that is available in the institution that you are about to be released from. I have learned that true discipleship and networking are often the most valuable tools that we as African-American males can utilize. Most prison ministries have a strong discipleship program made up of strong volunteers and brothers in the Lord—notably, ex-offenders. Who can better help guide and disciple you than one who has been through it?

Fourth, seek a personal relationship with the Lord. We often try everything under the sun only to finally realize that we have failed miserably. But God is gracious and merciful and abounding in forgiveness. Christianity adds to our manhood. Being a Christian in prison may not be easy, yet it is rewarding.

How does one accept Christ and begin a personal relationship with Him? The Bible is clear on this matter. It says that if we confess (agree) with our mouth the Lord Jesus and *believe* in our hearts that God has raised Him (Jesus Christ) from the dead, we shall be saved (Romans 10:9–10). Thus, if we say to God, "I believe in You and Your Son, Jesus Christ," we become a Christian.

CONCLUSION

The goal of this chapter has been to convey a message of hope and inspiration to those who may have been touched, in any way, by the criminal justice system. With the moral fabric of the United States at an all-time low, we will be faced within the next twenty years with a growing number of ex-offenders. This group will have survived the criminal justice system. Whether or not the survival was positive or negative will depend on their successful reentry into society and our willingness to assist them. This group will be mostly males between the ages of twenty-seven and forty who will come from varying sociological backgrounds and be overwhelmingly African-American. Consider the following statistics: The total population of the United States in 1990 was 248,709,873, according to the Census Bureau. In 1990, 2.35 percent of the adult population was under correctional supervision, that is, in prison, on probation, or on parole. African-American males, however, represented 1,634,000 or 38 percent of the total adult population under correctional supervision (Department of Justice 1990).

For most, your goals and aspirations will be unrealistic, having been shaped by the things that you have learned, heard, or seen during your years of incarceration. The things that you hold dear will have developed as a result of, or in response to, the treatment you did or did not receive while incarcerated. The most productive years of your lives will have been spent in prison. We must, however, believe that the billion-dollar structures we as taxpayers erect to house those who have been convicted (duly or otherwise) are filled with humans who can reenter society in a productive way.

REFERENCES

Allen, H. E., and C. E. Simonsen. 1992. *Corrections in America.* 6th ed. New York: Macmillan.

Inciardi, J. A. 1990. *Criminal justice.* 3d ed. Orlando, FL: Harcourt, Brace, Jovanovich.

Public Information and Communications. 1994. *Prisoners in Michigan.* Lansing: Michigan Department of Corrections.

Taylor, C. S. 1990. *Dangerous society.* East Lansing: Michigan State University Press.

U.S. Department of Justice. 1990. *Correctional populations in the United States.* Washington, DC: Office of Justice Programs–Bureau of Justice Statistics.

Webster's ninth new collegiate dictionary. 1985. Springfield, MA: Merriam-Webster.

PART 4

FACING
CONTEMPORARY
CHALLENGES

Warren E. Williams

Concepts
of
Manhood

WARREN E. WILLIAMS was born in and grew up in Houston, Texas. He earned a bachelor of science and a master of science degree in biology from Texas Southern University and a doctorate of philosophy degree from the University of Illinois, Urbana-Champaign. He is currently studying for a master of arts in theological studies at the Houston Graduate School of Theology. Warren was formerly Chair of the Department of Biology, and is currently a professor at Texas Southern University. He has published in the area of biology and has had several years of funded research from the National Institutes of Health. He is married to Dr. Patricia A. R. Williams, and they are the parents of Jerrel, Jaclyn, and Julian. Warren is a licensed minister and a member of the Wheeler Avenue Baptist Church in Houston, Texas. He and his wife work with the Wedding Council of the church, and they have conducted several Marriage Retreats for various churches.

Chapter 14

Warren E. Williams

Concepts of Manhood

When I was a child, I talked like a child, I thought like a child, I reasoned like a child. When I became a man, I put childish ways behind me. (1 Corinthians 13:11)

Over and over, today's male adolescents are exhorted by phrases such as "be a man," "take it like a man," "you're a man." In like manner, preadolescence offers no exemption. The phrase, *Momma's little man*, followed by a matronly hug is continually a source of embarrassment. For a young Black male, the thought that he is "not acting in a manly manner" (Andelin 1972) is considered to be a grave insult, the latter adjective not being coincidental.

This chapter offers an examination of Christian versus worldly values regarding the concept of manhood. In doing so, the example that will be highlighted will be that of Jesus Christ because the challenge confronting society today is how one develops into manhood generally and Christian manhood in particular.

THE MASCULINITY PATTERN

Simply inheriting x and y sex chromosomes and therefore being born male does not lead to an individual's becoming a man in the eyes of society or God. Genesis 1:27 states: "So God created man in his own image, in the image of God created he him, male and female created he them." Consider that Scripture, a glorious start filled with unlimited potential was given to humankind, and the male in particular, by God the Creator.

But with this beginning, a tremendous responsibility was also inherited. Perhaps the greatest unpursued questions in the world are: What ingredients were embodied in this created image? With what masculine traits did God endow man? and, How closely have we come to fulfilling this responsibility?

The thesis that I wish to set forth is this: The male of the species has fallen short of completing the tasks set forth for him by God because he has been diverted from his physical, mental, and spiritual inheritance. As a means of examining this thesis, one might consider what the world generally perceives as masculinity.

From the world's perspective, a masculine man is aggressive and decisive, and he possesses an excessive amount of drive. In addition to behavior patterns, a masculine man displays an impressive, muscular body that may be idolized by women and people in general. Being masculine, according to A. P. Andelin (1972) in *Man of Steel and Velvet* is to be characterized by qualities encompassed within the areas of physical traits, moral character, and marketablility.

First, with respect to physical traits, men should possess endurance and a masculine manner, the latter being especially derived from an inner attitude that is a trait to be elaborated upon in more detail.

Second, masculine traits of character—aggressiveness and drive—should not be an outgrowth of selfish intent. Personal goals, especially, should be approached with a sense of family or community good. While decisions should be made both firmly and promptly, they should always be based on an "in-depth knowledge of relevant facts and consequences of various alternatives" (p. 118). A man should not be "easily moved or shaken from his convictions or decisions" (p. 118), particularly when his thoughts or actions have been spiritually developed and weighed. As the leader of his family, a man should be determined and resolute, not easily deterred from his goals or objectives. He does not "give up, quit, relinquish, or surrender under pressure of individuals or circumstances" (p. 119). Thus, this characteristic is only fully realized in the face of opposition. A man should possess courage, that is, "that quality of mind which enables one to meet danger and difficulties with firmness and strength of spirit. He should be free of fear based upon experience or faith" (p. 115).

Third, a man should possess marketability. He should seek to master that "knowledge, skill and ability required to earn a living, to perform work skillfully and successfully lead his family. In a like manner, a man should bear tenderness, kindness, generosity and patience, be devoted to the care and protection of women and children, chivalrous, attentive and respectful to women, and humble" (Andelin 1972, p. 120).

The traits that Andelin identifies are those that correspond, primarily, with worldly expectations. The life of Christ, however, brings to bear a different "twist" on the concept of masculinity. This will be discussed in the next section.

JESUS CHRIST, THE SUPREME MODEL OF MANHOOD

Since God, according to the Bible, created man in His image, Jesus' masculine traits are indeed worthy of study. When we study Jesus, we find that He was decisive and direct when confronted with evil (John 9:14). He was always *firm* and *forthright* regarding His position on situations (Mark 2:10). When confronted with differences and possible conflicts, Jesus was honest and direct (Luke 22:48). Regarding courage and resoluteness, He had an earthly task to complete and its completion was to require physical bravery and suffering, but the necessity of the task (the Atonement, John 8:27ff.) and will of His Father buttressed His spirit (John 17:23ff.). Jesus displayed humility (Matthew 20:28) and consideration for the salvation of all (John 4:27; Matthew 19:14; Mark 9:37, 10:16). Andelin (1972, p. 14) notes regarding Jesus that

> Never did He lose sight of His responsibility to complete "the work He was sent to do." He maintained His devotion to it until the end when He said, "It is finished . . ." He had the moral courage to introduce ideals and standards which were in conflict with popular teachings of His day.
>
> He dedicated His life to the service and salvation of others, lifting people to higher planes of thought and living. He was indeed a builder of society for His day and for all eternity . . . His character was spotless . . . He was eager and enthusiastic about life. . . . He had humility . . . and with this humility there was a self-dignity which commanded respect.

THOUGHTS ON TEACHING MASCULINITY

If Jesus' masculinity is used as a model, then we must teach young males how to

• Be decisive and forceful in taking a stand against evil

- Operate in the context of established principles and be firm therein
- Be *honest* in relating to and representing themselves to others

Annetta Bridges (1973, p. 97) summarizes this need as follows:

> It takes men to build men ... genuine men who have proven their manhood and who don't need to go around parading it everyday ... [a genuine man who] doesn't have to bolster his courage with alcohol or to push his wife and children around; being considerate, protective, concerned and confident and by demonstrating it ... A boy should be taught self-respect and confidence so that he doesn't feel compelled to draw attention to himself the rest of his life.

One problem of developing young boys into godly men comes in determining who is to be the role model. Many youths of today are not in or are not placing themselves in an environment conducive to an initial appreciation for how the Jesus of the New Testament has any relevance to their day-to-day survival. Thus, Christian attributes must be found in men who are willing to be wherever the boy is to be found.

A. H. Bridges (1973, p. 98) suggests that "the only way he'll become a man is for somebody to show him the way." African-American men draw positive role examples from a variety of sources: A hard-working grandfather, a successful athlete on television, a dedicated social worker, a respected older brother, an involved community leader, a good neighbor, and last but not least, a dedicated churchman (Walker 1992, p. 25). This suggests that we need to establish mentoring between young males and mature godly men, be they churchmen or fathers in Christian homes.

THE MANHOOD PATTERN

William Lawson, pastor of Wheeler Avenue Baptist Church in Houston, sees biblical manhood as including three areas. First, according to Lawson (1994), man is defined as being part of a team. Thus, though man has been given the charge to provide and defend, he cannot bear or nurture life into being.

Second, man has been given, and must recognize, a mission or purpose. That is, he is never to operate on the basis of what he wants for himself. Of course, selfishness, wanting to run or be in charge of oneself and not allowing God's will to predominate is what was encompassed within the first sin. "Man at his worst is concerned about his own wealth, profit, or power. At his best, man views himself within his mission of 'Who I am in the realm of life,'" according to Lawson. Therefore, man is made to fulfill a purpose.

Our purpose or mission has also been shared with us in God's law, the Ten Commandments. There is nothing in the Ten Commandments that says for us to look out for number one. Rather we are advised as to our appropriate relationship to the one true God (Exodus 20:3–8; Acts 5:29; 17:29–31; James 5:12; Hebrews 10:25) and to our parents (Exodus 20:12, cf. Ephesians 6:1–3; Colossians 3:20), yielding to the basis for honorable family life and to one another (Exodus 20:13–17, cf. Romans 13:9–10; James 2:11; Ephesians 4:25; Romans 7:7; Ephesians 5:3–5; James 4:1–2). This has been summarized briefly but beautifully in Micah 6:8: "He has showed you, O man, what is good. And what does the Lord require of you? To act justly and to love mercy and to walk humbly with your God."

Third, man is seen as being responsible for the welfare of small ones, for a family, for providing a home and especially for the establishment of ideals and principles in that home. Again, quoting Lawson, "man is to see to it that families are produced and nurtured, yielding productive citizens" who individually have a mature relationship with God. Man is basically responsible for seeing to it that each succeeding generation is better than the preceding one. For as man seeks to truly know more of God, God reveals more of Himself to man. Accordingly, manhood involves fulfilling a purpose as part of a team with the aim of providing for the good of others.

THOUGHTS ON TRANSMITTING MANHOOD

Having outlined the biblical standard, how does one make such biblical concepts applicable or relevant to something as basic as personal survival, possibly from moment to moment? To be sure, the challenges and patterns in the worldly system direct us as men in a manner counter to the biblical standards. Writers agree that manhood cannot simply be left to rhetoric or an inward, nonactive desire. "You can't simply tell a kid," as Lawson states, that "he has been influenced for too long by someone else who has told him that you can make more money by selling drugs than you can by getting a job." The competition is too stiff. Most authorities agree that boys must have the opportunity to listen, to watch, and be led by men, specifically men who sincerely practice a Christian value system.

They do not automatically have an inner voice that says *No*. And the reason is that they have not been shown how to say no or why saying no is more profitable in the long run.

It should be emphasized that mentors should have a true concern. In most cases, there will exist an initial attitude of resentment or suspicion by the young male, and why should there not be? To a large extent, society in general, and Black society, in particular, has failed regarding this point because of chasing after the "dangling gold carrot." Thus, the values of the world are emphasized or embraced and the kid on the street who only wants to survive is but a victim of our selfishness.

USING THE RITES-OF-PASSAGE CONCEPT TO TEACH MANHOOD

The concept of a rite of passage is thousands of years old. As described by Oba Chapman, the director of the Rites-of-Passage Program at Wheeler Avenue Baptist Church (WABC), boys age ten to eleven were taken from their tribal villages to "bush camps" for a period of four to five rains (rainy seasons or years). There they were literally "educated" in the ways of a man. In this place, the "boy becoming man" is of highest priority.

As described by Jawanza Kunjufu (1989), such programs should include an understanding of African history, spirituality, economics, politics, career development, citizenship, community involvement, and physical development, and should operate within an African frame of reference and belief in *Nguzo Saba*—a Black value system.

Lawson, in analyzing WABC's and other similar programs, views them as providing harvest at the end of one, two, or three years (see Proverbs 22:6). The concepts of reverence, respect, and discipline are heard continuously by the boys—specifically, reverence for the God who has made and sustains you; respect for parents, women, and children; and discipline for yourself in becoming and existing according to God's will for you as a man "made in His own image." Thus, the developing man-child has a packet of values that he can systematize. Therefore, it is the hope that in due time, he chooses to invest in himself rather than to dilute himself with drugs, to choose marriage rather than to shack-up. While boys are not fully developed by such programs within two or more years, nevertheless a "seed package" is planted.

Lawson also states that everyone, Christian and non-Christian alike, is being tossed and thrown. The hope is that there will be a friendly receiver. Quite frequently, when life pitches us, an unfriendly receiver catches us and we are given a wrong set of values. But if Christian mentors are deliberately trying to position themselves, then when this boy or young man comes flying through life, they can catch him. Somebody will catch him, and somebody will influence him. Thus, we must be out there trying to catch that boy and assist him in becoming a man.

THE RULE OF SELF-ESTEEM AND SELF-DEVELOPMENT

In fully accepting and understanding our role as men, an in-depth awareness of our worth is of utmost importance. A man must therefore be secure in who he is (Romans 10:9; 1 Peter 2:9; Romans 8:17). It is difficult for an individual to have self-respect if the rest of the world seems to believe that he or she is dumb, ugly, lazy, boring, uncreative, or undesirable. Given the legacy of treatment in America, racial-ethnic groups have often felt that the rest of the world believed these negative things about them. Thus, Blacks often compartmentalize their self-esteem. Compartmentalizing enables one to accept himself or herself but reject their larger ethnic group, which is associated with the negative images that the dominant society has of them (Walker 1992).

Stated quite succinctly, Kunjufu (1989) indicated that until people know whose they are—God's child—and who they are—African or African-American—they will continue to exist in the wilderness of the world's value systems. Of course, the problem today is that too many young African-American males are not aware of their value to God and certainly not aware of their self-worth. This problem is compounded when this same individual becomes ashamed of himself, wherein he reverts to the solution of Adam and Eve, that of becoming hidden from himself and others (see Genesis 3:7–8).

William Hulme (1973, p. 21) has suggested three ways in which we try to protect ourselves from exposure. We all express profound distrust of human nature; i.e., others will hurt me if they can, therefore, I must not allow myself to become vulnerable. These three ways are

1. Withdrawal: You cannot see me if I do not get close to you, and if you cannot see me, you cannot hurt me. Here shaky confidence is hidden behind an "air of aloofness"; a true need for others is hidden behind a facade of self-sufficiency.

2. Servile Attachment: This individual concentrates on making friendly and helpful overtures to others, a process yielding a superficial loyalty and a smothered individuality.

3. Attack: Here, motivated by fear, one seeks to "go after others before they come after you." After all, this is the "way of the world." For if I am this way, then they must be this way also. Thus, life becomes merely a competitive business where survival is erroneously thought to depend on getting the best of someone else.

One possible understanding of this dilemma of not knowing ourselves has been offered by Kunjufu (1989) who lists the factors that best contribute to developing self-esteem: our relationship with God; unconditional love from parents; high expectations (from teachers, mentors, and so forth); feeling good about our race; and identifying talents, previous accomplishments, and career goals. The more of these factors we have working for us, the more stable and secure is our self-esteem.

How is a young male to know these things? The answer is that mentors must be present to guide our young males to a discovery of their true worth, especially in the eyes of God. Continuously the Bible admonishes us to "love your neighbor as yourself." Without the latter, the former cannot be accomplished. Also to be remembered is the fact that God accepts us in an imperfect state (John 13:20). In summarizing this dilemma, Jeremiah A. Wright Jr. (1993, p. 151) asks this question:

What makes you so strong, black people? No other race was brought to this country in chains. No other race had laws passed making it a crime to teach them how to read. No other race had skin color as the determining factor of their servitude and their employability. No other race was hounded and haunted when they wanted to be free. No other race was physically mutilated to identify them as property, not people. No other race was lied to and lied on like the African race. No other race had its names taken away in addition to its language and music. No other race has been denied more and deprived of more, treated as badly and treated as less than human. No other race was treated like the Africans were treated, and yet no other race has done so much after starting out with so little, defying all of the odds and breaking all of the records. What makes you so strong, black people?

But then Wright answers his own question by saying that "our strength comes from the Spirit of God." This, indeed, must be our source for the task of reminding today's youth of who they are in Christ.

SPIRITUAL DEVELOPMENT

Finally, if young males of today are to discover biblical standards of manhood, there must be the spiritual development of this "pro-man," or nascent, adult male. Again, God allows us to visit His perfect role model in knowing His Son:

> He knew who He was, what He was about, and what He was to accomplish. He could act with great gentleness and genuine compassion toward a widow, the sick, or needy; but, when confronted by bigotry and hypocrisy, His white-hot anger could blaze with righteous indignation. He was deeply rooted in prayer. He never compromised His submission to the will of His Father—Jesus' love knew no bounds and His forgiveness no limits. (Cole 1992, p. 30)

SUMMARY

This chapter has examined the world's standards of manhood and compared them with those revealed to us in Scripture. Problems of contrast were elucidated and suggested pathways leading to a rediscovery of the true role of men regarding their responsibility as "caretakers of creation" individually, as family leaders, and corporately were given. Jesus Christ is given as the ultimate example but the need for Christ-led "friendly receivers" (mentors) is also greatly stressed.

REFERENCES

Andelin, A. P. 1972. *Man of steel and velvet*. Pierce City, MO: Pacific Press Santa Barbara.

Bridges, A. H. 1973. Help your son become a man. In *For men only,* edited by J. A. Peterson. Wheaton, IL: Tyndale House.

Chapman, Oba. 1994. Co-director of the Rites of Passage program at Wheeler Avenue Baptist Church, Houston. Personal interview.

Cole, E. L. 1992. *On becoming a real man*. Nashville: Thomas Nelson.

1984. *The holy Bible: New international version*. Grand Rapids: Zondervan.

Hulme, W. 1973. Remove that wall. In *For men only*, edited by J. A. Peterson. Wheaton, IL: Tyndale House.

Kunjufu, J. 1989. *A talk with Jawanza: Critical issues in educating African American youth*. Chicago: African American Images.

Lawson, William A. 1994. Pastor of Wheeler Avenue Baptist Church, Houston. Personal interview.

Walker, C. 1992. *Biblical counseling with African-Americans*. Grand Rapids: Zondervan.

Wright, J. A., Jr. 1993. *What makes you so strong*? Valley Forge, PA: Judson Press.

John M. Wallace Jr.

Rebuilding
the Walls:
An Action Plan

JOHN M. WALLACE JR. was born and grew up in Pittsburgh, Pennsylvania. He received a bachelor of arts degree in sociology at the University of Chicago, a master of arts degree and a doctor of philosophy degree in sociology at the University of Michigan. Currently, John is Assistant Professor of Social Work and Research Associate at the Institute for Social Research at the University of Michigan, Ann Arbor. He is a member of Christian Love Fellowship (Ypsilanti, Michigan) and is involved with teaching and young-adult ministry. John is married to Cynthia and they have four children: Lauren, Linnea, and twins Lydia and John.

Chapter 15

John M. Wallace Jr.

Rebuilding the Walls:
An Action Plan

An endangered species is, according to Webster, "a class of individuals having common attributes and designated by a common name . . . [which is] in danger or peril of probable harm or loss." This description applies in a metaphorical sense to the current status of young Black males in contemporary American society. They have been mis-educated by the educational system, mishandled by the criminal-justice system, mislabeled by the mental-health system, and mistreated by the social-welfare system. All the major institutions of American society have failed to respond appropriately and effectively to their multiple needs and problems. (Gibbs 1988, pp. 1–2)

Rescue those being led away to death; hold back those staggering toward slaughter. If you say, "But we knew nothing about this," does not he who weighs the heart perceive it? Does not he who guards your life know it? Will he not repay each person according to what he has done? (Proverbs 24:11–12)

INTRODUCTION AND OVERVIEW

The quotes above present a tremendous challenge to Christians in general and to African-American Christians in particular. The first quote speaks to the status and well-being of African-American young men. If African-American males are an endangered species, as the quote states, the future of African-American families, African-American communities, and indeed, the future of America is endangered as well. While acknowledging the possible validity of Gibbs' quote, many people, both Black and White, Christian and non-Christian, have simply resigned themselves to accept its implied conclusion—the ultimate extinction of African-American men.

The second quote, the words of Solomon, provides the biblical response to the crisis presented in the first quote. Christians—followers of Christ—do not have the luxury of accepting the pronouncement concerning the extinction of African-American men. We are commanded by the Word of God to embark on a mission to rescue those whom much of society has written off as lost. In fact, on Judgment Day God will ask, "What did you do to rescue those being led away to death, what did you do to halt those staggering toward slaughter, what did you do to prevent the extinction of the endangered species." Proverbs 24:12 suggests that God will not accept excuses on that day; our reward will be contingent on our response to the needs of those headed for destruction. In sum, Gibbs speaks to what is; Solomon speaks to what, for Christians, must be.

In order to rescue African-American men, we, as African-Amercan men, must accurately assess and effectively eliminate the threats to our continued existence. With this goal in mind, the purpose of this chapter is threefold: (1) to discuss briefly a number of the problems indicative of the condition of African-American males; (2) to identify the root source of these problems; and (3) to present an action strategy to eliminate these problems and restorate African-American men, families, and communities.

Much of the following discussion is directed explicitly toward African-American males; nevertheless, it should be noted from the outset that the information transcends both gender and race. The true body of Christ has no color distinctions, only a commitment to Jesus Christ as Savior and Lord. As noted by the apostle Paul, "The body is a unit, though it is made up of many parts; and though all its parts are many, they form one body" (1 Corinthians 12:12). "If one part suffers, every part suffers with it . . ." (1 Corinthians 12:26). The suffering of the African-American male part of the body is to the detriment of the whole body; accordingly, the entire body has a vested interest in the salvation and restoration of African-American males.

SOCIAL PROBLEMS AND AFRICAN-AMERICAN MEN

Myriad problems disproportionately impact the lives of African-Americans generally and African-American men in particular. For example, research consistently suggests that Black male unemployment is two to three times that of White males (Farley & Allen 1989; Majors & Gordon 1994) and that this gap has increased over time. In light of the shift in our economy from manufacturing to service, the future looks bleak for African-American men, particularly those with limited education and few skills.

Linked to the substantial race difference in employment is the fact that Black males earn less than do White males within virtually every educational category. For example, the average income of a White male with a high school diploma is $26,526 compared with the Black male average of $20, 271. Related to differences in employment, earnings, and racist hiring practices of the past and present, there are substantial differences in net worth, where net worth is defined as the sum of one's assets minus one's liabilities. The average net worth for African-American families is $4,604 compared with $44,408 for White families (U.S. Census 1994).

Perhaps as a result of substantial race differences in socioeconomic status, employment, and related factors there are also substantial race differences in health (Williams & Collins 1995). For example, African-American men have life expectancies more than eight years shorter than White males as well as higher rates of sickness and death from virtually every major cause including heart disease, cancer, stroke, diabetes, and cirrhosis (National Center for Health Statistics 1993). African-American males are also much more likely than White males to die from two of the most socially stigmatized causes of death: HIV infection (twice as likely) and homicide (sixteen times as likely). In fact, an examination of death rates between 1900 and 1995 indicates that the difference between the Black and White male deaths has increased over time and currently is at its highest point (Williams & Collins 1995).

One of the most highly visible social problems as we approach the twenty-first century is the level of involvement of African-American men in the criminal justice system. For example, almost one in four African-American males between the ages of twenty and twenty-nine are involved with the criminal-justice system (i.e., in jail, in prison, on parole, or on probation) (Mauer 1994). Further, although African-American males make up only about 6 percent of the U.S. population, they comprise approximately

44 percent of all prisoners and 40 percent of those on death row (Mauer 1994). In addition to the social cost of removing these men from families and communities, the financial cost of supporting them in the criminal justice system is tremendous. Each year Americans spend more than $75.5 billion on police and corrections (i.e., $299 per year for every man, woman, and child in America); and in Washington, D.C., a city that is overwhelmingly African-American, this figure is $1,261 dollars per year (U.S. Census 1994). Although much of the race disparity in crime can be attributed to race differences in socioeconomic status, there is evidence to suggest that African-American men are more likely than White men to be arrested, incarcerated, and harshly punished for the same crime (Mauer 1994).

For virtually every indicator of mental, physical, economic, and social health and well-being, African-American males lag behind nearly every other group in society. For a detailed discussion of these and related issues I refer the reader to a number of publications (e.g., U.S. Census 1994 or the current edition; Farley & Allen 1987; Gibbs 1988; Majors & Gordon 1994).

THE ROOT OF THE PROBLEM

What is the solution to the following simple mathematical equation?

$$\frac{3}{2}$$

The answer, of course, depends on properly identifying the problem.

For addition-oriented persons, the answer is five. For those more inclined toward subtraction, the answer is one. For those with a proclivity toward multiplication, the answer would be six. Clearly, the solution to the problems of African-American men, our nation, and indeed the world, depends on the proper identification of those problems. The perspective of Christians is that while racism, addiction, unemployment, and other social problems may exist, they are ultimately the physical manifestation of an underlying spiritual problem. Based on the Word of God, humankind's root problem is sin—disobedience to God's law. The behaviors and conditions that we see manifested every day are simply the fruit of the root—symptoms of the underlying problem.

The origin of humankind's real problem, sin, can be traced back to the Garden of Eden. According to Scripture, God placed Adam and Eve in the Garden with only one restriction—not to eat from the tree of the knowledge of good and evil. When Satan deceived them into disobeying God and into eating from the tree, sin and its result, social problems and ultimately death, entered the world. Satan continues today to deceive humans, and the result is still the same. Homicide, substance abuse, broken families, racism, poverty, and society's other ills are all ultimately the result of man's violation of God's laws—sin.

Since Eden, Satan has used three primary weapons to cause humans to sin: (1) the lust of the flesh, (2) the lust of the eye, and (3) the pride of life. The lust of the flesh refers to a preoccupation with gratifying or fulfilling one's physical desires (e.g., food, sex, rest). The lust of the eye refers to a craving for material things (e.g., cars, clothes, jewelry). The pride of life refers to an inordinate concern with one's status, importance, and position in life (e.g., academic degrees, place of employment, business contacts).

The Bible provides numerous examples of Satan's use of one or more of these weapons; three are recounted here for illustrative purposes. The first recorded attack in which Satan utilized his arsenal is recorded in Genesis 3. Satan approached Eve with a very simple question, "Did God really say, 'You must not eat from any tree in the garden'?" Her response was that they were permitted to eat from every tree except one; eating from the forbidden tree would result in death. True to form, Satan refutes what God said and uses one of his three weapons—the pride of life—to tempt Eve to sin. He tells her that eating the fruit will not bring death, rather "when you eat of it [the fruit] your eyes will be opened, and you will be like God, knowing good and evil" (v. 5). Genesis 3:6 clearly summarizes the threefold temptation: "When the woman saw that the fruit was good for food [lust of the flesh], and pleasing to the eye [lust of the eye], and also desirable for gaining wisdom [pride of life], she took some and ate it. She also gave some to her husband, who was with her, and he ate it." As a result of breaking God's law, humankind became estranged from God. As a direct result of Adam's sin the world is in its present condition.

The second example of Satan's effective use of his tripartite weapon is the life of Solomon. Despite the fact that God blessed Solomon with wisdom, knowledge, riches, wealth, and honor greater than that of any ruler before or after (see 2 Chronicles 1), Solomon fell prey to Satan's strategies and turned his heart away from God.

The books of Kings and Chronicles provide just a glimpse at the extent of Solomon's wisdom, wealth, and power. For example, according to 1 Kings 11, Solomon had one thousand wives (seven hundred wives and three hundred concubines [secondary wives]). Second Chronicles 9:23 says that "all the kings of the earth sought audience with Solomon to hear the wisdom God had put in his heart." Further, Solomon made silver in Jerusalem, where he lived, as common as stones (v. 27). The account of Solomon's wealth and power recounted in 2 Chronicles 9 far exceeds anything ever described on *Lifestyles of the Rich and Famous*! Solomon actually lived the life that many people only dream of. Clearly, if anyone should have been content with life and its pleasures it should have been Solomon; his desire for sex (lust of the flesh), wealth (lust of the eye), and power (pride of life) had been met. In his own words, "I denied myself nothing my eyes desired; I refused my heart no pleasure. . . . Yet when I surveyed all that my hands had done and what I had toiled to achieve, everything was meaningless, a chasing after the wind; nothing was gained under the sun" (Ecclesiastes 2:10–11). Based on the results of Solomon's life there should be little doubt that the pleasures of the world are insufficient to truly satisfy our needs. Rather these pleasures and desires are potential weapons for Satan's destruction of our lives.

A third example of Satan's attempt to use the "big three" is found in Luke 4. Satan's intended victim in this instance was Jesus Himself. Jesus' response to Satan provides the model for us to follow when we are attacked. Jesus had just completed a forty-day fast in preparation for beginning his ministry when Satan approached him and said, "If you are the Son of God, tell this stone to become bread" (v. 3). This is a clear appeal to the desire of the flesh. Jesus had just gone forty days without food, so Satan sought to attack Jesus' hunger. Satan's second attack attempted to appeal to the desires of the eye. The Bible says that Satan took Jesus to a high place and showed him all the kingdoms of the world and promised Jesus that all of their splendor and power would be His if He would only worship him. In his final attack Satan attempted to appeal to the pride of life. He took Jesus to the top of the temple and suggested to Him that if He was really the Son of God, if He was really the Man, then He would jump off, knowing that God had promised that the angels would not let Him even hit His foot against a stone. Unlike Adam and Eve, Solomon, and every man since, Jesus successfully withstood every one of Satan's attacks. In each instance, Jesus responded to Satan's deception with the truth found in the Word of God. Jesus was tempted in all the ways in which we are tempted and yet He did not sin (Hebrews 4:15). Jesus' life provides encouragement to us and the message that we too must know and utilize the Word, the commands, instruction, and promises of God to defeat Satan and thwart his attack on our lives, families, and communities.

Ephesians 6 provides explicit instruction in how to defend against Satan's attack: "Put on the full armor of God so that you can take your stand against the devil's schemes" (v. 11). This passage also tells us that we are engaged in open, hostile conflict (i.e., war) not with men, the man, or the brothers, but rather with satanic forces in spiritual realms. Accordingly, the weapons necessary to engage in the battle are not natural, rather, they are spiritual. In light of the perspective provided through the above examples, Ephesians 6, and numerous other passages throughout the Bible, it is clear that many of the difficulties, challenges, and problems that we as African-American men experience individually and collectively, are actually physical manifestations of spiritual phenomena. When we recognize the source from which these problems emanate, we can then begin to fight effectively against them, and we can respond in ways that will impact the spiritual realm. Perhaps no passage in Scripture manifests this principle more poignantly than does the rebuilding of the wall of Jerusalem as written in the book of Nehemiah. It is from the autobiography of Nehemiah that the principles for rebuilding African-American men, their families, and communities will be drawn.

REBUILDING THE WALLS

Historical Background

Because the people of Judah were disobedient, God allowed the Babylonians to destroy their capital city, Jerusalem, and to send the Jews into exile. After King Cyrus of Persia conquered the Babylonians, he issued a decree that all exiles could return to their homelands. Although some Jews did travel back to Jerusalem, many remained in various places throughout the Persian Empire. Under the leadership of Ezra, the Jews who returned to Jerusalem rebuilt the temple and reestablished their relationship with God.

Nehemiah was one of the Jewish exiles who had remained in the Persian Empire. In fact, Nehemiah had risen to a position of prominence; he was the king's cupbearer. The role of cupbearer was not that of a servant, rather, given the cupbearer's daily direct access to the king, it was a position of great prestige and influence.

The book of Nehemiah begins with Nehemiah's brother and a number of other Jews bringing him news about the condition of Jerusalem. The news was that although the temple had been rebuilt, the city remained without walls. At that time, walls not only served to protect the city but they also symbolized the strength and well-being of a city or community. Accordingly, being without walls was a symbol of weakness and poverty and was a source of great shame and distress.

Today, the strength or the "walls" of a community are often perceived to be the level of business activity, political involvement, and physical appearance and infrastructure. In reality, these are merely an outgrowth or reflection of the true walls—the strength, stability, and level of responsibility assumed by its men. Based on the high rates of father absence in African-American homes, divorce rates in our families, failure rates in our schools, incarceration rates in the nation's prisons, and crime rates in our cities, the walls of many African-American families and communities have been torn down and are in disrepair. Like Jerusalem, our lack of walls should be a source of sorrow and disgrace, but more importantly, as it was for Nehemiah, the condition in which we find our walls, our men, should be the impetus for action.

A Strategy for Action

I believe that the book of Nehemiah outlines ten principles that Nehemiah used to rebuild the wall of Jerusalem. These same principles can be used for the rebuilding of African-Americans walls—our men, our families, and our communities.

1. Become Informed About the Condition of the Community

The book of Nehemiah begins with Nehemiah's inquiring of a group of Jews from Jerusalem about the condition of the city and its inhabitants. The report that Nehemiah received is recorded in chapter 1, verse 3, "those who survived the exile and are back in the province are in great trouble and disgrace. The wall of Jerusalem is broken down and its gates have been burned with fire." Before Nehemiah could take any steps to resolve Jerusalem's problem, he had to become informed that a problem existed.

Recall that Nehemiah occupied an important position in the Persian Empire; he was the cupbearer to the king. As a result of his elevated position, Nehemiah was largely unaware of the condition of his Jewish brothers and sisters who lived in Jerusalem. Accordingly, as America increasingly becomes a nation of haves and have nots, there are many African-Americans who are living in the "palace" and are really not aware of the magnitude of the problem at "home in Jerusalem" because we no longer physically live there or because we have become totally engulfed in the pleasures of so-called palace living. As in the book of Nehemiah, before any steps can be taken to rebuild our men, families, and communities, we must know their condition.

It is interesting to note that one of the exiles who informed Nehemiah about the condition of Jerusalem and its people was his own brother. Like Nehemiah, many of us no longer live in "Jerusalem" conditions but we continue to have brothers, sisters, mothers, fathers, and other relatives who do. As a result of these continued ties we are very much aware of the problems. And so while information about the condition of our men is necessary prior to beginning the restoration effort, it is not sufficient. It is our response to the information that is of the utmost importance. Nehemiah's response to the news concerning the condition of Jerusalem must be our response to the condition of our walls.

2. Develop a Sensitivity and Burden for the Problem

The second point that we can learn from the story of Nehemiah is found in chapter 1 verse 4: "When I heard these things, I sat down and wept." As a result of his love for his people, news of their dire condition moved him to tears. Nehemiah's tears demonstrate his sensitivity toward and burden for the condition of his brothers and sisters.

Nehemiah's response is a stark contrast to present-day responses to the poverty, violence, addiction, and other problems that plague African-Americans. Not only does the dire condition in which many African-Americans find themselves not cause us deep grief and sorrow, these things have actually become a multimillion-dollar source of "entertainment." Movies, news reports, magazines, songs, and even video games sensationalize and glorify problems that destroy us as African-American males. These various media sources, artists, and companies exploit the deterioration of African-American men, families, and communities for economic gain. Further, as a result of our constant exposure to violence and the destruction of life in the media, many of us have become desensitized to human pain and suffering, even when those who are suffering are our own flesh and blood.

248 MEN TO MEN • Part 4: Facing Contemporary Challenges

As Christians and as African-Americans we must pause and ask if there is something wrong with us when we use money that God blesses us with for "entertainment" that depicts murder, adultery, senseless violence, the profane use of God's name, and other behaviors contrary to God's Word. We must ask if there is something wrong with us when the sight of homeless children, the homicide of African-American boys, the impregnation of African-American girls, and the physical abuse of African-American women do not cause us to cry. Unfortunately, there are many Christians, both Black and White, who because of their pursuit of personal pleasure and their lack of communication with God through prayer and His Word, are unmoved by the bleak situation that faces a significant portion of the African-American community.

3. Mourn, Fast, Pray, and Seek God's Direction

After Nehemiah became aware of the condition of the exiles who had returned and he had mourned their plight, he fasted and prayed, seeking God's direction with regard to His plan to restore the walls of Jerusalem. Although Nehemiah was a man of action, he recognized that without supernatural intervention, he would be unable to achieve the task of rebuilding the wall.

In verses 5–11 of chapter 1, Nehemiah presents a model of prayer for us as we seek God's direction and wisdom for the difficult task of rebuilding our walls. The prayer consisted of several distinct components: worship, confession, reminding God of His Word, and petition. Nehemiah's prayer begins with worship—recognizing and exalting God for who He is. He then confesses his sins as well as the sins of the entire Israelite community. Next, knowing that God is faithful and cannot lie, Nehemiah reminds God of His promise to restore His people if they seek Him and follow His commands. Finally, Nehemiah petitions God, asking God for what he needs to rebuild the wall.

It is interesting to note Nehemiah's request. He did not ask that God send "someone" to "bless those abroad," but rather his prayer reflected a specific request that he might go and do the work that had to be done. During the time that Nehemiah had been fasting and praying, God had revealed to him the plan to rebuild the walls. While Nehemiah was very clear about the plan, he also recognized that in order to execute this plan he would have to have the favor and support of the king. That he might receive this favor and support was his prayer.

Fasting, denying ourselves food for the purpose of increasing our spiritual sensitivity and growth, is foreign to many Christians. Nevertheless, Nehemiah's example as well as Christ's admonition and example (see Matthew 17:2) suggest that this is a spiritual discipline with which we must become acquainted to be fully tuned into God's leading.

Along with fasting, prayer is a critical component for rebuilding ourselves and other African-American men. Nehemiah's prayer teaches us the importance of worshipping God simply for His being God, and of confessing and repenting of our individual and corporate sins. The effectiveness of this strategy is elucidated in 2 Chronicles 7:14, where God says, "If my people, who are called by my name, will humble themselves and pray and seek my face and turn from their wicked ways, then will I hear from heaven and will forgive their sin and will heal their land."

One of the most important things for us to learn from Nehemiah's prayer is that our prayer should be motivated by our intention to *do* something. Prayer is a necessary prerequisite to action, not a substitute for it. God's work on earth must be accomplished by people. We must pray for wisdom, knowledge, and direction that we may know, not what God is going to come down and do but rather what He wants to do through the work of our hands.

4. Obtain the Resources Necessary to Do the Work

Nehemiah was aware of the problem that faced Jerusalem, he had sought and received God's direction concerning the solution to the problem, and he was willing to implement God's plan. There was simply one drawback—he lacked the resources necessary to execute the plan. For these resources, Nehemiah turned to the king. Chapter 2 of Nehemiah begins approximately four months after he had become aware of conditions in Jerusalem. During this four-month period, I believe that Nehemiah was seeking God and preparing a proposal for the king.

One day while Nehemiah was serving the king, the king noticed sadness in Nehemiah's face and asked why he was sad. Nehemiah told the king that he was sad because of the condition of Jerusalem, the place where his ancestors were buried. At this point Nehemiah's opportunity came; the king asked Nehemiah what he wanted. The second half of verse 4 of chapter 2 tells us that Nehemiah sent a quick prayer to God and then presented his proposal. In verses 5–9 Nehemiah presents his goal to rebuild Jerusalem, a timeline in which the work would be accomplished, a request for letters guaranteeing his safe passage through various parts of the kingdom, and a request for timber with which to build. Clearly, this was no spur-of-the-moment request! Nehemiah, under God's direction, had determined what was needed in order to accomplish the work and waited for God to provide the opportunity to present the request.

The message of this section of Nehemiah is clear—rebuilding our walls will require that we plan and that we identify and obtain the material resources necessary to do the work. Although this step may not seem spiritual, the reality is that the work will require an explicit plan with specific goals, measurable objectives, a projected timeline for completion, a list of materials, and the expected cost. It has been said that when you fail to plan, you plan to fail. Although this statement is not scriptural it certainly is accurate.

Too often we begin a work without any planning with the expectation that "God will provide." While it is true that God will provide, it is important that we identify to the best of our ability what it is that we need Him to provide. Luke 14:28–30 emphasizes the need for planning: "Suppose one of you wants to build a tower. Will he not first sit down and estimate the cost to see if he has enough money to complete it? For if he lays the foundation and is not able to finish it, everyone who sees it will ridicule him, saying, 'This fellow began to build and was not able to finish.'"

The story of Nehemiah suggests that the failures and difficulties that many of us have experienced in the past as we have sought to do God's work have not been because we were out of God's will, nor that we had not fasted and prayed. Our failure resulted because we failed to create and follow a solid plan.

5. Examine the Magnitude and Extent of the Problem

Nehemiah left the palace with the specific goal to rebuild the wall of Jerusalem. When he arrived in Jerusalem, however, he did not tell anyone what his intention was; rather, he went out at night and inspected the walls to ascertain the extent of the problem. As a result his meeting with his brother back in the palace, Nehemiah knew in a general sense that the walls of Jerusalem had been torn down. Nevertheless, it was necessary for him to identify the actual level of need so that he could refine his plan and enlist the necessary support to begin the actual work.

In present-day language, Nehemiah performed a local needs assessment. While it is useful to know general information, like that presented in the first part of this chapter about the condition of African-American men, this information is of relatively little use for local planning and initiative. In order to be effective at the local level, we must assess the problems that are most pressing in the specific location where we have been led to work. This local planning should force us to identify realistic and manageable goals. Identifying realistic and manageable goals will better enable us to address the most pressing needs, not only in prayer but also in deeds.

Another point to be gleaned from this section of Nehemiah is that no matter how wonderful Nehemiah's plan was, it was absolutely useless until he left the palace and went to the place where the work had to be done. Similarly, addressing the problems that face our men, families, and communities will require that we leave the king's court (the boardroom, the executive suite, the ivory tower of academe) every once in a while and go where the problems are. Before we can rebuild our walls, we will have to stop talkin' in the palace and start walkin' in the rubble.

6. Articulate the Plan to Those Who Will Be Involved in the Work

After Nehemiah had assessed the actual magnitude of the work, he finally presented the plan to the people, "'You see the trouble that we are in: Jerusalem lies in ruins, and its gates have been burned with fire. Come, let us rebuild the wall of Jerusalem, and we will no longer be in disgrace.' I also told them about the gracious hand of my God upon me and what the king had said to me" (2:17–18). Nehemiah did not come in as the outside expert with lofty ideas, misconceptions, and a lot of work for other people to do. Nehemiah had informed himself about the problems of the community even before he had arrived, he had obtained a plan from God to deal with the problem, he acquired the material resources necessary to do the work, he assessed the actual magnitude of the work that had to be done, and he strengthened his hands for the work.

In order to be received by African-American men and in African-American communities of which we are not residents or in which we have not been actively involved, we too will have to be informed about their conditions, obtain a plan from God to address a specific problem, acquire resources necessary to implement the plan, effectively articulate the plan to those who will be involved, and prepare ourselves to get busy.

7. Build Teams and Coalitions to Implement the Plan

Nehemiah presented his plan to the priests, the nobles, the various city officials, and the common people of Jerusalem. The response to

Nehemiah's thorough presentation at the "Rebuilding the Wall Summit Meeting" is found in Nehemiah 2:18: "Let us start rebuilding."

Nehemiah realized that the task before him was impossible for him to accomplish alone. Accordingly, it was necessary to incorporate as many people as possible in order to do the actual work. In his presentation, he emphasizes the terms *we* and *us* in referring to the condition that Jerusalem was in and what the inhabitants would have to do to address the problem. By focusing on his shared concern about Jerusalem and his commitment to its well-being, he was able to develop a city-wide building campaign that involved virtually everyone in the community. A description of the work effort is presented in chapter 3.

There are several notable points in chapter 3 that bear significance for current efforts to rebuild our walls. One point is found in verse 1. The first group mentioned to be working on the wall was the priests. An effort to address the needs of the African-American community must begin with and be initiated by the priests—the religious leadership in our community. Our pastors, ministers, and other church officials must lead the way as we lay the spiritual foundation upon which to rebuild our men, families, and communities.

A second important point made in chapter 3 is that everyone's help was needed. Verse 12 points out that the ruler of half of Jerusalem and his *daughters* actively worked on the wall. Although we do not typically think of wall repair as so-called women's work, this passage makes clear that the seriousness of the job demanded that all hands were needed to accomplish the mission. This point is further supported by the fact that there were those from outside the community who helped in the work. While the work and responsibility for rebuilding the wall was primarily that of the inhabitants of the city, there were those from outside the community who actively participated. Similarly, while much of the work that needs to be done in our communities will be done by African-American men, African-American women as well as people from outside the African-American community will have to be involved in the work. This is particularly true for Christians. Differences in race, gender, social class, and so forth, cannot separate us with regard to the work that must be done.

Another key point found in chapter 3 that is applicable to present circumstances is the fact that most people were assigned to rebuild the section of the wall in front of their own homes. This was a brilliant strategy that guaranteed that people would do a good job because it focused their efforts on their self-interests. Today this strategy might mean encouraging people to work in their own local communities or to be involved in projects for which they have specialized training, skills, gifts, or interests.

Another extremely important point presented in chapter 3 was the fact that those rebuilding the walls reused the old stones from the original walls. As we seek to rebuild African-American communities and African-American young men in particular, we must use and reinstill the "old stones" (e.g., respect for women and the elderly, responsibility, commitment to family, love, discipline, spirituality, and the value of hard work).

8. Pray, Persist, and Remain Focused on the Plan

From the time that Nehemiah arrived in Jerusalem until the wall was completed, there were those who opposed his efforts. The enemies' initial response to Nehemiah's effort was simply verbal ridicule. However, as it became clear that the inhabitants of Jerusalem were going to be successful in their effort to rebuild the wall, ridicule in the form of joking about how weak the Jews were turned to persecution and even threats of war. In typical fashion, Nehemiah sought God in these situations, but he also took action. According to Nehemiah 4:9, "we prayed to our God and posted a guard day and night to meet this threat."

At one point, persecution by their enemies, coupled with the fatigue of the workers, caused the work on the wall to cease. At this time Nehemiah gathered the people together in families, placed them on battle alert and used the opportunity to encourage them. Specifically, in chapter 4, verse 14, Nehemiah tells the people, "don't be afraid of them. Remember the Lord who is great and awesome, and fight for your brothers, your sons and your daughters, your wives and your homes." As a result of this gathering, the workers were encouraged and their enemies were discouraged. From this time on, however, the men working on the wall worked with one hand and kept a weapon in the other. In the final verse of chapter 4 Nehemiah notes, "Neither I nor my brothers nor my men nor the guards with me took off our clothes; each had his weapon, even when he went for water."

Those of us committed to improving the condition of African-Americans should not be surprised when those outside the community question the motives of our efforts. Historically, most efforts by African-Americans for self-definition and empowerment have been met with fierce resistance from factions within the community and from a variety of sources from without. Undoubtedly, there will be enemies to the effort; nevertheless, the message of Nehemiah is one that we must grasp—we too must be willing to fight for our families. When persecution arises we must first deal with it in the spiritual realm with our spiritual weapons as outlined in Ephesians 6. Having prayed, we, like Nehemiah, must then post a guard and prepare for war. We must be willing to persist despite persecution, fatigue, and even threats.

9. Make Personal Financial Sacrifices to Complete the Work

In chapter 5, Nehemiah becomes aware of the practice of some of the Jews of charging their poorer brothers and sisters interest on money they had borrowed during this difficult period. While the exiles had become free from foreign rule, many had been reenslaved by their own people. Nehemiah condemns this practice and demands that the land be given back to its owners and that Jews not charge interest to other Jews. Further, Nehemiah sacrificed his own rights for the sake of the work in that he did not acquire any land and refused to take food and taxes from the people, even though he was entitled to them as governor. Rather than take money, Nehemiah gave it away. During the period in which the wall was being rebuilt, Nehemiah fed 150 people every day out of his own resources.

Nehemiah's example of the sacrifice of his own material gain is an important message for those of us today who plan to be involved in rebuilding our walls. Too often excellent efforts that are effectively reaching the needs of the disadvantaged are discontinued because of insufficient funds to pay for staff, supplies, and other materials necessary to continue the work. When we begin the work of restoration, we may have to sacrifice our personal resources for its existence. This type of sacrificial giving will require that we remember that all we have comes from God and that it is for Him to use as He sees fit. As the parable of the talents reminds us, we are merely stewards, or managers, of that which is owned by God.

10. Expect and Prepare for a Life of Continued Watchfulness and Self-Sacrifice

The final principle that can be abstracted from the book of Nehemiah emerges after the wall is completed. Nehemiah placed his brother and Hananiah, "a man of integrity" and one who "feared God more than most men do," in charge of Jerusalem. Nehemiah established rules surrounding the times when the gates of the city should be opened, when they should be closed, who should guard the gates, and who should guard the rest of the city. The implication here was that although the walls had been successfully built, the city still was not completely safe from attack. Accordingly, it was necessary for the people to remain in a state of constant watchfulness, readiness, and self-sacrifice.

So it is with us. As we begin to use Nehemiah principles to rebuild our walls, we will undoubtedly experience many of the challenges, problems, and difficulties that he encountered. Using these principles will result in our success also. Despite our successes, however, we must remain on constant alert and be prepared to wage spiritual warfare. Also, we should not take for granted the advances that we make. They must be constantly protected and guarded.

SUMMARY

Numerous social problems have acted to damage and destroy African-Americans' walls—our men, our families, and our communities. The book of Nehemiah provides at least ten principles for us to follow as we seek to rebuild these walls. Current efforts to address these issues typically include numerous meetings, summits, special commissions, and a variety of other forums in which the problems are discussed but little effort is expended with regard to implementing solutions.

The book of Nehemiah offers a viable model with solutions at its core. Nehemiah's first meeting was with his brother and a number of exiles from Jerusalem. This first meeting provided Nehemiah with information about the existence of the problem. In the second meeting, Nehemiah presented an action plan for dealing with the problem to those who would do the work. The third meeting occurred during the process of repairing the wall to make those involved aware of their collective progress, to encourage and motivate them to persist with their work despite the challenges that they faced, and to prepare them to fight for their families. The fourth meeting also occurred during the building process. During this meeting Nehemiah rebuked those who exploited their brothers for their personal gain and encouraged them to sacrifice their material possessions for the common good.

Nehemiah provides the model for those of us who have the intent and desire to rebuild our walls. Now is the time to implement the Nehemiah plan, remembering that God will hold us accountable for what we have and have not done. When we use the scriptural principles outlined in the book of Nehemiah, we will experience good success and the world will know that "this work had been done with the help of our God" (Nehemiah 6:16).

REFERENCES

Farley, R., and W. R. Allen. 1989. *The color line and the quality of life in America.* New York: Oxford University Press.

Gibbs, J. T. 1988. *Young, Black and male in America: An endangered species.* Dover, MA: Arbor House.

1984. *The holy Bible: New international version.* Grand Rapids: Zondervan.

Majors, R. G., and J. U. Gordon. 1994. *The American Black male: His present status and his future.* Chicago: Nelson-Hall.

National Center for Health Statistics. 1993. *Health 1992.* Hyattsville, MD: Public Health Service.

U.S. Bureau of the Census. 1994. *Statistical abstract of the United States: 1994 (114th ed.).* Washington, DC: U.S. Bureau of the Census.

Williams, D. R., and C. A. Collins. 1995. U.S. socioeconomic and racial differences in health: Patterns and explanations. *Annual Review of Sociology* 21: 349–86.

Lee N. June

African-American, Afrocentric (Africentric), Christian, and Male?

LEE N. JUNE is a professor at Michigan State University and currently serves as Assistant Provost for Student Academic Support Services, Racial, Ethnic, and Multicultural Issues, and is Interim Vice President for Student Affairs and Services. He was director of a university counseling center for eight and a half years. Born and reared in Manning, South Carolina, Lee holds a bachelor of science degree from Tuskegee University, a master of education degree in counseling, a master of arts degree in clinical psychology, and a doctor of philosophy degree in clinical psychology from the University of Illinois (Champaign-Urbana). He did postgraduate study in psychology at Haverford College (1966–67) and was a special student during a sabbatical leave at the Duke University Divinity School (1981). He is editor of *The Black Family: Past, Present, and Future* (Zondervan, 1991). A member of the New Mount Calvary Baptist Church (Lansing, Michigan), Lee is married to Shirley Spencer June, and they have two sons, Stephen and Brian.

Chapter 16
Lee N. June

African-American, Afrocentric (Africentric), Christian, and Male?

The purpose of this chapter is to explore the relationship between and issues associated with being African-American, Afrocentric/Africentric (these terms are often used interchangeably), Christian, and male. This question is important particularly to the African-American Christian because of how Christianity is often portrayed by the broader Christian community and by those who are African-American and outside the Christian community.

In exploring this topic, the specific challenges that face the African-American Christian male will be discussed and solutions will be presented. The areas to be discussed are

1. Being an African-American male
2. The issue of the color and race
3. The issue of the color of Jesus Christ
4. Afrocentricity
5. Contributions of Black male Christian American writers to Christianity
6. Blacks and Black males in the Bible
7. The Christian "Right"

CHALLENGES OF BEING AN AFRICAN-AMERICAN MALE

As African-American males, we face many challenges regardless of our religious affiliations and beliefs. As we develop as men, we often experience a hostile environment, some form of which has existed since we arrived on the American shores in large numbers.

"Real Black masculinity" is often not viewed as compatible with Christianity. Lincoln and Mamiya (1990, p. 391) have noted how other religions, particularly Islam, have increased in appeal to Black males. They state:

> The attraction of Islamic movements to black males may be due to several reasons, among them the legacy of the militant and radical black nationalist Malcolm X has been a profound influence on these young men. As a culture hero, Malcolm X was seen as the uncompromising critic of American society. Another reason is that the Muslims project a more macho image among black men. The Qur'an advocates self-defense while the Christian Bible counsels turning the other cheek. The *lex talionis*, "an eye for an eye, a life for a life," has a persuasive appeal to the oppressed whose cheeks are weary of inordinate abuse. Black sport heroes such as Muhammad Ali and Kareem Abdul-Jabbar have further legitimated the Islamic option by converting to Islam and taking on Muslim names. Black parents who are not Muslims frequently give their children Muslim names as a statement of solidarity with some features of Islam and as a way of announcing their independence from Western social conventions, or as a means of identifying with an African cultural heritage. Finally, many black men have been attracted to Islamic alternatives because the Muslims have been very active in working in prisons and on the streets where they are, a ministry which is not pronounced in most black Christian churches.

Lincoln and Mamiya estimate that in the late 1980s there were six million Muslims in America, the second largest religion in America after Protestant and Catholic Christianity.

Jawanza Kunjufu (1994) discusses twenty-one reasons why most Black men do not go to church and offers a solution to these issues. These reasons were gathered through survey and focus-group discussions. Of the twenty-one reasons, the two most germane to our discussion are that the church is too Eurocentric, and there is a lack of Christian role models.

In regard to the first reason that Black men do not go to church because the church is too Eurocentric, Kunjufu states:

> The brothers discussed the issue of Eurocentrism for almost four hours. I eventually had to conclude the discussion, because everyone

had something to say about the White, blond, blue-eyed image of Jesus proudly displayed in the church sanctuary. One brother said, "I will go to church when that lying image comes down. I'm not worshipping no White man. I'm not worshipping anybody that does not look like me ... I got a problem with those movies on television, where Moses, Cleopatra, Jesus, and everybody else is White...." One brother said, "that's why I like Minister Farrakhan, because in the mosque you don't see those images. Islam is the original religion of the Black man." (pp. 60–61)

In regard to the issue of lack of Christian role models, Kunjufu states:

I chose to go around the room so that they could see for themselves, and it was amazing, not one of them had a male that had been in their home who was saved and went to church. One brother said, "it should be obvious why we're here. Can you be anything that you have not seen? Can you be a Black man if you have not seen a Black man? Can you be a saved Black man if you haven't seen a [saved] Black man? If you haven't seen a Black man tithe, if you haven't seen a Black man in your house pray, it's going to be difficult if not impossible to emulate him." (pp. 69–70)

I am happy to be able to report that there are solutions to both of these two concerns. Kunjufu discusses them and they will be further explored later in this chapter. Suffice it to say at this point that a church does not have to be Eurocentric and there is a growing number of Black Christian role models.

THE ISSUE OF COLOR AND RACE

In America, color and race historically have been, and are currently, very important. Much attention has focused on this question as it relates to Jesus Christ. The attack on Christian symbols and images have focused particularly on Jesus Christ who is portrayed in most churches as a blond, blue-eyed White man, as the earlier quote from Kunjufu shows. Na'im Akbar (1984), in his book *Chains and Images of Psychological Slavery,* states:

For African-Americans racial religious imagery is even more devastating. We have demonstrated that the one who sees himself in the Divine image is given an unnatural and a very inflated notion of what he or she is, which develops a kind of egotistical maniac. What is even worse, though, is what happens to the one who is not portrayed in the Divine imagery, and who worships a non-self in the image. In Judeo-Christian imagery, this means that the Caucasian bows down and worships himself, and the African-American worships the Caucasian as a God as well. (p. 52)

Once you begin to believe that the deity is somebody other than you, then you are put into a psychological dependent state that renders you incapable of breaking loose until you break the hold of that image. (p. 60)

The image of the Creator sets the tone for the potential of creativity in the human sphere. Those who are alienated from the concept of being in the image of the Creator do not attribute the characteristic of creativity to themselves.

Therefore, productivity can at best be imitative of those who are viewed to be in the image of the Creator. Again, the problem stems from a stifled independence based upon the psychological straight-jacket of seeing God portrayed as other than the self. (p. 63)

The real challenge, however, is to remove the racial images of Divinity from our minds. . . . But, we must also take self-affirmative steps to transform our own world. We must carefully monitor the images that we expose ourselves to which perpetuate this destructive influence. For example, we might choose to refrain from uncritically watching a movie such as "The Bible" which depicts the entire religious history of the Judeo-Christian world in Caucasian flesh. (p. 70)

William Mosley (1987, p. 7), also speaking to the issue of a non-Caucasian Jesus, states:

Let us look to biblical history to piece the puzzle together. If we acknowledge the archeological findings that earliest man originated in northeastern Africa, then what is written [in] the Bible as it pertains to the creation of man and the Garden of Eden is confirmed. In establishing exactly where the Garden was, the book of Genesis cites the [sic] four rivers—Gihon (in the land of Kush-Ethiopia), Tigris and Euphrates—which run through Syria and Iraq. These two countries were also connected to Africa before the construction of the Suez Canal.

So if the original Hebrews were a non-White stock, we may conclude that the original Israelites were considerably more Black at the time of the Exodus than present-day Israelis.

Furthermore, the historical record says that ancient Israel, Egypt, and Ethiopia were not only close geographically, but were also close socially, culturally, economically, and politically.

Both sacred and secular writing describe the presence of Ethiopian peoples in Egypt and Israel from the Exodus to the birth of Jesus of Nazareth. Also, the Ethiopian peoples of ancient times were comparable to present-day Sudanese people; that is, they were Africans that anthropologists would call the Negroid type: full-blooded, black skinned, broad-featured.

In short, if there was an assimilation of Black peoples among the Israelites, and there was; and if Jesus was an Israelite, and He was; then Jesus might very well have inherited genes from Ethiopian ancestors, which would have made him Black.

As Lincoln and Mamiya (1990) indicated, most of the popular role models of young African-Americans are Blacks who are seen as "defiant" in some way. Thus, the last thing one would want is to be identified with a religion that fits the description of a "White man's religion" with its corresponding images and symbols.

As a result of the challenges launched by many, including Akbar and the Association of Black Psychologists, including Mosley and Kunjufu, many African-American churches have removed the European images of Jesus Christ and the Last Supper. Likewise, we have begun to see a greater sensitivity to the color of biblical personages as presented in publications geared toward African-American audiences. A leader in this regard has been Urban Ministries publications of Chicago, Illinois. *The Original African Heritage Study Bible* (1993) does so also. There is also evidence that some Black Christian churches are increasingly growing and attracting African-American males. However, these churches tend to be the ones that are more Afrocentric and are labeled "liberation" churches and/or churches that have *focused* ministries geared toward the African-American male (see Richardson 1991; Kunjufu 1994).

THE ISSUE OF THE COLOR OF JESUS CHRIST

While one may not be able to be as certain about the *exact* color of Jesus, what is clear from the Bible and the available and evolving literature is that Jesus was not White as has been historically portrayed. The Bible, itself, describes Jesus in this manner:

> And I turned to see the voice that spake with me. And being turned, I saw seven golden candlesticks;
>
> And in the midst of the seven candlesticks one like unto the Son of man, clothed with a garment down to the foot, and girt about the paps with a golden girdle.
>
> His head and his hairs were white as wool, as white as snow; and his eyes were as a flame of fire;
>
> And his feet like unto fine brass, as if they burned in a furnace; and his voice as the sound of many waters.
>
> And he had in his right hand seven stars; and out of his mouth went a sharp two edged sword: and his countenance was as the sun shineth in his strength.
>
> And when I saw him, I fell at his feet as dead. And he laid his right hand upon me, saying unto me, Fear not; I am the first and the last:
>
> I am he that liveth, and was dead; and behold, I am alive for evermore, Amen; and have the keys of hell and of death. (Revelation 1:12–18)

The above description does not fit a White person. However, we must note that this is a postresurrection description.

There are no clear-cut physical descriptions of the earthly Jesus recorded in the Bible. But as Mosley (1987), McCray (1990a, 1990b), and Felder (1993) have stated, based on the geography of where Jesus lived and his ancestral lineage, he was not the color that American Christians have used to depict Him. As we continue to explore the issue of color, however, it may be well to remember and reflect on the apostle Paul's comments on Mars' Hill.

> Then Paul stood in the midst of Mars' Hill, and said, Ye men of Athens, I perceive that in all things ye are too superstitious.
>
> For as I passed by, and beheld your devotions, I found an altar with this inscription, TO THE UNKNOWN GOD. Whom, therefore, ye ignorantly worship, him declare I unto you.
>
> God that made the world and all things therein, seeing that he is Lord of heaven and earth, dwelleth not in temples made with hands;

Neither is worshipped with men's hands, as though he needed any thing, seeing he giveth to all life, and breath, and all things;

And hath made of one blood all nations of men for to dwell on all the face of the earth, and hath determined the times before appointed, and the bounds of their habitation;

That they should seek the Lord, if haply they might feel after him, and find him, though he is not far from every one of us:

For in him we live, and move, and have our being: *as certain also of your own poets have said,* For we are also his offspring.

Forasmuch then as we are the offspring of God, we ought not to think that the Godhead is like unto gold or silver or stone, graven by art and man's device.

And the times of this ignorance God winked at; but now commandeth all men every where to repent:

Because he hath appointed a day in which he will judge the world in righteousness by that man whom he hath ordained; whereof which he hath given assurance unto all men, in that he hath raised him from the dead. (Acts 17: 22–31, emphasis mine)

AFROCENTRICITY

Molefi Asante (1990, pp. 6–7) introduced the concept of Afrocentricity. In defining the concept, he states:

Afrocentricity is the belief in the centrality of Africans in post modern history. It is our history, our mythology, our creative motif, and our ethos exemplifying our collective will ...

Afrocentricity does not convert you by appealing to hatred or lust or greed or violence. As the highest, most conscious ideology, it makes it a point, motivates its adherents, captivates the cautious by the force of its truth. You are the ultimate test. You test its authenticity by incorporating it in your behavior. At the apex of your consciousness, it becomes your life because everything you do, it is ...

... with Afrocentricity you see the movies differently, you see other people differently, you read books differently, you see politicians differently, in fact, nothing is as it was before your consciousness. Your conversion to Afrocentricity becomes total as you read, listen, and talk with

266   MEN TO MEN • Part 4: Facing Contemporary Challenges

others who share the collective consciousness. It supersedes any other ideology because it is the proper sanctification of your own history.

The momentum for the evolution of Afrocentricity occurred parallel to other Black movements and within the context of several scholarly works that have gradually shown the positive and more complete contributions of Black people to world civilization. This movement was a natural next step given the changes that were then occurring on the world scene. Among the scholarly works that helped to launch, anchor, and sustain Afrocentricity are books such as *The Destruction of Black Civilization: Great History of a Race—From 4000 B.C. to A.D. 2000* (Williams 1976), *Civilization or Barbarism* (Diop 1974), *The African Origin of Civilization* (Diop 1991), *Pre-colonial Black Africa* (Diop 1976), *They Came Before Columbus* (Van Sertima 1976), and *Black Athena* (Bernal 1987). These books, and many others, present clear documentation of what Blacks did prior to their encounter with America. In these writings, we are portrayed as kings, queens, the builders of the pyramids, the discoverers of iron and democracy, the inventors of trial by jury, and so forth.

The Afrocentric movement, in combination with other movements of similar types, has been able to show that many Black behavior patterns and traditions seen throughout the world can be traced to ancient African traditions. It also shows that on the world scene, we are actors and not merely subjects.

While there are many positive aspects to the Afrocentric movement, there are also some areas of caution as well as areas that need to be further explored. Afrocentricity, at its core, has led to a necessary paradigm shift in how to more accurately view history and study African peoples. It tells us that in any study of African people, Africa must be placed at the center (Asante 1988). This means that if we are to understand Africans fully, wherever we are in the Diaspora, we must center us in Africa and look at the developments that have contributed to our current situation. To understand us, African lenses must be used.

This paradigm shift is positive. Using African lenses, lenses consistent with African traditions, is necessary for an accurate historical, sociological, psychological, political, and economic understanding and description. The caution (tension points), however, also lies in the full definition of Afrocentricity as offered earlier by Asante (1990). Maybe unintended, though nevertheless present, Asante in defining Afrocentricity stated that "at the apex of your consciousness, it becomes your life because everything you do, it is ..." (p. 6). He further states that "it supersedes any other ideology because it is the proper sanctification of your own history" (p. 7).

The solution for the African-American Christian male who is Afrocentric is that *God must be at the apex of our consciousness, He must become our life.* Additionally, *God and the Bible must supersede any other ideology where there is conflict or incompatibility*. Afrocentricity, for us, must be limited to being an important tool and a necessary lens to fully understand us in world history. Any ideology that excludes God or relegates Him to second place must be resisted and ultimately rejected and abandoned.

One of the areas that needs further study and scholarship is ancient Egyptian religion vis-à-vis the Old and New Testament Christianity that places Jesus Christ as necessary for salvation and a proper connection to God. Thus, while I am male, African-American, and appreciative of the contributions of Afrocentricity (and thus am Afrocentric in the more narrow sense as I defined it earlier), I am careful when embracing some of the writings in the area of ancient religions vis-à-vis the Bible. As we read these books, we must discern and appreciate the actual scholarship but ask questions when it becomes ideology about the place Jesus Christ holds in their articulated worldview.

Afrocentricity, the development of Black scholarship, the genesis of various professional Black disciplinary associations, such as the Association of Black Psychologists, have all resulted in an increase in scholarly works that show the strengths and historical contributions of Blacks to the world. This scholarship has also pervaded the area of religion and Christianity.

It is beyond the scope of this chapter to fully explore all of these works and their development. However, I will share some of the critical evolutionary works by Black Christians that evolved during this period of exploding scholarship.

CONTRIBUTIONS OF BLACK MALE CHRISTIAN AMERICAN WRITERS TO CHRISTIANITY

While the "Black Power" movement was developing in the 1960s and the book by Stokely Carmichael and Charles Hamilton entitled *Black Power: The Politics of Liberation in America* (1967) was published, there were Blacks who were writing in reference to Christianity.

This is important to remember and recognize because the struggle for identity and proper recognition was also occurring in Christian circles. For instance, William Pannell wrote *My Friend, The Enemy* (1968), Tom Skinner wrote *Black and Free* (1968), and James Cone wrote *Black Theology and Black Power* (1969). In the 1970s the writing continued. Tom Skinner wrote *Words of Revolution* (1970) and *How Black Is the Gospel* (1970), while the interracial team of Columbus Salley and Ronald Behn wrote *Your God Is Too White* (1970). James Cone wrote *A Black Theology of Liberation* (1970), A. G. Dunston wrote *The Black Man in the Old Testament and Its World* (1974), and C. Eric Lincoln contributed with *The Black Church Since Frazier* (1974). Cone's works were key in the evolution of the Black-theology movement.

In the 1980s and 1990s we have seen the works of Mosley (1987), McCray (1990a, 1990b), June (1991), McKissic and Evans (1994), and Felder (1989, 1991, 1993), just to name a few. I expect to see further such books in the future.

BLACKS AND BLACK MALES IN THE BIBLE

As one now looks at the contributions of Blacks, both in general history and in biblical history, one must wonder why there was ever any reason for our not showing the visibility of our presence and the richness of our contributions. For example, prominent throughout the Old Testament is the continent of Africa. Over and over again we see the interaction of the Israelites with Egypt. Abraham went to Egypt. Joseph became a prominent ruler in Egypt under the Pharaoh. The Hebrew people as a nation spent more than four hundred years there. Moses spent forty years there. Moses married an African woman (Zipporah). One of Abraham's wives was an African (Hagar). The Garden of Eden is situated in that region.

In the New Testament, there is also an African presence. Jesus Himself went to Africa (Egypt) with his parents to escape the decree given by Caesar to kill the young boys under the age of two. We see the conversion of the Ethiopian eunuch. On the day of Pentecost, the Bible indicates that there were people present from every nation.

These facts are evident even from a cursory reading of the Scriptures. One now sometimes wonders why there was ever the assertion that Christianity was (is) a White man's religion when it is clear that Blacks were integral to God's plan all along and involved with Christianity from its inception.

The works of Alfred Dunston (*The Black Man in the Old Testament and Its World,* 1974), Walter A. McCray (*The Black Presence in the Bible,* 1990a, 1990b), L. H. Carter (*Black Heroes of the Bible,* 1989), and Cain H. Felder (*The Original African-American Heritage Study Bible,* 1993) contain additional evidence of our contributions in biblical history. While there may be some controversy over whether some of the individuals referred to were Black, there is no question that there is a prominent Black male and female presence in the Bible in both the Old and New Testaments. Among the many males listed in the Old Testament as being Black are Adam, Ham, Cush, Melchizedek, Ephron the Hittite, Ebed-melech the Ethiopian, and Nimrod. The reader is encouraged to consult the above works for a more detailed listing.

Martin Delaney (1879), in *The Origin of Races and Color,* states the following:

> "There is no doubt that, until the entry into the Ark of the Family of Noah, the people were all of the One Race and Complexion: which leads us to the further inquiry, What was that Complexion? It is, we believe, generally admitted among linguists, that the Hebrew word Adam (*ahdam*) signifies *red*—dark red as some scholars believe. And it is, we believe, a well-settled admission that the name of the original man was taken from his complexion. (p. 11)

> Shem, Noah's son, settled in Asia, peopling the country around the center of where the ark landed. Ham went to the southwest, and Japheth to the northwest. It will not be disputed that, from then to the present day, the people in the regions where those three sons are said to have located—the three grand divisions of the Eastern Hemisphere: Asia, Africa, and Europe—are, with the exceptions to be hereafter accounted for, of the distinct complexions of those attributed to Shem, Ham, and Japheth: yellow, black, and white. The subsequent confusion of tongues and scattering abroad in the earth were the beginning and origin of the races. (p. 19)

In the New Testament, among the males believed to be Black are Simone of Cyrene and the Ethiopian eunuch.

Why is it so important to clearly show that Blacks in general and Black males in particular are represented in the Scriptures and made important contributions to Christianity? There are several reasons. Among them:

- All of us profit from having access to the truth.
- It debunks the idea that Christianity is a White man's religion.
- It shows that Blacks were integrally involved with Christianity from its inception.
- It provides Black role models to African-Americans.
- It takes away any validity to the argument that Christianity is not a valid religion for Black people.

THE CHRISTIAN RIGHT

A movement that gained attention during the late 1970s was the Moral Majority. Originally headed by Jerry Falwell, this movement attempted to influence the political agenda of the nation. The successor to this movement in the 1990s is the Christian Coalition, led by Ralph Reed. Its adherents pride themselves as being evangelical Christians.

What makes the movement problematic for African-Americans is its staunch political conservatism that is antithetical to the interests of most Black people. The movement raises *some* issues that any evangelical Christian, regardless of race, can embrace but its silence on issues of social justice is appalling. It appears that a political and cultural agenda rather than a pure biblical agenda is being advanced, and this is embarrassing for me as a Black Christian. What demonstrated clearly the political nature of the movement was its embracing of Ronald Reagan for president in 1980 over Jimmy Carter. Jimmy Carter was clearer and bolder in admitting that he was a born-again Christian, yet he was not embraced.

The Christian Right is a clear contrast to the Civil Rights Movement of the 1950s and 1960s, which saw massive Black church involvement in the political arena. This movement, in my opinion, focused on issues of social justice in the tradition of the Old Testament prophets. It was not pushing a "culture agenda" as the Christian Right seems to be trying to advance.

Those of us, as Black males, who are put off by the agenda of the Christian Right must remember that there have always been factions throughout history within the Christian church. We must constantly search for the biblical Jesus (and accept Him when we find Him) and challenge the Christian Right to do the same. We must see the true role models in our midst who continue to pursue a true biblical agenda.

CONCLUSION

This chapter has explored the possibility of and the issues associated with being African-American, Christian, Afrocentric, and male. I have concluded that it is possible to be African-American, Christian, Afrocentric, and male depending ultimately upon one's definition of Afrocentricity. Several challenges to and solutions for African-American Christian males were presented and discussed.

REFERENCES

Akbar, N. 1984. *Chains and images of psychological slavery*. Jersey City, NJ: New Mind Productions.

Asante, M. K. 1988. *The Afrocentric idea*. Philadelphia: Temple University Press.

_____. 1990. *Afrocentricity*. Trenton, NJ: Africa World Press.

Bernal, M. 1987. *Black Athena*. New Brunswick, NJ: Rutgers University Press.

Carmichael, S., and C. V. Hamilton. 1967. *Black power: The politics of liberation in America*. New York: Vintage Books.

Carter, L. H. 1989. *Black heroes of the Bible*. Columbus, GA: Brentwood Christian Press.

Cone, J. H. 1970. *A Black theology of liberation*. Philadelphia: Lippincott.

_____. 1969. *Black theology and Black power*. New York: Seabury.

Delaney, M. R. 1879. *The origins of races and color*. Philadelphia: Harper and Brothers.

Diop, C. A. 1991. *Civilization or barbarism*. Trenton, NJ: Lawrence Hill.

_____. 1990. *The cultural unity of Black Africa*. Chicago: Third World Press.

_____. 1987a. *Black Africa: The economic and cultural basis for a federated state*. Trenton, NJ: Lawrence Hill.

_____. 1987b. *Precolonial Black Africa*. Trenton, NJ: Lawrence Hill.

_____. 1974. *The African origin of civilization*. Trenton, NJ: Lawrence Hill.

Dunston, A. G., Jr. 1974. *The Black man in the Old Testament and its world*. Philadelphia: Dorrance.

Felder, C. H. 1989. *Troubling biblical waters*. Maryknoll: Orbis.

Felder, C. H., ed. 1993. *The original African-American heritage study Bible*. Nashville: James C. Winston.

_____. 1991. *Stony the road we trod*. Minneapolis: Fortress.

June, L. N., ed. 1991. *The Black family: Past, present, and future*, edited by L. N. June. Grand Rapids: Zondervan.

Kunjufu, J. 1994. *Adam! Where are you: Why most Black men don't go to church*. Chicago: African-American Images.

Lincoln, C. E. 1974. *The Black church since Frazier*. New York: Schocken.

Lincoln, C. E., and L. H. Mamiya. 1990. *The Black church in the African American experience*. Durham, NC: Duke University Press.

Mbiti, J. S. 1975. *Introduction to African religion*. Oxford: Heinemann.

_____. 1970. *African religions and philosophy*. Garden City, NY: Doubleday.

McCray, W. A. 1990a. *The Black presence in the Bible*. Vol. l. Chicago: Black Light Fellowship.

_____. 1990b. *The Black presence in the Bible and the table of nations*. Vol. 2. Chicago: Black Light Fellowship.

McKissic, W. D., Sr., and A. T. Evans. 1994. *Beyond* Roots II: *If anybody ask you who I am*. Wenonah: Renaissance.

Mosley, W. 1987. *What color was Jesus*. Chicago: African-American Images.

Pannell, W. E. 1968. *My friend, the enemy*. Waco: Word.

Richardson, W. 1991. Evangelizing Black males: Critical issues and how tos. In *The Black family: Past, present, and future*, edited by L. N. June. Grand Rapids: Zondervan.

Salley, C., and R. Behm. 1970. *Your God is too White*. Downers Grove, IL: Intervarsity Press.

Skinner, T. 1970. *How Black is the gospel*. Philadelphia: J. B. Lippincott.

_____. 1970. *Words of revolution*. Grand Rapids: Zondervan.

_____. 1968. *Black and free*. Grand Rapids: Zondervan.

Van Sertima, I. 1976. *They came before Columbus*. New York: Random House.

Williams, C. 1976. *The destruction of Black civilization*. Chicago: Third World Press.

Wilmore, G. S. 1989. *African-American religious studies*. Durham, NC: Duke University Press.